TV
Typewriter
Cookbook

by

Don Lancaster

Howard W. Sams & Co., Inc.
4300 WEST 62ND ST. INDIANAPOLIS, INDIANA 46268 USA

International Standard Book Number: 0-672-21313-3
Library of Congress Catalog Card Number: 75-46215

Printed in the United States of America.

Preface

This book shows you how to put your own words and pictures on ordinary tv sets. It's also a book on cheap things that can be connected to a microprocessor to get it to do genuinely useful tasks. If you are a computer hobbyist with a home-brew lashup, a serious professional data processor concerned with low-cost small machine systems, a video games freak, or a ham working with rtty, you will find in depth information on tv typewriter technology, which today represents the only truly low-cost ($30 to $150) microcomputer and small-systems display interface. If you are a software specialist, we will be showing you the hardware that makes your software work, giving you the depth of background you will need for effective and efficient small-systems coding. If you are teaching micro-processors, you will find this book useful as a primary or supplemental text on the high school through university levels. If you are into video recording, cable tv, or studio broadcasting, you will find techniques here for low-cost titling and annotation of existing program material, as well as the means for video art synthesis. And, if you are an electronics technician, herein lies the answers on the standard ASCII code; serial transmission formats; keyboards and encoders; Teletype, cassette, and modem techniques; along with many of the integrated circuits and systems concepts that back them up.

We start in Chapter 1 with some basics—what a tv typewriter is and what are its uses, configurations, and operating principles. After this, we take a quick look at the fundamentals of television raster scanning, followed in turn by the standard computer codes and their formats. A collection of essential terms involved with tvt's and microcomputer interface then follows.

Chapter 2 is a catalog of integrated circuits you will find useful in tvt and interface work. It is organized in much the same way as the similar device chapter of the *TTL Cookbook*, also published by Howard W. Sams & Co., Inc.

Memory is the topic of the next chapter. We consider three basic types: you-program PROMs, including a seven-segment calculator interface and a Selectric converter; factory-programmed ROMs, including particularly the dot-matrix character generator; and read-write or RAM technology that lets you selectively store and retrieve information. The 2102-style devices and their improved offspring are emphasized because of their ultralow cost, extreme simplicity of use, and microprocessor compatibility.

Basic concepts of tvt system design appear in Chapter 4, including such things as timing-chain design and line-lock and EIA sync techniques. Cursor and update circuitry, which is usually the hardest-to-design part of a stand-alone tvt, is covered in Chapter 5. Cursor techniques range from the traditional count and compare and the ultrasimple McFadden system, to dedicated "super front panel" tvt's that work directly with microcomputers. Update systems include both frame-rate and direct memory access (DMA) systems.

Keyboards and encoders follow in Chapter 6, with a number of basic encoding techniques, key arrangements, and circuits shown.

An extensive review of serial interface centered around the UART, or universal asynchronous receiver transmitter, is presented in Chapter 7. Here we also look at the bit boffer software-independent, speed-tolerant cassette storage system, along with Teletype and standard interfaces and various types of modems.

The care and feeding of the tv set are next in Chapter 8, which shows us both the rf and direct-video methods, along with several ways of extending video bandwidth for long line-length displays. We end the chapter by looking at color subcarrier techniques—simple ways of adding one or more colors to your system for video games or art synthesis, or for other applications where you want to use color for added emphasis or value.

Our last chapter is on hard copy (printed records) and color graphics. The full gamut of hard copy is covered, from computer Teletypes, Baudot Teletypes, and economical Selectric office typewriter conversions, to ink squirters and special paper systems that include the electrosensitive, thermal, impact, and photographic systems. Our color graphics section shows you both ultracheap ways of converting an ordinary tvt into a limited-performance graphics mode and into a sophisticated 96 × 96 color matrix system that includes "chess" and "pong" interchangeable software. Finally, we take a quick look at where you can go from here—what is needed now in the way of further tvt-related development in which you can play an important part.

DON LANCASTER

This book is dedicated to an amplifier with nothing to amplify.

Contents

CHAPTER 1

Some Basics

A tvt, or *tv typewriter*, is any low-cost way of displaying lots of words, numbers, or graphics on an ordinary tv set. The single most important use for a tvt is that of an input/output device for a microprocessor or microcomputer, but the concept of using a low-cost, mass-produced display to present locally generated and used information is incredibly broad. It is so broad that tvt techniques represent a totally new communications media—a decentralized media that is based on the fast and easy transfer of information rather than the difficult and energy-intensive moving of physical objects, particularly cars and people.

So, what can we do with a $30 to $150 machine that puts words and pictures on a tv set? Some of the uses we know of today include:

* Computer terminals
* Video games
* Microprocessor "super front panels"
* Video titling
* Deaf communications
* Calculator readouts
* Advertising displays
* Touch typing learning aids
* Teaching machines
* Electronic notebooks
* Remote message centers
* Cable tv response units
* Mailing list generators
* Word processing and editing systems

* Color graphics displays
* Political polling
* Ham rtty
* Phototypesetting
* News, weather, and stock displays
* Community direct-information access systems

There are several overlapping ways we can classify the different types of tvt that are available:

A *stand-alone* tvt does just that. It can interface with any source of information, with or without a microprocessor, and contains its own cursor, update, storage, and modification circuitry.

A *dedicated* tvt is usually intimately associated with a microprocessor or other devices that make the tvt a component part of a larger system. Typical dedicated applications include tvt's used as microprocessor *super front panels*, on which the tvt can display every memory location in the entire computer system on a page-at-a-time basis; word-processing applications in which extensive editing, rearranging, or format changes are needed; and "pong" and chess-style games in which move computation is needed.

A *utility* tvt usually displays 16 lines of 32 characters at a time, most often in an uppercase-only 5 × 7 dot-matrix character format. This type of tvt has very simple timing requirements, a minimum memory cost, and is cheap to build, interface, and use. Often a second *page* of memory is internally provided to increase the total display to 1024 characters on a selected basis.

A *premium* tvt can display more information and uses fancier character presentations that include lowercase and that have better character definition. These presentations can display as many as 4000 characters simultaneously, and a quarter of a million or more resolvable elements in graphic displays. Premium tvt's almost always need a modified tv set that has additional display bandwidth. They are usually associated with larger memories, faster components, higher cost, and more critical timing.

Since a television set has no internal way to store information for more than a tiny fraction of a second, a memory, often called a *refresh memory*, is needed and must somehow be associated with the tvt. A tvt with *dedicated internal memory* has its own internal storage available only for its own use.

A *shared internal memory* tvt has its own memory but makes it available to other circuits on a DMA, or *direct memory access*, basis. This is handy for games and calculator displays.

An *external memory* tvt simply borrows the information it needs from a microcomputer, microprocessor, or other system memory any time a display is needed.

An *input/output*, or i/o, tvt has ways of both accepting and re-turning information. If we have a cassette storage interface, a modem, or a hard copy (printer) associated with the tvt, or if we have the ability to retransmit the tvt screen or to sense a portion of it with a *light pen*, we have an i/o tvt.

A *read only*, or RO, tvt can only accept and display information without electronically returning any of it. Typical examples are a microprocessor memory readout and a game graphics display.

Fig. 1-1. The tvt-1 using TTL and shift-register memory.

Figs. 1-1 through 1-3 show some typical early stand-alone tvt's representing three generations of design. Sources of tvt's include *Polymorphic Systems, Processor Technology,* and *Southwest Technical Products.* Fig. 1-4 shows the typical display of a 16 × 32 utility tvt.

ORGANIZATION

The arrangement of our tvt system is very much a dynamic and changing process, owing to the recent (at this writing) dramatic cuts in memory components and microprocessor circuits. Fig. 1-5 shows one possible block diagram of a tvt.

Courtesy Southwest Technical Products Co.

Fig. 1-2. The tvt-2 system.

Courtesy Synergetics

Fig. 1-3. The tvt-3 uses CMOS and RAMs; it is 8-bit microprocessor DMA compatible.

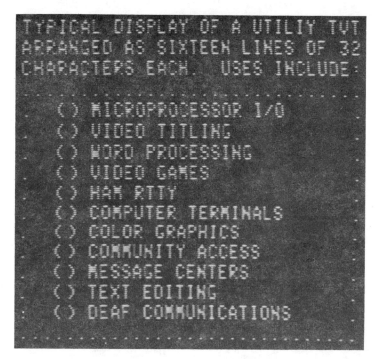

TYPICAL DISPLAY OF A UTILIY TVT
ARRANGED AS SIXTEEN LINES OF 32
CHARACTERS EACH.   USES INCLUDE:

( ) MICROPROCESSOR I/O
( ) VIDEO TITLING
( ) WORD PROCESSING
( ) VIDEO GAMES
( ) HAM RTTY
( ) COMPUTER TERMINALS
( ) COLOR GRAPHICS
( ) COMMUNITY ACCESS
( ) MESSAGE CENTERS
( ) TEXT EDITING
( ) DEAF COMMUNICATIONS

Fig. 1-4. Typical page display of utility tvt.

A memory is an essential part of a tvt. The memory has to store the characters for us, delivering them to the tv as needed to generate the desired display. As we have seen, this memory can be a dedicated internal memory, an internal memory accessible from the outside, or an external microprocessor or minicomputer memory. The memory is often arranged as 1024 words of 8 bits each, with one memory word associated with each displayed character or a close grouping of graphic display dots. The 2102-style MOS random-access memory or one of its improved offspring is often a good choice for tvt memory. We will be looking at these devices briefly in the next chapter and will take a detailed look at them in Chapter 3.

Our tvt has to have some *system timing* that converts and presents information in such a way that a television set is able to use it. The system timing is usually faster than can be handled by early microprocessors and is often done by a half dozen or so dedicated integrated circuits, which are often stock TTL or CMOS chips. System timing also provides for line locking to eliminate weaving or "seasick" displays, and optionally allows us to lock onto an existing program for titling annotation, or adding the scores to a graphic

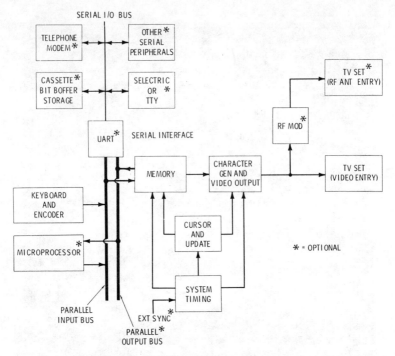

Fig. 1-5. Block diagram of typical tvt system.

game display. Chapter 4 covers many of our system timing problems and solutions.

The *character-generator and video-output* block converts the six to eight bits worth of character stored in the memory into an expanded group of dots that we see as a character on the screen. We have the options of using *direct video* that is wired into the tv set or using an *rf modulator* that gives us clip-on antenna entry to an unmodified tv. Details on these particular circuits appear in Chapters 3 and 8.

A *cursor and update* circuit takes care of adding new material to the memory and the display. The cursor itself is usually a blinking box, underline, or overline that shows the user where a new character is to go. Cursor updating can be done with a frame-rate system that takes 1/30 or 1/60 of a second to enter a single character, or with *direct memory access* (DMA) that lets us fill the entire screen in 1/60 of a second or so. Direct memory access is obviously much faster but is usually more complex and not directly compatible with the speeds associated with cassette data recorders, modems, and hard-copy devices. We have the option of building the cursor into the tvt or doing it externally under microcomputer control.

Related to the cursor circuits is an optional *screen-read* circuit through which the formatted, corrected, and otherwise edited screen display can be retransmitted or sent along to another system in *parallel* or *serial* form. This is particularly useful for assembling blocks of data for cassette recording. Chapter 5 covers cursor techniques in depth.

Normally, tvt's are set up to accept their input words in *parallel* form (all the bits at once). Parallel form is cheaper and faster, and is convenient to use with keyboards and microprocessor data buses. Details on keyboards and encoders appear in Chapter 6.

Another convenient input form is *serial* data, in which the bits march down a single line in sequential order at a specified rate. Since tvt's are basically parallel devices, they must be converted to and from serial form with a suitable *serial interface*. A special, low-cost integrated circuit called a *universal asynchronous receiver transmitter* (UART) usually does the conversion for us. This lets us input or output tvt information to a cassette data recorder, a telephone *modem*, a Teletype, a remote keyboard, or another communications channel. Chapter 7 covers these serial interface techniques in detail.

Our final concern is the tv itself. While a clip-on rf entry at the antenna of a stock set is ideal from a convenience standpoint, this approach both restricts the length of character line and needs FCC approval. The alternative is *direct video* entry, which requires set modification and can prove a problem on hot-chassis style tv sets. Chapter 8 shows what we need to know for the care and feeding of a tv set, along with the modifications we can make for direct video, extended response, and multiple color displays.

Two add-on output options for a tvt system are hard-copy (printed records) and color graphic displays. These take a slightly different type of system timing and are covered in the final chapter.

SOME TV FUNDAMENTALS

The main purpose of a tvt is to convert stored, compactly coded characters located in a memory, into a repetitive form that a tv set can understand and use.

A television set is a *raster scan* device. It puts a dot of light on its screen and moves the dot around rapidly to generate a composite picture. The dot is moved in an orderly manner called a *scan*, starting the upper left-hand corner and going rapidly to the right and slowly downward. Two types of raster scan are the *interlaced* and *noninterlaced* scans shown in Fig. 1-6.

An interlaced system is normally used with tv broadcasts. The horizontal scan rate is 15,750 Hz for black and white and 15,735 Hz for color. Two trips, or *fields,* are made down the screen for one composite *frame* or single picture. One trip starts at the upper left; the second in the upper center, overlapping or interlacing the two fields into a single frame. There are 262½ horizontal lines per field and a total of 512 lines per frame. The field rate is 60 Hz, and the frame rate is 30 Hz. This interlace system is normally used to minimize flicker and blur, particularly when associated with fast screen motions.

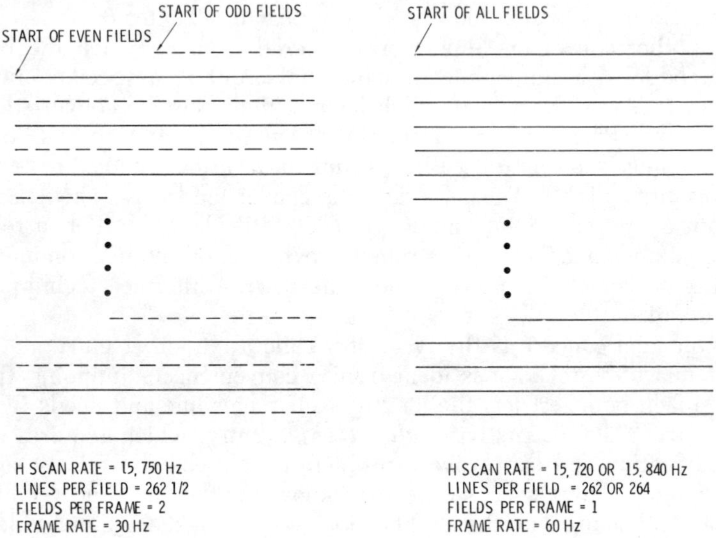

H SCAN RATE = 15, 750 Hz
LINES PER FIELD = 262 1/2
FIELDS PER FRAME = 2
FRAME RATE = 30 Hz

H SCAN RATE = 15, 720 OR 15, 840 Hz
LINES PER FIELD = 262 OR 264
FIELDS PER FRAME = 1
FRAME RATE = 60 Hz

(A) Interlaced, used in broadcasting and tvt titling.

(B) Noninterlace, used in most other tvt applications.

Fig. 1-6. Television raster scan.

Interlace is rarely needed for tvt use. The only exceptions are in video titling and other applications in which you are going to *superimpose* a message on top of an existing interlaced program. Instead of interlace, we use a noninterlaced scan as shown in Fig. 1-6B. Often we use either 262 or 264 horizontal lines per scan. We hold the frame rate (which is also the field rate) to *exactly* 60 Hz, so the horizontal scan rate changes to 15,720 Hz or 15,840 Hz. The reason the frame rate *must* be held to 60 Hz is that the poor shielding and excess hum in many television sets will cause a weaving or otherwise seasick display as a result of being slightly off frequency and slowly slipping power line cycles. Often our tvt circuitry will *lock* itself to the power line, an existing EIA-standard video program, or a crystal.

So far we have talked only about dot motions. These motions are controlled by *scanning circuits* that *deflect* the spot to a desired position. Scanning is normally continuous, but we can *synchronize* the start of each horizontal scan and the start of each frame with external *sync* signals. Normally, these horizontal- and vertical-sync signals must be locked together and must be very stable. They do *not* start and stop the scan—all they can do is shorten or lengthen existing scan motions to lock them to an input for synchronization.

The brightness of the spot is controlled by *video* circuits and *blanking* circuits. Blanking turns the spot off for the return trip on each horizontal scan and frame. Since the corners of a tvt message are just as important as the middle, and since most stock tv sets overscan badly (the scan wraps itself around the side to prevent a black bar, particularly at line-voltage extremes), it is common to use *one third to one half* the scan time for blanking in the horizontal direction. The video circuits determine *how bright* the spot is to be. In broadcasting, variable-level signals are routed to the video amplifier circuitry to provide gray levels. In most tvt's, simple on-off or white-black levels may be supplied instead, to provide dots or no dots as needed.

There is a limit to the number of dots the tv video can handle. This is called the *video bandwidth* or the video response limit. The video portion of a quality color set is some 3 MHz in bandwidth; a black-and-white set can handle 3.5 MHz. Details on where these figures come from appear in Chapter 8. The number of dots per second roughly equals twice the video bandwidth, so a color set can handle six million dots per second, and a black-and-white set can handle seven million dots per second. This sounds like a lot, but if you divide this by the horizontal scan time and allow for blanking and retrace, *the response of an ordinary tv set very much limits the line length and quality of characters you can present*. To beat this problem, you can usually modify the tv, using direct video entry and extending the video response as shown in Chapter 8. It is usually not possible to use clip-on rf entry with long line lengths for this same response-limiting reasoning.

DOT-MATRIX SCANNING

The important thing to note about television scanning is that *we cannot send the dot anywhere we like—all we can do is wait till it comes by and then use it*. This is unlike oscilloscopes and premium X-Y displays and is one of the reasons why some tv sets cost much less than some oscilloscopes. We can control only three things: (1) how bright the spot is, (2) when the spot begins the horizontal scan, and (3) when the spot begins a new frame. In fact, (2) and

(3) are further limited in that they must be locked together and cannot be changed much. So, we have to pick a means of character generation that is compatible with the television's normal scanning.

One good approach is called the *dot-matrix* system. Each character is put down as a group of dots or undots. Most tvt's use either a 35-dot character, five dots wide by seven dots high, or a 63-dot character, seven dots wide by nine dots high, with suitable extra undots between characters and character lines.

Fig. 1-7 shows how we dot-matrix scan several letters of a message. On a certain horizontal scan, we put down the top five dots or undots of the first character, skip one or more undots and then put down the top five dots or undots of the second character, and so on across the screen.

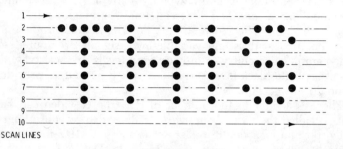

SCAN LINES

Fig. 1-7. Dot-matrix characters on a raster scan.

On the next scan, we put down the five dots or undots of the *second* row of dots in each character, until all our characters are complete. *Note that it takes eight to twelve raster lines to present a single row of characters.* Also note that we must be able to get each character back at least seven times on successive raster scans, and must be able to do this sixty times over for each second of display time.

This sure seems like a complicated setup, just to keep one tv set happy. However, it really works out rather simply as the rest of the book will show. Fortunately, we have an integrated circuit, called a *dot-matrix character generator,* that converts the characters, stored in a compact code in the memory, into the dot patterns. This circuit is easily told which portion of which character to get back at any time. The memory normally consists of a random-access memory (RAM). This type of memory is easily told to get characters back, over and over again in the proper sequence needed. As we will see later, what looks like a complex repeat timing problem is solved simply by skipping three outputs on a timing chain divider, and is almost free.

THE ASCII COMPUTER CODE

There is a standard code that all microprocessors, tv typewriters, and other computer peripherals use. This code is called ASCII, which is short for the American Standard Code for Information Interchange. This code is shown in Table 1-1.

The full ASCII code is normally used as an 8-bit word, either in parallel form by itself or in serial form with additional start and stop bits. The last of these eight bits is reserved for a *parity*, or error-testing, bit. Optionally, this last bit can be used as a cursor or a flag signal, or can be simply ignored.

That leaves us with seven bits. Seven bits can represent 2^7, or 128 different things. In ASCII, we group these 2^7 possible codes into

Table 1-1. The Standard ASCII Code Generated by Most Keyboards

b_7	b_6	b_5	b_4	b_3	b_2	b_1	COLUMN → / ROW ↓	0	1	2	3	4	5	6	7
								0	0	0	0	1	1	1	1
								0	0	1	1	0	0	1	1
								0	1	0	1	0	1	0	1
		0	0	0	0		0	NUL	DLE	SP	0	@	P	`	p
		0	0	0	1		1	SOH	DC1	!	1	A	Q	a	q
		0	0	1	0		2	STX	DC2	"	2	B	R	b	r
		0	0	1	1		3	ETX	DC3	#	3	C	S	c	s
		0	1	0	0		4	EOT	DC4	$	4	D	T	d	t
		0	1	0	1		5	ENQ	NAK	%	5	E	U	e	u
		0	1	1	0		6	ACK	SYN	&	6	F	V	f	v
		0	1	1	1		7	BEL	ETB	'	7	G	W	g	w
		1	0	0	0		8	BS	CAN	(	8	H	X	h	x
		1	0	0	1		9	HT	EM	)	9	I	Y	i	y
		1	0	1	0		10	LF	SUB	*	:	J	Z	j	z
		1	0	1	1		11	VT	ESC	+	;	K	[	k	{
		1	1	0	0		12	FF	FS	,	<	L	\	l	¦
		1	1	0	1		13	CR	GS	–	=	M	]	m	}
		1	1	1	0		14	SO	RS	.	>	N	^	n	~
		1	1	1	1		15	SI	US	/	?	O	–	o	DEL

four groups of 32 characters each. Depending on our system complexity, we may or may not use all four of these 32-character groups.

The two groups in the middle of the table make up the upper-case alphabet, the numbers, and some frequently used punctuation. These two groups are sometimes called an ASCII-6 *subset*. They take only six bits to represent their $2^6 = 64$ different characters. For instance, an ASCII uppercase *H* is coded 00-1000. This is read with the least significant bit (or bit number 1) on the right and the most significant bit (or bit number 6) on the left.

NUL	NULL	**DLE**	DATA LINK ESCAPE
SOH	START OF HEADING	**DC1**	DIRECT CONTROL 1
STX	START TEXT	**DC2**	DIRECT CONTROL 2
ETX	END TEXT	**DC3**	DIRECT CONTROL 3
EOT	END OF TRANSMISSION	**DC4**	DIRECT CONTROL 4
ENQ	ENQUIRY	**NAK**	NEGATIVE ACKNOWLEDGE
ACK	ACKNOWLEDGE	**SYN**	SYNCHRONOUS IDLE
BEL	BELL	**ETB**	END TRANSMISSION BLOCK
BS	BACKSPACE	**CAN**	CANCEL
HT	HORIZONTAL TAB	**EM**	END OF MEDIUM
LF	LINE FEED	**SUB**	SUBSTITUTE
VT	VERTICAL TAB	**ESC**	ESCAPE
FF	FORM FEED	**FS**	FORM SEPARATOR
CR	CARRIAGE RETURN	**GS**	GROUP SEPARATOR
SO	SHIFT OUT	**RS**	RECORD SEPARATOR
SI	SHIFT IN	**US**	UNIT SEPARATOR

Fig. 1-8. ASCII machine commands.

There are several interesting things to note about this ASCII-6 subset. One is that the all zeros 00-0000 code is an "@." When we want a blank or space, either we use the ASCII 10-0000 space code or we disable or blank something between the code and its ultimate output. The second thing to note is that the four least significant bits of the numbers are the same in ASCII, in binary, and in binary-coded decimal (bcd). Thus, to get from a "6" in binary, or a bcd 0110, we simply "hard wire" two additional ones in front, giving us an ASCII "6," or 11-0110. Note that we need only six bits for the ASCII-6 subset. If we use seven bits instead, the seventh bit is simply the *complement* of bit six, being a one when six is a zero and vice versa.

The first 32 code groups in ASCII are called *machine commands* or *control functions*. These are always identified by both bits six and seven being zeros. Machine commands are not usually intended to appear in print or on a screen. Instead, they provide control functions of the support circuitry at either end. These control functions are identified in Fig. 1-8. Typical examples are a carriage return (CR); a backspace (BS); a bell (BEL); an escape (ESC) command that breaks us out of ASCII; and available, but unspecified, direct control lines DC1, DC2, DC3, and DC4.

Generally, tvt's use only a few control functions, so we have the option of choosing how many machine commands we are going to recognize in our system. These options can range from calling *any* machine command a carriage return, through decoding a few needed commands, on up to a complete decoding of all the possible commands. Chapter 5 takes a closer look at these options.

Our final 32 characters are the lowercase alphabet and some infrequently used punctuaion. These are identified by bits six and seven both being a one. These lowercase characters can be used only in a system that has the capability to display lowercase. Note that lowercase characters do not automatically get read as uppercase equivalents if we simply ignore the seventh bit. A simple, logical code change involving bits 6 and 7 (Fig. 6-7) *must* be made if the full ASCII code is input to an uppercase-only output device.

BAUDOT AND SELECTRIC CODES

There are two lesser used and specialized codes that sometimes crop up in tvt use. While they are not directly equivalent to ASCII, it is possible to convert them to and from ASCII, with some add-on "repairs" and definitions.

The first of these is the 5-bit *Baudot* code of Table 1-2. Baudot is an obsolete code used with early Teletype machines. It still sees some use in ham rtty and deaf communications systems.

There are only 32 possible code combinations. To get more characters, there are two *shift* commands—a *letters* shift and a *figures* shift. These almost double the number of available characters, but you have to keep track of what the past history of the code was. You have to shift to letters for letters and figures for figures. Baudot is further complicated by the punctuation symbols, which differ, depending on whether the machine was originally used by the military, the weather service, telex, twx, or stock quotation services. More

Table 1-2. Baudot Code

5	4	3	2	1	Letters	Figures	5	4	3	2	1	Letters	Figures*
0	0	0	0	0	Blank	Blank	1	0	0	0	0	T	5
0	0	0	0	1	E	3	1	0	0	0	1	Z	"
0	0	0	1	0	Linefeed	Linefeed	1	0	0	1	0	L	)
0	0	0	1	1	A	—	1	0	0	1	1	W	2
0	0	1	0	0	Space	Space	1	0	1	0	0	H	#
0	0	1	0	1	S	Bell	1	0	1	0	1	Y	6
0	0	1	1	0	I	8	1	0	1	1	0	P	Ø
0	0	1	1	1	U	7	1	0	1	1	1	Q	1
0	1	0	0	0	Car. Ret.	Car. Ret.	1	1	0	0	0	O	9
0	1	0	0	1	D	$	1	1	0	0	1	B	?
0	1	0	1	0	R	4	1	1	0	1	0	G	&
0	1	0	1	1	J	'	1	1	0	1	1	Figures	Figures
0	1	1	0	0	N	,	1	1	1	0	0	M	.
0	1	1	0	1	F	!	1	1	1	0	1	X	/
0	1	1	1	0	C	:	1	1	1	1	0	V	;
0	1	1	1	1	K	(	1	1	1	1	1	Letters	Letters

* "Figures" punctuation may vary, depending on original use of machine.

Table 1-3. Selectric Code

R5 →				0	0	0	0	1	1	1	1
T1 →				0	0	1	1	0	0	1	1
T2 →				0	1	0	1	0	1	0	1
S	R2A	R2	R1								
0	0	0	0	−	b	w	9				
0	0	0	1	y	h	s	φ	/	l	o	4
0	0	1	0								
0	0	1	1								
0	1	0	0	q	k	i	6	,	c	a	8
0	1	0	1	p	e	'	5	;	d	r	7
0	1	1	0	=	n	.	2	f	u	v	3
0	1	1	1	j	t	½ !	z	g	x	m	1
1	0	0	0	_	B	W	(				
1	0	0	1	Y	H	S	)	?	L	O	$
1	0	1	0								
1	0	1	1								
1	1	0	0	Q	K	I	¢	,	C	A	*
1	1	0	1	P	E	"	%	:	D	R	&
1	1	1	0	+	N	.	@	F	U	V	#
1	1	1	1	J	T	¼ °	Z	G	X	M	‡ [

lowercase (rows 0···)

UPPERCASE (rows 1···)

 = REDUNDANT OR NOT USED

details on this code and its conversion to and from ASCII appear in the last chapter.

The Selectric code of Table 1-3 is associated with the Selectric office typewriters and the Selectric computer i/o machines, and is important whenever you are adapting an office typewriter for tvt hard copy, following the guidelines of Chapters 3 and 9. There are seven bits to this code, but not all possible code combinations are used. One of these bits is called a *shift* bit. It gives us the ability to handle uppercase or lowercase information, usually with a 180° rotation of the typing ball. The remaining bits in the code are named after their effect on ball positioning and are coded by the Selectric code bails. These are called Rotate 1, 2, 2A, 5, and Tilt 1 and 2.

Unlike ASCII, machine commands are external to this code. They include space, return, backspace, tab, bell, and index. Note that space is treated as a character in ASCII and as a machine command in Selectric.

SOME TERMS

Let's now take a quick look at some of the concepts, terms, and acronyms that are associated with tvt systems:

address—A particular *location* in a memory.

ASCII—An acronym for American Standard Code for Information Interchange. Standard code used in tvt's, microcomputers, and peripheral devices. See Table 1-1.

ASR33—Automatic Send-Receive Computer Teletype. See Chapter 9.

asynchronous—A form of serial data transmission in which the spacing between words can be random and unpredictable. Asynchronous transmission is commonly used with tvt interfaces. Start and stop bits must be added to a character before transmission. See Chapter 7.

baud rate—The speed at which 1's and 0's are sent through a serial interface. Common baud rates are 110, 150, 300, 600, and 1200 bits per second.

Baudot—An obsolete 5-bit Teletype code. See Table 1-2 and Chapter 9.

bit position error—A displacement of a received data bit, in which the data bit is ahead of or behind where it is expected to be. Often caused by group delay distortion in modem channels.

bit rate error—A received data bit stream that is faster or slower than it is expected to be. Often caused by speed variations in cassette recorders.

blanking—Making a display black by turning off the video. Used during retrace and to format data.

bounceless contact—A mechanical contact that has been conditioned with a flip-flop or monostable to eliminate all contact noise during make and break.

bus organization—A system sharing a common set of communications lines among several devices. In a *unidirectional bus system,* signals from one or more sources, *activated one at a time,* drive a common load or loads. Addressing a tvt memory internally, from a cursor or from an external microcomputer, is one example. A *bidirectional bus system* lets signals go either way on the bus, again activated only one at a time. Most microprocessor data buses are bidirectional.

character generator—A circuit that converts characters stored in ASCII into dot patterns suitable for tvt display.

class-1 tv device—Legal classification of clip-on rf entry modulators. See Chapter 8.

CMOS—An acronym for Complementary Metal-Oxide Semiconductor. A micropower logic family that is widely available and low in cost.

code converter—A read-only memory or other system set up to convert one code to another. Typical examples are ASCII/Selectric, Baudot/ASCII, and ASCII/ Baudot conversions.

color subcarrier—A 3.58-MHz signal added to the composite video whose phase sets the received color and whose amplitude sets the color saturation.

cursor—A circuit used to keep track of which character is entered next in a tvt and to display that character location. Typical cursors include the *count and compare,* the *McFadden,* and *microprocessor-based systems.*

data—The information that is to be displayed on a tvt.

DMA (direct memory access)—Any system for rapidly changing the contents of a memory by means of an external set of control signals.

direct video—Presenting information to a tv set by entering it into the video circuitry, usually by way of an added jack and changeover switch.

dot matrix—A method of generating characters by converting the ASCII code into a suitable group of dots arranged in a 5×7, 7×9, or other suitable patterned array.

encoder—A circuit used to convert the single switch closures of a keyboard into a composite ASCII or other code.

EPROM—A read-only memory that can be both programmed and erased in the field. Bulk erasure is often done with strong ultraviolet light.

full duplex—Operating a communications channel in both directions at the same time without interference.

graphics—Using a tvt to display lines, patterns, art forms, and symbols, rather than its standard alphanumeric letters and numbers mode. Both modes can be combined.

group delay distortion—A hard-to-eliminate filter property that speeds up or slows down 1's with respect to 0's in a communications channel. A key design problem in modems.

half duplex—Taking turns operating a communications channel in one direction at a time.

handshaking—A communications interface in which the receiver asks for a signal, accepts it, and then acknowledges it. Handshaking prevents ignored and overrun signalling between devices.

hard copy—Any reasonably permanent form of printed data or other record.

hardware—The physical circuitry of a tvt or microcomputer.

hot chassis—A television set that has its chassis connected to one side of the power line, thus creating a safety hazard. See Chapter 8.

interface—A circuit used to get between two systems having different requirements. Serial interface is often used to communicate with cassette systems, modems, and Teletypes.

i/o—Input/output.

k—Symbol for 1024 bits. A 4k memory has 4096 bits.

keyboard—Standard method of manual data entry into a tvt. See Chapter 6.

mark—A digital logic 1 or a shorted transmission line.

memory—Circuits capable of remembering data or sequential operating procedures.

microprocessor—A "computer-on-a-chip" integrated circuit usually set up to move information from inputs, into and out of related memory circuits, and then to feed it into one or more *peripheral* devices, usually following a specified sequence or program.

microprogramming—Any "hard-wired" way of carrying out a sequential routine on a computer, microcomputer, or microprocessor. The alternative is software programming in which stored but changeable instructions are used.

modem—Acronym for *mo*dulator-*dem*odulator. A means of getting data onto and back from a telephone line or other communications channel.

MOS—*M*etal-*O*xide *S*emiconductor. A family of integrated circuits and their technology that lends itself well to tvt and microcomputer uses. They are normally used in larger subsystems called LSI, or large-scale integration, and have very high input impedances and medium speeds.

page—A full screen of tvt information.

parallel—An arrangement of data or addresses in which all the bits are simultaneously available on multiple lines.

parity—An error-testing technique. An extra bit called a parity bit is added to a word. The parity bit makes each of the 1's in the word an even number. After transmission and reception, parity can be tested. An error has happened if the 1's are now odd. Alternatively, a system can be set up for odd parity with the same results. Simple parity can indicate but not repair errors.

peripheral device—A device that attaches to a computer or microprocessor, letting it perform useful tasks. Typical examples are tvt's, hard-copy printers, modems, cassette storage, etc.

phase-locked loop—A circuit that locks some system timing to an externally provided reference. Used in tvt's to lock system timing to the power line for a stable display or to an existing video program for titling and annotation.

programming—Defining the operating sequences that a computer or microprocessor is to follow.

PROM—Acronym for *P*rogrammable *R*ead-*O*nly *M*emory. An integrated circuit that can have its internal memory patterns changed in the field but is otherwise nonvolatile. See Chapter 3.

RAM—Acronym for *R*andom-*A*ccess *M*emory. An integrated circuit that can have its internal memory patterns rapidly changed at system speeds in any sequence. Normally volatile. See Chapter 3.

raster—The repetitive sequence of scan lines on a television set. See Fig. 1-6.

read—To interrogate the contents of a memory without changing the contents, or to provide an output *from* memory or another source.

refresh—To make information available over and over again as needed to meet the timing needs of a dynamic memory or a tv raster scan display.

rf entry—Presenting information to a tv set by entering it into the tuner via the antenna terminals, usually by way of a class-1 tv device.

rollover—A keyboard encoding technique that minimizes errors. Two-key rollover allows any two keys to be down at once without error. N-key roll-over allows any number of keys to be down at once without error but is complex and has system limitatitons. See Chapter 6.

RS232C—A very old EIA interface standard that is commonly used by peripheral devices on larger computer systems. See Chapter 7.

screen read—An optional tvt circuit that allows the displayed message to be retransmitted to a microcomputer or peripheral device. Used to format data for cassette storage and to edit programs.

Selectric—IBM office typewriter or computer input/output device using the Selectric code of Fig. 1-9.

serial—An arrangement of data or characters in which the bits are made sequentially available on a single line.

sidetone—"Hear yourself" feedback common in phone systems. A serious problem in modern design. See Chapter 7.

software—The programming, documentation, and specified paper sequences of operation that allow a computer or microcomputer system to work.

space—A digital logic 0 or an open transmission line.

speed tolerant—A type of cassette recording system that allows changes in recorder speed from machine to machine or from time to time as batteries age or as line voltages change, and that does so without introducing errors.

start bit—A signal bit, usually a 0, that precedes a word to be sent in an asynchronous data system.

stop bit—One or more signal bits, usually a 1, that follow a word just sent in an asynchronous data system.

sync—The vertical and horizontal synchronizing pulses that tell a tv display when to start each horizontal line and each frame.

synchronous—A form of serial data transmission in which the spacing between words is locked to system timing and a constant. Not commonly used in tvt work.

system timing—The TTL or CMOS integrated circuitry that converts characters stored in a memory into a repetitive form that a tv set can use.

TTL—Acronym for transistor-transistor logic. A fast digital-logic family that is widely available and low in cost. See the *TTL Cookbook,* also by this author and published by Howard W. Sams & Co., Inc.

tvt—Abbreviation for a tv typewriter. Any low-cost way of displaying lots of words, numbers, or graphics on an ordinary tv set.

UART—Acronym for *U*niversal *A*synchronous *R*eceiver *T*ransmitter. An integrated circuit used to convert data from parallel to serial form and back again. Covered in detail in Chapter 7.

update—To change part or all of the message displayed on a tvt. A frame-rate update usually adds or drops one character per frame. A DMA update usually changes the entire screen in one frame time.

video—The brightness and color information fed to a television set.

video bandwidth—The maximum number of dots per second that a television set can display. The video bandwidth for an unmodified color tv is 3 MHz, while the bandwidth of an unmodified black-and-white tv is 3.5 MHz. These correspond to 6 and 7 million dots per second, respectively. See Chapter 8.

word—A grouping of bits representing a character or command. Most tvt systems use words of six to eight bits.

write—To place information into a memory, changing the memory contents. To provide an input from another source *to* memory.

CHAPTER 2

Integrated Circuits for TVT Use

In this chapter, we will take a detailed look at some representative samples of integrated circuits suitable for tvt uses. The seven basic types of circuits that we will be looking at are *baud-rate generators, character generators, keyboard encoders, line drivers and receivers, programmable read-only memories, random-access memories,* and *serial interface UARTs.*

Besides these devices, there are other types of integrated circuits that you will often be using in tvt circuits. A general-purpose digital logic family such as TTL or CMOS is almost essential for system timing and to "glue" the rest of the works together. CMOS is often the best choice for new designs.

Dedicated integrated circuits are also available that are intended to work within a specific microprocessor family. Often these are simply modifications of the ICs we will be looking at in this chapter. More details on these specialized circuits are available from their respective manufacturers.

Sources for the circuits in this chapter and alternates to them appear in Chart 2-1. Always be sure to have manufacturers' data sheets on hand whenever you are testing or using these devices.

BAUD-RATE GENERATORS

Baud-rate generators are used to provide the reference frequencies needed by serial interface devices, such as UARTs, telephone modems, Teletypes, and cassettes. They have the advantages of adjustment-free crystal stability and multiple output frequencies that are easily changed.

Chart 2-1. Some Integrated Circuit Manufacturers

Advanced Micro Devices
901 Thompson Place
Sunnyvale, CA 94086

American Microsystems, Inc.
3800 Homestead Road
Santa Clara, CA 95051

Cal-Tex Semiconductor
3090 Alfred Street
Santa Clara, CA 95950

Cermetek, Inc.
660 National Avenue
Mountain View, CA 94040

Electronic Arrays, Inc.
550 East Middlefield Road
Mountain View, CA 94043

Exar Integrated Systems, Inc.
750 Palomar Avenue
Sunnyvale, CA 94086

Fairchild Semiconductor
464 Ellis Street
Mountain View, CA 94040

General Instrument Corporation
600 West John Street
Hicksville, NY 11802

Harris Semiconductor
Box 883
Melbourne, FL 32901

Intel Corporation
3065 Bowers Avenue
Santa Clara, CA 95051

Intersil, Inc.
10900 North Tantau Avenue
Cupertino, CA 95014

Monolithic Memories, Inc.
1165 East Arques Avenue
Sunnyvale, CA 94086

MOS Technology, Inc.
950 Rittenhouse Road
Norristown, PA 19401

Mostek Corporation
1215 West Crosby Road
Carrollton, TX 75006

Motorola Semiconductor
  Products, Inc.
Box 20912
Phoenix, AZ 85036

National Semiconductor
2900 Semiconductor Drive
Santa Clara, CA 95051

Nitron Corporation
10420 Bubb Road
Cupertino, CA 95014

RCA Solid State Division
Somerville, NJ 08876

Rockwell International
  Microelectronic Device Div.
3310 Miraloma Avenue
Anaheim, CA 92803

Signetics
811 East Arques Avenue
Sunnyvale, CA 94086

SMC Microsystems
35 Marcus Boulevard
Hauppauge, NY 11787

Synertek
3050 Coronado Drive
Santa Clara, CA 95051

Texas Instruments
Box 5012
Dallas, TX 75222

Western Digital Corporation
3128 Red Hill Avenue
Newport Beach, CA 92663

The 5016 is a Standard Microsystems product in an 18-pin package that produces a selected pair of standard 16× reference frequencies. The 14411, made by Motorola, comes in a 24-pin package. It simultaneously produces 16 different reference frequencies, available as 1×, 8×, 16×, or 64×.

CHARACTER GENERATORS

Character generators convert a stored ASCII character and some timing commands into a group of dots suitable for raster scan tv display.

The 2513 is a utility 5 × 7, 64-character device by Signetics and General Instruments. The GI device needs only a single +5-V supply but may not be compatible with a CMOS video output shift register working on a higher supply voltage or on a split +5-V, −5-V supply. The 5004 is a Standard Microsystems product. It works on a single +5-V supply and has internal storage and output registers. It provides a premium 7 × 9 dot matrix of uppercase and lowercase characters. The 6072 is a very fast, single-supply 7 × 9 matrix of 128 characters offered by Monolithic Memories.

KEYBOARD ENCODERS

Keyboard encoders convert single-contact closures of a keyswitch into a composite, debounced, and properly shifted ASCII code. Output is usually in parallel form with parity.

The 2376 is an 88-key encoder with two-key rollover and a choice of uppercase only or uppercase plus lowercase output. The 3600 is a 90-key encoder that allows true n-key rollover, provided diodes are added to each keyswitch. Both devices are available from General Instruments and Standard Microsystems.

LINE DRIVERS AND RECEIVERS

Line drivers and receivers are used to "amplify" 1's and 0's so that lots of loads can be driven and so that wiring capacitance and cable runs do not adversely slow down system speeds. They are also used to send signals long distances over wired serial interfaces.

There are many of these devices available. The major manufacturers include Advanced Micro Devices, Fairchild, National, Texas Instruments, Motorola, and Signetics.

The 26S10 is a quad bidirectional bus transceiver user for two-way microprocessor interface by Advanced Micro Devices. Similar devices are the Motorola 3443 and the Texas Instruments 75138, while the National 8838 does the same thing with a different pinout.

The 1488 and 1489 are an older pair of devices for RS232-C interfacing. The 1488 is a quad-line driver, while the 1489 is a quad-line receiver. Suppliers include Advanced Micro Devices, Motorola, and Texas Instruments.

The 75107 and 75109 are dual receivers and transmitters for differential data transmission over long distances. Suppliers include AMD and TI.

PROGRAMMABLE READ-ONLY MEMORIES

Programmable ROMs are used for storing microprocessor programs, for code conversions, and for customized, "you-program-it," nonvolatile logic arrays.

The 1702 is a 2048-bit MOS programmable read-only memory organized as 256 eight-bit words. It can be electrically bulk-erased by placing it under intense ultraviolet light. Sources include Intel and Advanced Micro Devices. A similar device is the National 5202.

The 5600 is an Intersil bipolar programmable read-only memory arranged as 32 eight-bit words and having a 50-ns access time. Similar devices include the National 5330, the Texas Instruments 74188, and the Harris 8256.

RANDOM-ACCESS MEMORIES

We use random-access memories, or RAMs, for character storage in tvt's and for microprocessor data storage. Static 1024-bit devices are often the best choice for these applications.

The 2101 is arranged as 256 four-bit words and is in a 22-pin package. It has separate input and output leads. It is made by Intel, Advanced Micro Devices, and Synertek. The Texas Instruments 4039 is a similar device.

The 2102 is arranged as 1024 one-bit words and is in a 16-pin package with separate input and output leads. Sources include Intel, Advanced Micro Devices, Fairchild, and Synertek. It is also known as the Intersil 7552, the Signetics 2602, and the Texas Instruments 4033.

The 2111 is arranged as 256 four-bit words and is in an 18-lead package. It has common input/output leads and an output disable. Sources include Intel, American Micro Devices, and Synertek, along with the Texas Instruments 4042.

The 2112 is similar to the 2111 except that it is in a 16-pin package and has no output disable. Sources are similar to the 2111 except that the Texas Instruments part number is 4033 and it is also offered by Signetics as a 2602.

The Intel 5101 is a premium micropower 2101 using CMOS technology. It is useful for nonvolatile memory systems using standby battery-power backup.

SERIAL INTERFACE UARTS

A UART, or *universal asynchronous receiver transmitter,* is used for serial-to-parallel and back again conversion to interface a serial-operating device, such as a Teletype, a cassette storage system, or a modem, with the parallel input/output lines of a tvt or a microcomputer.

The 1013 is a general instruments device. It is also available as a 1014 working off a single 5-V supply. Other similar devices include the American Microsystems S1883, the Signetics 2536, the Standard Microsystems 2502, the Texas Instruments 6012, and the Western Digital 1602.

5016
BAUD-RATE GENERATOR

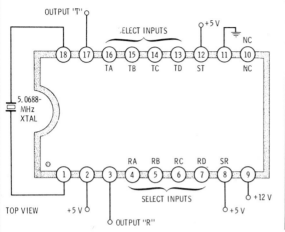

SELECT PROGRAMMING	
D C B A	BAUD RATE
0 0 0 0	50
0 0 0 1	75
0 0 1 0	110
0 0 1 1	134.5
0 1 0 0	150
0 1 0 1	300
0 1 1 0	600
0 1 1 1	1200
1 0 0 0	1800
1 0 0 1	2000
1 0 1 0	2400
1 0 1 1	3600
1 1 0 0	4800
1 1 0 1	7200
1 1 1 0	9600
1 1 1 1	19,200
ALL OUTPUTS ARE 16X BAUD RATE	

This integrated circuit simultaneously generates two reference frequencies useful in tvt, serial interface, and microprocessor applications. The two selected frequencies may be rapidly changed either by manual control or under software control.

In normal operation, pins 2, 8, and 12 are made +5 V, and +12 V is applied to pin 9. A 5.0688-MHz crystal is connected as shown. Output frequencies are selected by the A, B, C, and D inputs following the chart at the right. A 0 is a grounded input; a 1 is +5 V. Each output can drive two TTL loads or any number of CMOS loads.

The transmitter side of a serial interface is normally associated with the higher or T pins, while the receiver side uses the lower or R pins. This choice is arbitrary.

Select inputs need not be applied continuously if a latched mode is used. To latch, bring pins 8 and 12 low. Apply the A,B,C,D code and briefly bring pin 8 or 12 high, returning it to ground after selection. The chip will now hold the selected code. Pin 8 low holds the T selection; pin 8 high follows the T selection. Pin 12 does the same for the R selection.

All outputs are symmetrical 50-50 duty cycle except for 9600, which is 48-52. *All outputs are sixteen times the baud rate.* Slight frequency errors exist on the 134.5, 2000, and 19,200 baud-rate outputs; these are rarely used.

Supply current is 10 mA from the +12-V supply and 28-mA from the +5-V supply.

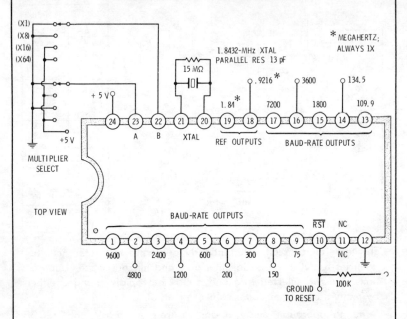

14411
BAUD-RATE GENERATOR

This integrated circuit simultaneously generates 16 reference frequencies useful in tvt, serial interface, and microprocessor applications.

In normal operation, pins 10 and 24 are made +5 V. Pins 22 and 23 are programmed as shown, to output frequencies that are 1X, 8X, 16X, or 64X those shown on pins 1 through 9 and 13 through 17. Each of these outputs can drive one TTL load or any number of CMOS loads.

Frequency is set by the parallel-resonant 1.8432-MHz crystal and bias resistor on pins 20 and 21. The crystal frequency appears as an output on pin 19, and half that frequency appears at pin 18, independent of the multiplier settings. These outputs are useful for microprocessor clocks, both single and two-phase.

All outputs may be reset to zero by bringing pin 10 low. In normal operation, pin 10 must be held high.

Typical supply current is 2 mA plus one additional milliampere for each output connected to a TTL load.

All outputs are symmetrical with a 50-50 duty cycle.

CHARACTER GENERATOR
(5 X 7, Row Scan, Uppercase Only)

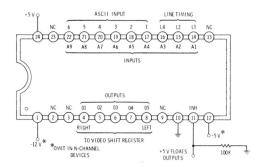

This circuit provides the dot-matrix patterns needed for raster scan display of ASCII characters. It uses a 5 × 7 matrix of uppercase-only characters and is a *row scan device* intended for normal tv use.

In normal operation, supply power is applied as shown and pin 11 is allowed to be at ground. The ASCII code is input to pins 17 through 22. Line timing is applied to pins 14 through 16. A 000 on these lines selects all blank outputs. A 001 on these lines puts out the dots for the first, or *top,* row of the character. A 010 puts out the second from the top row of dots, continuing to a 111 output that puts out the bottom, or seventh, row of dots.

The output is routed to a video shift register, arranged so that the left-most dot, 05, goes nearest the serial *output* of the shift register.

The N-channel versions of this device need no −5-V or −12-V supplies but are unable to accept or provide outputs that swing below ground.

Access time is 400 ns after all address inputs are stable.

Placing +5 V on pin 11 floats the output. This produces a white or 1 output when connected to TTL. It produces a white or 1 output when connected to CMOS with pull-up resistors, and produces a black or 0 output when connected to CMOS with pull-down resistors.

Operating current is 25 mA for a 5-V device and 12 mA from each supply for the +5-V, −12-V devices.

Note that loading of the output character must be delayed from the input address changes by at least the access time. Chapters 3 and 4 have more-detailed information on using character generators.

CHARACTER GENERATOR
(7 X 9, Row Scan, Choice of Case, Serial Output)

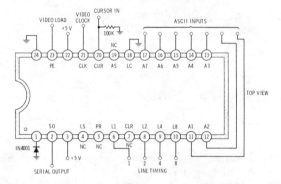

This is a premium dot matrix, row-scan character generator. It has its own internal shift register and directly produces output serial video.

In normal operation, a video clock that sets the dot rate is input to pin 21. A normally low video load command is input to pin 23, which briefly goes high whenever you want to transfer a new set of dots to the output register. The video clock should be eight times the frequency of the video load for one undot between characters, nine times for two undots, and ten times for three undots.

Line timing is applied weighted 1, 2, 4, 8 as shown, and the ASCII code is input on the A1 through A7 lines. Serial video, ready for sync combination, appears as an output on pin 2.

There are many use options. The line timing may be strobed into the chip by grounding pin 4 during the hold times. The ASCII character may be strobed into the chip by grounding pin 19. Lowercase may be inhibited by making pin 18 positive. A positive input to pin 20 replaces the character with a cursor box.

Access time is typically 750 ns. Power-supply current is 75 mA.

Note the unusual supply connections, particularly the ground on pin 24. Pin 1 controls an internal charge pump to bias the substrate at −0.6 V.

Pin 5 will force the output high. Pin 7 will force the output low. Pins 5 and 7 high together will float the output. This can simplify video combination.

CHARACTER GENERATOR
(7 X 9, Row Scan, Uppercase and Lowercase

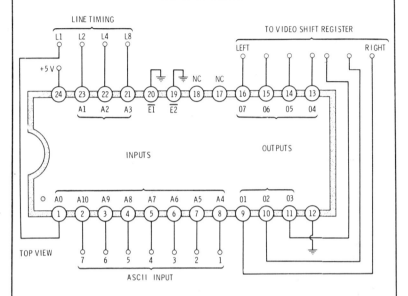

This is a premium device that provides the dot-matrix patterns needed for raster scan display of ASCII characters. It uses a 7 × 9 matrix of uppercase and lowercase characters and is a *row scan device* intended for normal tv use.

For normal operation, the ASCII code is routed to pins 2 through 8, and line timing signals weighted 1, 2, 4, 8 are routed to pins 1, 23, 22, and 21. Pins 20 and 19 are grounded, and supply power is applied to pin 24. The line timing selects which line of character dots is to be output.

The output dot combinations appear on pins 9, 10, 11, 13, 14, 15, and 16 in the order noted. They are routed to a video-output shift register for serial conversion.

This is a bipolar device and has a 175-ns access time. Current is 90 mA from the single +5-V supply.

KEYBOARD ENCODER, 2KRO

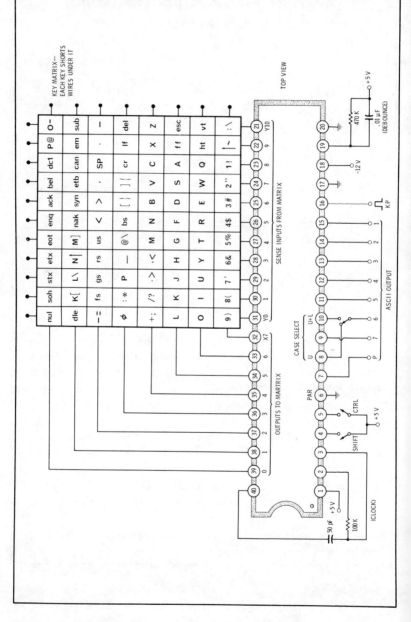

This is a scanning keyboard encoder that samples 88 keys and provides a parallel ASCII output with parity. Two-key rollover is inherent in the circuit.

For normal operation, $+5$-V and -12-V supplies are provided as shown. The left network sets the clock to a 50-kHz frequency. The right network sets the debounce time to approximately 8 ms.

Keys are continuously scanned till a closed key routes a matrix output to a sense input. At that time, the scanning stops and the ASCII code, modified by the SHIFT and CTRL keys, is output.

Uppercase-only or uppercase plus lowercase coding may be selected as shown. The output code can be inverted by making pin 20 positive. The parity sense can be changed by making pin 6 positive.

Note that a random and constantly changing output code is provided between key closures. Only when a key is pressed does a stable output result. Circuits downstream from the encoder must ignore the output code between valid keypressed times.

Note further that a shorted key or a short on the key matrix will stop scanning and make the chip look defective. If pin 16 is positive, the chip thinks a key is pressed and will output the code for that key.

A space during clear output can be obtained by shorting X2 to Y8 during the clearing time. This clear should be latched or otherwise held as long as needed to guarantee system clearing.

Typical power-supply current is 5 mA from each supply. Each output will drive one TTL load.

3600

KEYBOARD ENCODER, NKRO

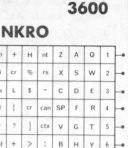
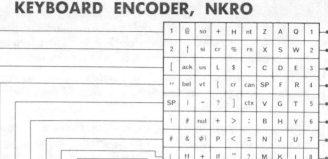

This is a scanning keyboard encoder with latch that samples 90 keys and provides a parallel ASCII output with parity. N-key rollover is possible if diodes are added to each key.

The left network sets the clock to 50 kHz. The capacitor on pin 31 sets the debounce time to about 8 ms. Every time a key is *first* pressed, it changes the output to its ASCII code as modified by the SHIFT and CTRL keys.

Scanning is continuous, and the output latches store the last key pressed at all times. Uppercase only or lowercase plus uppercase can be selected as shown. Two-key rollover is provided unless diodes are added to the keys. With diodes, n-key rollover results.

Pin 4 is an optional, "any key down" output.

A space during clear output can be obtained by shorting X3 to Y3. The space output will be held till any new key is pressed.

Typical power-supply current is 8 mA from each supply. Each output will drive one TTL load.

26S10
QUAD BIDIRECTIONAL BUS TRANSCEIVER

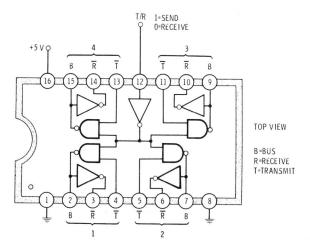

T/R   1=SEND
O   0=RECEIVE

TOP VIEW

B =BUS
R =RECEIVE
T =TRANSMIT

The 26S10 contains four transceiver circuits that let you get data on to or off of a bidirectional data bus. The circuit has a very high bus drive capability and provides good noise immunity.

To send, make the T/R input on pin 12 high. Data input on any T input will be inverted and will drive the respective bus output. This data will also appear noninverted at the $\overline{R}$ output.

To receive, make the T/R input on pin 12 low. Data input will be ignored, and the state of the bus, driven from another source, will appear on the $\overline{R}$ output. Note that both the transmitted and received data are inverted by this circuit.

Input current to the T/R or any T input is 0.5 mA and is CMOS or TTL compatible. Output drive current from a $\overline{R}$ output is 20 mA in the low state and 1 mA in the high state. This output can drive at least 10 TTL loads or any number of CMOS loads.

The bus output can source or sink up to 200 mA, and terminating resistors on the bus can be as low as 100 ohms. Receiver switching takes place at 2 V.

Power-supply current is 45 mA from a +5-V supply. All switching times are under 15 ns.

On any bus system, be certain to enable only one transmitter at a time. Note that signals are inverted going on to and off of the bus. Both package grounds must be used.

QUAD RS232 DRIVER

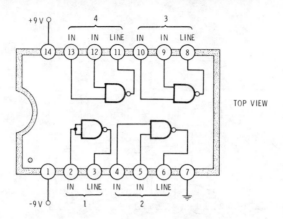

This package converts input TTL logic levels into bipolar voltages suitable for driving an RS232-C interface. There are four separate drivers. One has a single input. The others have dual NAND inputs.

A digital logic 0 at the input is inverted to a 1 and converted to a +9-V line voltage. A digital logic 1 at the input is inverted to a 0 and converted to a −9-V line voltage.

The inputs are TTL compatible and need 1.6 mA of input current in the low state. CMOS logic having this much output sinking current may also be used.

A capacitor of not less than 330 pF must be placed on each output to limit the slew rate to values within the RS232 spec.

Series power diodes on both supply lines are recommended for fail-safe operation.

Power-supply current from each supply is 20 mA.

QUAD RS232 RECEIVER

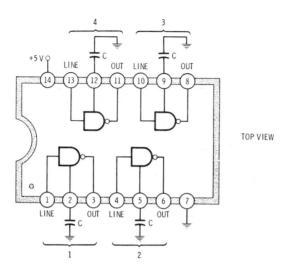

This package converts four separate bipolar RS232-C input logic swings into TTL logic levels. Each of the four separate receivers inverts its logic sense.

On any single receiver, a negative input voltage greater than −3 V will be read as a logic 1. A positive input voltage greater than +3 V will be read as a logic 0.

The capacitors may be used to minimize impulse noise. A value of at least 330 pF is normally used. Resistive connection of this terminal to an external power supply can also be used to shift the trip points and hysteresis of the receiver.

The output can drive up to 10 TTL loads and any number of CMOS loads.

Power-supply current is 25 mA.

DUAL BALANCED-LINE RECEIVER

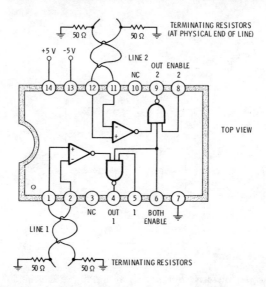

This IC accepts balanced currents from a twisted-pair transmission line and converts them into output TTL logic swings. There are two separate receivers in the package.

For normal operation, pins 5, 6, and 8 are made positive. If the line connected to pin 1 is sourcing current and the line connected to pin 2 is sinking current, a logic 1 will appear at pin 4. If the reverse is true, a logic 0 will appear at pin 4.

Similarly, a sourcing current on 12 and a sinking current on 11 will produce a logic 1 at pin 9 and vice versa.

Grounding pin 6 tri-state disables both outputs, reverting them to a high impedance. Selectively grounding pin 5 disables output 1, and selectively grounding pin 8 disables output 2.

The outputs can drive up to 10 TTL loads. They may drive any number of CMOS loads if a 2.2K pull-up resistor is provided.

Note that resistors are added to ground at both ends of the transmission line. These resistors are usually set to one half the characteristic impedance. A typical value for a 100-ohm transmission line is 50 ohms.

Response time is typically 17 ns. Supply current is 18 mA from the positive supply and 9 mA from the negative supply.

DUAL BALANCED-LINE DRIVER

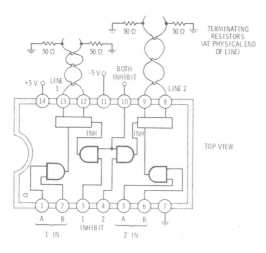

This IC accepts TTL logic swings and converts them into balanced currents for a twisted-pair transmission line.

For normal operation, pins 2, 3, 4, 5, and 10 may be grounded. A digital logic 1 on pin 1 will cause pin 13 to source 6 mA and pin 12 to sink 6 mA, driving a transmission line balanced with respect to ground. A similar input to pin 6 will cause pin 9 to source 6 mA and pin 8 to sink 6 mA. A digital logic 0 on either input will reverse the sense of the currents, with the original source being a sink and vice versa.

Inputs 2 and 5 may be logically ANDed to inputs 1 and 6, respectively, for two-input operation. Pin 3 positive will inhibit the first driver, dropping both outputs to a zero current and a high output impedance. This makes the device transparent to the line so that another driver may be used. Pin 4 positive will inhibit the second driver, while pin 10 positive will simultaneously inhibit both drivers.

Inputs are TTL compatible and may also be driven by a CMOS stage capable of sinking 3 mA of current.

Resistors are added to ground at both ends of the transmission line. These resistors are usually set to one half the characteristic impedance. A typical value for a 100-ohm transmission line is 50 ohms.

Response time is typically 9 ns. Typical power-supply current is 30 mA from each supply.

1702

PROGRAMMABLE READ-ONLY MEMORY
(256 X 8, MOS, Bulk UV Erasable)

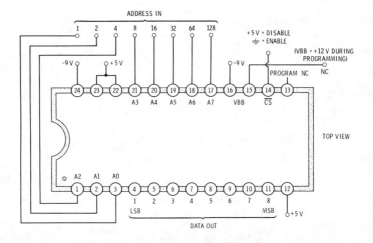

This is a nonvolatile memory that may be field-programmed to output any of 256 eight-bit words. The device is bulk-erasable in strong, short-wavelength ultraviolet (uv) light.

In normal operation, pin 14 is grounded, and the binary address selecting 1 of 128 words is applied to the address inputs. The data outputs for that word are then activated.

Inputs and outputs are TTL and CMOS compatible. Outputs will drive one TTL load. Making pin 14 positive will tri-state disable the outputs, reverting them to a high impedance. Any number of outputs can be paralleled between devices, provided only one chip select is enabled at any one time.

Programming consists of applying excess output voltage to set internal charge layers. As received or erased, all output bits are in the 0, or low, state. Consult individual data sheets for programming and erase information. The use of a programming machine or a programming service is strongly recommended.

Note that bulk uv erasure clears the entire device. There is no means to correct a single-bit error, short of total erasure and reprogramming.

Typical access time is 1 μs. Power-supply current is 35 mA from both supplies.

5600

PROGRAMMABLE READ-ONLY MEMORY
(32 X 8, Bipolar, not Erasable)

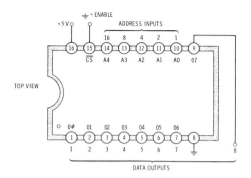

This is a nonvolatile memory that may be field-programmed to output any of 32 words of eight bits each.

In normal operation, pin 15 is grounded, and the binary address selecting 1 of 32 words is applied to the address inputs. The data outputs for that word are then activated.

Input and output currents will vary with the manufacturer. All inputs are TTL compatible. Most newer inputs require less than half a milliampere and are also CMOS compatible. Outputs can normally drive 10 TTL loads.

There are two types of outputs, again depending on the manufacturer and part number. An open circuit output needs a pull-up resistor and can drive either TTL or CMOS loads. A tri-state output can directly drive TTL but needs a pull-up resistor, often 2.2K to drive CMOS loads.

Pin 15 will allow the memory to function when it is grounded and will provide an open-circuited or a tri-state high-impedance output when positive. Any number of outputs can be paralleled, provided only one chip is enabled at a time. When open collector devices are used, only one pull-up resistor is needed for each set of paralleled outputs.

Programming consists of applying excess output voltage to blow internal fuses. A blown fuse corresponds to a 1 output. Consult individual data sheets for programming information. The use of a programming machine or a programming service is strongly recommended.

Typical access time is 60 ns. Supply power is 80 mA.

45

STATIC RANDOM-ACCESS MEMORY
(256 X 4, Separate I/O, 22 Pin)

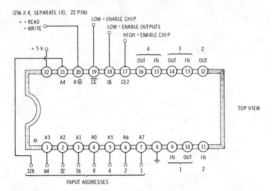

This is a static random-access memory organized as 256 × 4 in a narrow 22-pin package with separate input and output leads. Information may be rapidly read into, and nondestructively read out of, memory at system speeds. No clocking or refresh is needed. Storage is volatile with data being held only as long as supply power is applied.

To read, pins 18 and 19 are grounded and pins 17 and 20 are made positive. A binary address applied to the eight input address pins will select four internal storage cells and output the data in those cells on the four output lines.

To write, pins 18 and 19 are grounded, and pins 17 and 20 are made positive. The write input, pin 20, is then brought low and returned high. *All address lines must be stable immediately before, during, and immediately after the low state on pin 20.*

All inputs and outputs are TTL and CMOS compatible. Making pin 19 positive or grounding pin 18 will float the outputs and ignore write commands. Making pin 18 positive will float the outputs but still allow writing into memory. These extra pins are handy for common bus and multiple-chip systems.

Access time varies with the manufacturer and the grade of the device. An 800-ns read time and a 400-ns write time are typical for a nonpremium unit. Supply power is typically 60 mA, less with premium units.

Note that input addresses may be redefined in any manner convenient for circuit layout.

STATIC RANDOM-ACCESS MEMORY
(1024 X 1, 16-Pin, Separate I/O)

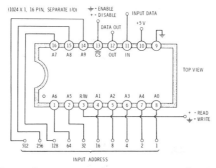

This is a static random-access memory organized as 1024 × 1 in a 16-pin package with separate input and output leads. Information may be rapidly read into, and nondestructively read out of, memory at system speeds. No clocking or refresh is needed. Storage is volatile with data being held only as long as supply power is applied.

To read, pin 13 is grounded and pin 3 is made positive. A binary address applied to the ten input address pins will select an internal storage cell and will output the data in that cell.

To write, pin 13 is grounded and pin 3 is made positive. A binary address is applied to the ten input address pins to select an internal storage cell. The write input, pin 3, is then brought low and returned high. *All address lines must be stable immediately before, during, and immediately after the low state on pin 3.*

All inputs and outputs are TTL and CMOS compatible. The output will drive one TTL load. Making pin 13 positive will float the outputs and ignore write commands. Any number of outputs from separate devices may be connected in parallel as long as only one circuit is enabled at a time.

Access time varies with the manufacturer and the grade of the device. A 800-ns read time and a 400-ns write pulse are typical for a nonpremium unit.

Supply power is 70 mA or less, again depending on the grade of the device and the manufacturer.

Note that input addresses may be redefined in any manner convenient for circuit layout.

2111

STATIC RANDOM-ACCESS MEMORY
(256 X 4, 18 Pin, Common I/O)

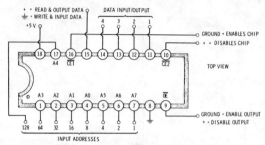

This is a static random-access memory organized as 256 words of four bits each in an 18-pin package with common input/output leads. Information may be rapidly read into, and nondestructively read out of memory at system speeds. No clocking or refresh is needed. Storage is volatile, with data being held only as long as supply power is applied.

To read, pins 9, 10, and 16 are grounded. A binary addess is applied to the eight address pins to select four internal storage cells. The data selected appears on the four i/o lines. *Nothing else may be connected to the i/o lines that sources data during the read time.*

To write, pins 10, and 16 are grounded, and pins 9 and 15 are made positive. A binary addess is similarly applied to the address pins, and an outside source of data is enabled and data is presented to the input pins. Pin 15 is then brought low and back high again. *All address lines must be stable immediately before, during, and immediately after the low state on pin 15.* After the data source is disabled, pin 9 may be grounded to allow reading.

Inputs and outputs are TTL and CMOS compatible. Outputs drive one TTL load. Making pins 10 or 16 positive floats the outputs and ignores write commands. Making pin 9 positive floats the outputs, allowing writing but not reading, or allowing the tri-state bus combination of several devices on the i/o line. *Note that only one enabled source can exist on the i/o line at any single time.*

Access times of 500 ns and less are typical. Consult specific data sheets for timing restrictions on i/o operation. Typical supply current is 60 mA.

Note that input addresses may be redefined in any manner convenient for circuit layout.

48

STATIC RANDOM-ACCESS MEMORY
(256 X 4, 16 Pin, Common I/O)

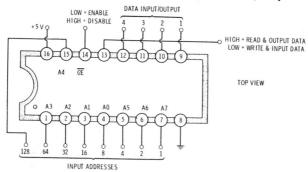

This is a statis random-access memory organized as 256 words of four bits each in a 16-pin package with common input/output leads. Information may be rapidly read into, and nondestructively read out of, memory at system speeds. No clocking or refresh is needed. Storage is volatile, with data being held only as long as supply power is applied.

To read, pin 14 is grounded and pin 13 is made positive. A binary address is applied to the eight address pins to select four internal storage cells. The data selected appears on the four i/o lines. *Nothing else may be connected to the i/o lines that sources data during the read time.*

To write, pin 14 is grounded and pin 13 is made positive. A binary address is similarly applied to the address pins. The write input, pin 13, is brought low and back high again, *at the same time enabling an external source of data for only the time the write input is low.* All address lines must be stable immediately before, during, and immediately after the low state on pin 13.

Inputs and outputs are TTL and CMOS compatible. Outputs drive one TTL load. Making pin 14 positive floats the outputs and ignores write commands. Note that very careful managing of the input/output lines is needed to make sure only one source exists at any particular time. This i/o management is eased in the 18-pin 2111.

Access times of 500 ns and less are typical. Consult specific data sheets for timing restrictions. Supply current is typically 60 mA.

Note that input addresses may be redefined in any manner convenient for circuit layout.

STATIC RANDOM-ACCESS MEMORY, CMOS
(256 X 4, 22 Pin, Separate I/O, Micropower)

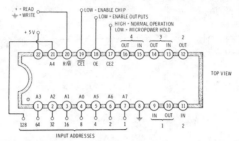

This is a static random-access memory organized as 256 × 8 in a narrow 22-pin package with separate input and output leads. Information may be rapidly read into, and nondestructively read out of, memory at system speeds. No clocking or refresh is needed. Nonvolatile, permanent storage can be simulated by retaining supply power in a micropower holding mode.

To read, pins 18 and 19 are grounded, and pins 17 and 20 are made positive. A binary address applied to the eight input address pins will select four internal storage cells and will output the data in those cells on the four output lines.

To write, pins 18 and 19 are grounded, and pins 17 and 20 are made positive. A binary address is then applied to the eight input address pins. The write input, pin 20, is then brought low and returned high. *All address lines must be stable immediately before, during, and immediately after the low state on pin 20.*

All inputs and outputs are TTL and CMOS compatible. Making pin 19 positive will float the outputs and ignore write commands. Making pin 18 positive will float the outputs but still allow writing into memory. Grounding pin 17 drops the chip into a micropower hold mode in which only 15 μA of supply power are needed but all other read, enable, and write commands are ignored.

Access times of 650 ns for read and write are typical. Operating supply current is 13 mA in the normal mode and 15 μA in the storage mode. This latter current is easily provided by a small battery in the system. Supply voltage changeover must be transient free for data holding.

Note that input addresses may be redefined in any manner convenient for circuit layout.

UNIVERSAL ASYNCHRONOUS RECEIVER TRANSMITTER (UART)

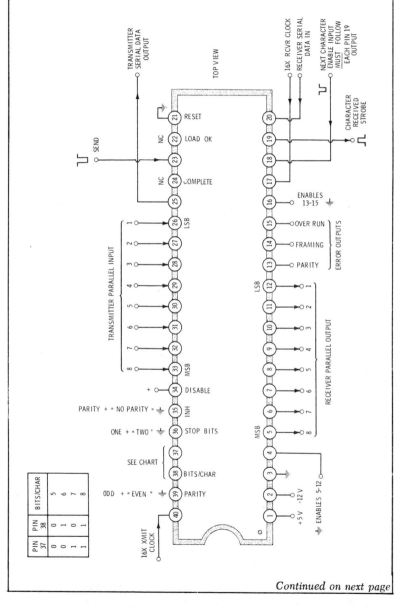

PIN 37	PIN 38	BITS/CHAR
0	0	5
0	1	6
1	0	7
1	1	8

Continued on next page

This integrated circuit is used to convert data from parallel to serial form in its *transmitter* section and to convert data from serial asynchronous form to parallel form in its *receiver* section. Operation of this device is detailed in Chapter 7.

The receiver and transmitter portions are programmed to a common format with pins 34 through 39. Pin 34 is usually positive. Pin 35 provides a parity bit if grounded. Grounding pin 36 produces one stop bit; making it positive produces two. Pins 37 and 38 select the number of bits per character, according to the chart at upper left. Note that the parity bit is one more *than* the bits per character, if it is used. Pin 39 sets odd parity if grounded and even parity is positive.

To transmit a serial signal, program the circuit for the desired format. Apply a clock of 16 times the baud rate to pin 40. Apply five to eight data bits to the transmitter parallel inputs, right justified. Bringing pin 23 briefly to ground and then returning it to positive will transmit the character as serial output. Load OK and Send OK flags appear on pins 22 and 24, respectively.

To receive a serial signal, program the circuit for the desired format. Note that this must be identical to the transmitter format. Apply a clock of 16 times the receiver baud rate to pin 20. Briefly bring pin 18 low. When complete, the received word will appear right justified on pins 5 through 12, and the character-received strobe will go high on pin 19. *Note that the next character enable input to pin 18 must go low and then high again after each received character to allow reception of the next character.* A brief 3-microsecond glitch may be present on pin 19 if it is not reset after each character.

Receiver parity, framing, and overrun error flags appear on pins 13 through 15. Making pin 4 positive tri-state disables the receiver outputs. Making pin 21 positive resets the entire chip for initialization. Supply current is 20 mA from +5 V and 7 mA from −12 V.

CHAPTER 3

Memory

Low-cost and compact memory components are the key to simple, reasonably priced tv typewriter systems. Today there are many ICs available that will cram thousands, or more, bits of storage into a single package at a cost of a fraction of a cent per bit. The problem is to pick the memory components that are the cheapest and the easiest to use, and have the least number of unpleasant surprises.

What does memory do for us? Well, it remembers. We can usually sort our memory needs into two basic types.

One type is the *permanent* memory that does not change throughout the usage life of the circuit. The most important example of this is the *character-generator* memory that converts the ASCII (American Standard Code for Information Interchange) code into a group of dot patterns suitable for video use. The same type of memory might be used to change the keyboard switch closures and shift combinations into selected ASCII codes. We also use permanent memory for *code conversion,* such as from ASCII to Selectric, and permanent memory is usually used to store the program and control commands for a microprocessor or microcomputer based system.

This particular type of memory is called a *read-only memory* (ROM). Once programmed, it does the same thing forever, even if supply power is repeatedly applied and removed. There are several ways this type of memory can be programmed. One is to use a *factory-programmed* mask at the time of manufacture. Another is to use a *field-programming* technique such as melting internal silicon or metallic fuses. This is handy whenever you are doing a special, low-volume code or program, or whenever you are not sure that what you are doing is really what you want to end up with. *Field program-*

ming also allows later customizing for special uses. Some premium field-programmed memories can be bulk-erased by exposing them to strong ultraviolet light. This type is more properly called a *read-mostly memory*. It is erased and reprogrammed only when you want to change what the memory is going to do or when you have made a programming error.

The second main type of memory is one that stores *changing* information for us. We can put data into it or get it back at system timing rates. The *screen-refresh* or *character-store* memory is the main example we have of this type, although an associated microprocessor will also use this type of memory for data and program storage. The *random-access memory* (RAM), particularly the static versions based on the 2102 family by Intel, are very often the top memory choice for this type of storage.

Unfortunately, there is no memory system available today that will both remember information forever *and* be able to read and write information rapidly, cheaply, and with reasonable timing signals. This is called the *volatility* problem.

A memory is *nonvolatile* if it remembers forever. A *volatile* memory loses its contents if you remove supply power or fail to observe any timing restrictions it might have.

One older and nonvolatile memory system is magnetic core. The problem with magnetic core is that much of its support circuitry (including sense amplifiers, write after destructive read circuits, system timing generators, power-down interrupts, etc.) make magnetic core highly impractical for small-scale tv typewriter and terminal-refresh systems.

Sometimes you can gain nonvolatility in a volatile memory by using some system-level tricks, such as a power-down technique that holds a low voltage from a battery applied to the memory when the main supply power goes away. Newer CMOS random access memories consume almost negligible power in the standby mode and lend themselves well to this. You can also transfer data to some nonvolatile outside storage, such as a cassette recorder or a magnetic disc.

Let's take a closer look at these two most common types of tv typewriter memory:

READ-ONLY MEMORIES

Most read-only memories can also be called *code converters* or *table look-up* devices, and are usually organized as shown in Fig. 3-1. Each ROM is a fixed logic block that has several inputs and several outputs. For every possible input *address* combination of 1's and 0's, some unique combination of output 1's and 0's will result. There does not have to be any rational relationship between these two code words. Either you or the manufacturer decides what these combinations are going to be at the time the ROM is *programmed*. A ROM is completely universal; it is inherently set up to provide *all possible* combinations of input/output word arrangements. When you program a ROM, you limit these combinations to the single specific word exchange that you want.

One popular small ROM arrangement is called a 32 × 8 ROM. This means you can program thirty-two 8-bit words. Since 32 words can be represented with binary combinations on five lines, this particular ROM has five input lines and eight output lines. There are 256 possible memory locations. At each and every location, we have the option of permanently or semipermanently placing a 1 or a 0. This leaves us with 2^{256} possible programs we can teach our ROM, an incredibly large number. The only thing that changes with a particular program is where you put the 1's and 0's. The rest of the circuit stays the same.

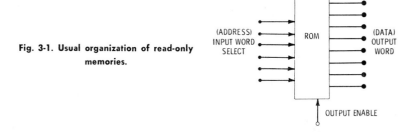

Fig. 3-1. Usual organization of read-only memories.

ROMs work by decoding each and every possible input state into a one-of-n code and then recombining certain selected combinations of decodings into output words using OR circuits. The decoding combinations that you use determine what the output word is going to be.

There are several ways to program a ROM. It can be done at the factory where metal jumpers are provided or omitted to produce, respectively, holes or no holes in a mask. Factory programming is cheap, but it must be done with a high-volume product that has one internal code that lots of users can agree to use. Dot-matrix character generators, some keyboard encoders, trig look-up tables for calculators, and so on are typical factory-programmed ROMs. *Field-programmable* ROMs are programmed by the user or by a distributor or some one else who is set up to do programming. A programmable ROM arrives from the factory either all 1's or all 0's, depending on the type. You then do something to change the bits to suit your code. In one type of ROM, fusible links are melted. These links are made of a metal, such as nichrome, or of a semiconductor, such as silicon. These techniques are most commonly used on *bipolar* or TTL-like ROMs. These ROMs are usually fast and relatively small. Another type of programming injects large voltage pulses that avalanche-charge storage areas, electret style. This type of programming is used on MOS read-only memories. They are usually slower but have more bits available per package.

Some premium ROMs are *reprogrammable*. In one type, there is a quartz window above the circuit. The ROM can be bulk erased with strong, short-wavelength ultraviolet light, but otherwise holds data indefinitely. This type is sometimes called an EPROM for *Erasable and Programmable Read Only Memory*. Normally these devices are bulk erased, resetting the entire chip to logical 0's. Ordinary, strong ultraviolet sources such as direct sunlight, poster UV lamps, mercury vapor lamps, and fluorescents will not affect the storage. Erasure takes special short-wavelength lamps without filters. Some "rockhound" mineral lamps will work. Two sources of erasing machines are Ultra Violet Products, 5114 Walnut Grove Avenue, San Gabriel, CA 91775; and Prometrics Inc., 5345 N. Kedzie Ave., Chicago, Ill., 60625.

Other types of reprogrammable ROMs can have 1's or 0's selectively and more or less permanently written into them, and can have their data selectively altered after programming but not at system speeds. EPROMs often cost more than PROMs but have the obvious advantage that they can be used over. More importantly, if you make a programming mistake, you can reuse or correct the same chip, correcting the error later on.

We can also classify ROMs as *general-purpose* devices and *dedicated* ones. A general-purpose ROM can be made into whatever you like and used for just about anything, such as for code conversion or for storing programs for a microcomputer or microprocessor. Dedicated ROMs are usually part of a larger integrated circuit and have very specific uses. Typically they can be used in a dot-matrix character generator, as the word converter in a premium keyboard encoder, and as the program storage in many calculator integrated circuits.

To see how ROMs work and what devices are available, let's look at three important tv typewriter (tvt) uses for ROMs—a seven-bar to ASCII converter that can be used to tie a calculator into a tv typewriter, an ASCII to Selectric code converter that lets us drive a Selectric typewriter with a tvt, and the character generators that do the essential ASCII to dot-matrix conversion for use. Later on in Chapter 9, we will also look at ROMs for ASCII-Baudot and Baudot/ ASCII code conversion.

Seven-Segment Converter

The output of many calculator chips is a seven-segment code that is not directly tvt compatible unless it is changed to a binary-coded decimal (bcd) or ASCII coding. While several conversion ICs exist, at this writing they are neither cheap nor readily available. Can we do the job with a read-only memory?

At first glance, it would seem that we would need a ROM with seven inputs or $2^7 = 128$ words minimum. But, as with practically every ROM application, a little bit of rethinking can often drastically cut down the size and cost of the ROM we will need. For instance, Fig. 3-2 shows how we can simply ignore the bottom and

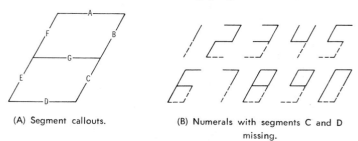

| (A) Segment callouts. | (B) Numerals with segments C and D missing. |

Fig. 3-2. Removing redundant information from the 7-bar calculator display.

bottom-right segments ("C" and "D") of the segment code and still have ten distinct and identifiable characters. This cuts the size down to 32 words, which means we can get by with five inputs and a ROM only one fourth the size of the one we started with.

Fig. 3-3 shows how we might build our own "pseudo-ROM" by using some CMOS gates and decoders. While you would rarely want to go this route, it is useful to look at it since it shows how the real ROMs work inside. You might occasionally use a circuit like this to verify programs and truth tables since it is easy to change.

The five input lines (ignoring the redundant C and D segments) are decoded to a 1-high-out-of-32 code. For every possible input combination, one and only one of the horizontal rails goes to a 1; the rest stay low. The OR gates on the output encode this into a 1-2-4-8 binary-coded decimal code. We decide what the OR gates do by where we put the dot connections between the horizontal and vertical rails. To get from bcd to ASCII, we can simply tack a *hard-wired* 011 in front of the bcd word.

While we could possibly dream up a simpler "logical minimum" circuit to do the same job, this particular circuit has a unique advantage—if our OR gates are wide enough, it will convert *any* five-bit input word into *any* four-bit output word, *with no change in hard-*

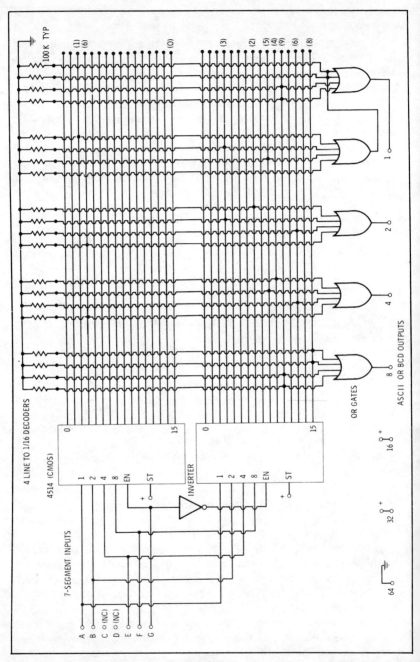

Fig. 3-3. ROM-organized logic to convert 7-segment calculator code to bcd or ASCII code.

58

ware. All that changes is the positions of the dots. This is the beauty of the read-only memory—only a single integrated circuit is needed to do an incredible variety of specialized jobs, depending only on how you program it.

Fig. 3-4 shows how we take a stock 32×8, 256-bit programmable read-only memory (PROM) and do the whole job with one integrated circuit. Since we have extra outputs left over, we can use one for a "valid keypressed" output that can tell the difference between a 0 code and no keypressed. The remaining three outputs can be used for detecting a 9 output or for doing other housekeeping that is handy when you demultiplex the scanning digit outputs of the calculator IC. To program the ROM, the *truth table* of Fig. 3-4B is entered into the integrated circuit, and the 1's and 0's are selectively programmed in as needed.

Working With PROMs

Table 3-1 is a listing of some currently available PROMs. Where two numbers are shown, one usually has open collection outputs; the other tri-state outputs. At this writing, PROMs cost from $3 upwards, with surplus versions starting as low as $2. *Bipolar* PROMs are based on TTL technology, usually work off a single +5-V supply, and are rather fast, typically 50 to 70 ns access time. MOS PROMs often take two power supplies (usually +5 and −12 V) and are slower than bipolar PROMs, typically having a one-microsecond access time. MOS devices are often cheaper *per bit*, and many MOS types are bulk-erasable by exposure to strong ultraviolet light. A few ultrafast emitter-coupled logic. PROMs also exist, but these are reserved for special uses and are expensive.

Two good choices for tvt use are the 32×8 bipolar PROM, such as the Intersil 5600 or the Signetics 8223, and the 256×8 erasable MOS versions, including the Intel 1702 and its second sources.

While you can program your own PROM with nothing but a power supply and a meter, the "zero-defects" nature of this work and its frustrating aspects turn the job into quite a hassle. Even with bulk-erasable PROMs, a mistake on bit number 1874 of a 2-k PROM can be enough to ruin your whole day. Instead of trying to do your own programming, you can buy programming services at very low cost from many electronic parts distributors, as well as from surplus and computer hobbyist supply houses. Programming machines that simplify the job are available for several hundred dollars. A good "first project" for the microcomputer hobbyist is a PROM programmer using software.

When you design your own PROM circuit, be absolutely sure that your truth table is correct before you order any programming. The program service will only guarantee that what you send in is

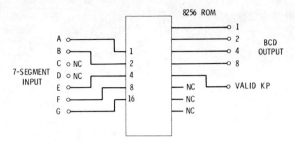

(A) Circuit using 32 × 8 ROM.

INPUT					NUMERAL	OUTPUT				
G	F	E	B	A		KP	8	4	2	1
0	0	0	0	0	-	0	0	0	0	0
0	0	0	0	1	-	0	0	0	0	0
0	0	0	1	0	1	1	0	0	0	1
0	0	0	1	1	7	1	0	1	1	1
0	0	1	0	0	-	0	0	0	0	0
0	0	1	0	1	-	0	0	0	0	0
0	0	1	1	0	-	0	0	0	0	0
0	0	1	1	1	-	0	0	0	0	0
0	1	0	0	0	-	0	0	0	0	0
0	1	0	0	1	-	0	0	0	0	0
0	1	0	1	0	-	0	0	0	0	0
0	1	0	1	1	-	0	0	0	0	0
0	1	1	0	0	-	0	0	0	0	0
0	1	1	0	1	-	0	0	0	0	0
0	1	1	1	0	-	0	0	0	0	0
0	1	1	1	1	0	1	0	0	0	0
1	0	0	0	0	-	0	0	0	0	0
1	0	0	0	1	-	0	0	0	0	0
1	0	0	1	0	-	0	0	0	0	0
1	0	0	1	1	3	1	0	0	1	1
1	0	1	0	0	-	0	0	0	0	0
1	0	1	0	1	-	0	0	0	0	0
1	0	1	1	0	-	0	0	0	0	0
1	0	1	1	1	2	1	0	0	1	0
1	1	0	0	0	-	0	0	0	0	0
1	1	0	0	1	5	1	0	1	0	1
1	1	0	1	0	4	1	0	1	0	0
1	1	0	1	1	9	1	1	0	0	1
1	1	1	0	0	6	1	0	1	1	0
1	1	1	0	1	6	1	0	1	1	0
1	1	1	1	0	-	0	0	0	0	0
1	1	1	1	1	8	1	1	0	0	0

(B) Programming.

Fig. 3-4. Single IC 7-segment code converter uses 32 × 8 read-only memory.

Table 3-1. Some Commercially Available Programmable ROMs

Manufacturer	Part	Bits	Org.	Type	Erasable?
American Micro Devices	57S08,09	256	32 × 8	BIPOLAR	NO
	27S10,11	1024	256 × 4	BIPOLAR	NO
	1702	2048	256 × 8	MOS	YES
Harris Semiconductor	1256	256	256 × 1	BIPOLAR	NO
	8256	256	32 × 8	BIPOLAR	NO
	0512	512	64 × 8	BIPOLAR	NO
	1024	1024	256 × 4	BIPOLAR	NO
	2048	2048	512 × 4	BIPOLAR	NO
Fairchild	93421	256	32 × 8	BIPOLAR	NO
	93416,26	1024	256 × 4	BIPOLAR	NO
	93436,46	2048	512 × 4	BIPOLAR	NO
Intel	3601	1024	256 × 4	BIPOLAR	NO
	3602,22	2048	512 × 4	BIPOLAR	NO
	1702	2048	256 × 8	MOS	YES
	3604,24	4096	512 × 8	BIPOLAR	NO
	2704	4096	512 × 8	MOS	YES
	2708	8192	1024 × 8	MOS	YES
Intersil	5600,10	256	32 × 8	BIPOLAR	NO
	5603,23	1024	256 × 4	BIPOLAR	NO
	5604,24	2048	256 × 8	BIPOLAR	NO
Monolithic Memories	6330,31	256	32 × 8	BIPOLAR	NO
	6300,01	1024	256 × 4	BIPOLAR	NO
	6305,06	2048	512 × 4	BIPOLAR	NO
	6340,41	4096	512 × 8	BIPOLAR	NO
National	8573,74	1024	256 × 4	BIPOLAR	NO
	5202,03	2048	256 × 8	MOS	YES
	5204	4096	512 × 8	MOS	YES
Nitron	7002	1024	512 × 2	MOS	YES
	7002	1024	1024 × 1	MOS	YES
Signetics	8223	256	32 × 8	BIPOLAR	NO
	82126,29	1024	256 × 4	BIPOLAR	NO
	82130,31	2048	256 × 8	BIPOLAR	NO
	82115	4096	512 × 8	BIPOLAR	NO
Texas Instruments	74188	256	32 × 8	BIPOLAR	NO
	74186	512	64 × 8	BIPOLAR	NO
	74287	1024	256 × 4	BIPOLAR	NO

what you get back, and nothing more. They have no way of second guessing what you really wanted.

If you do a PROM design and end up with a very large number of bits, you can almost always go through a rethinking and reduction process that will minimize things. Leaving off the two redundant segments of a seven-bar code is one obvious example. Other possibilities are to put simple logic *outside* the PROM—often a gate or two can significantly reduce the PROM size. Bypassing control commands around a PROM is one way to do this. Sometimes symmetry and mirror techniques can be used, particularly when you are working with trig waveforms, music waveshapes, and other data tables that have some sort of symmetry. In PROM microcomputer programs, programming tricks can often drastically cut the number of steps needed; extensive use of subroutines is one route to this end.

In *code converter* and *table look-up* applications, you usually address the PROM in a random fashion and you have no way of knowing what is going to be needed next. There are other ways to address ROMs that open up other types of applications. For instance, if you *sequentially* clock the PROM, changing the address one bit at a time at a constant rate, you can generate an output sine wave or a musical timbre waveform. The clocking rate will select the output frequency, and you can get a symmetrical output by using an up/down counter driving the address inputs. Variable-rate clocking can also be used to produce exponential waveforms. Another possibility is to let the PROM output set its own next *input* address, or at least influence it. Some outside latch or storage is needed to prevent an unchecked race, but this is easily added.

This particular technique is called *microprogramming* and is the key to calculator and microcomputer operation. Even without a CPU (central processing unit), a PROM can be used by itself as a programmable controller. Loops and branches are easily added by using external gating and extra PROM inputs. Several additional details on PROM and ROM design appeared in the February 1974 issue of *Radio Electronics* magazine.

ASCII-Selectric Code Conversion

A ROM or PROM can be used to change ASCII coded signals into Selectric outputs suitable for the hard-copy techniques of Chapter 9. While a few ICs are commercially available to do this job (such as the Fairchild 3512 and the National 4230), at this writing it is much cheaper and simpler to program your own PROM. You can also add custom features of your own, such as conversion of the ASCII ↑ command into a capital "E" and so on.

Fig. 3-5 shows a circuit that needs only a 512-bit ROM and a few gates to do the one-way conversion for us. The PROM basically

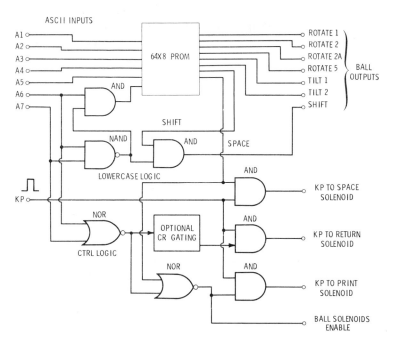

Fig. 3-5. ASCII to Selectric interface using PROM.

works with the ASCII-6 code of uppercase alphabets, numbers, and punctuation. It converts these ASCII commands into the seven Selectric shift, rotate, and tilt ball commands. The program appears in Table 3-2. We have shown it in octal coding to make it more compact.

Most of the characters are directly converted from ASCII to their Selectric equivalents. ASCII < and > become the Selectric ½ and ¼, respectively, the ASCII \ becomes the Selectric ¢, and opening and closing brackets are disallowed and produce question marks. ASCII ↑ become a capital "E" to indicate exponentiation, particularly when you are using the Basic language on a computer display.

The eighth output of our PROM is used to detect an ASCII space and break it out of the code; a Selectric space is a *machine* command, and an ASCII space is a *printing character*. If a space is detected, the keypressed output is diverted to the space solenoid and the ball-moving solenoids are disabled.

If a lowercase alphabet is provided, the input logic on bits A6 and A7 detects lowercase and converts it to its equivalent uppercase ASCII six-bit *input* code and at the same time forces the shift *output* line to the lowercase low state. This is a good example of how a quarter's worth of gating can cut the size of a ROM in half.

Table 3-2. Octal Programming for Fig. 3-5 PROM

ASCII Input	Character	Selectric Output	ASCII Input	Character	Selectric Output
00	@	166	40	Space	200
01	A	134	41	!	177
02	B	140	42	‖	125
03	C	154	43	#	176
04	D	155	44	$	171
05	E	145	45	%	135
06	F	116	46	&	175
07	G	117	47	'	025
10	H	141	50	(	160
11	I	124	51	)	161
12	J	107	52	*	174
13	K	144	53	+	106
14	L	151	54	,	014
15	M	137	55	—	000
16	N	146	56	.	026
17	O	131	57	/	011
20	P	105	60	0	061
21	Q	104	61	1	077
22	R	135	62	2	066
23	S	121	63	3	076
24	T	147	64	4	071
25	U	156	65	5	065
26	V	136	66	6	064
27	W	120	67	7	075
30	X	157	70	8	074
31	Y	101	71	9	060
32	Z	167	72	:	115
33	[(?)	111	73	;	015
34	\ (¢)	164	74	< (½)	027
35	] (?)	111	75	=	006
36	↑ (E)	145	76	> (¼)	127
37	—	100	77	?	111

	ASCII					Selectric								
6	5	4	3	2	1		SP	SH	T2	T1	R5	R2A	R2	R1	← Bits
0	1	0	1	0	1	U	0	1	1	0	1	1	1	0	← Binary
	2			5		U		1		5			6		← Octal

Reading Octal

The only other Selectric machine command we really need is a *return* command. This can be detected with the lower left NOR gate and used to divert the keypressed output to the carriage-return (CR) solenoid, at the same time disabling the ball-moving solenoids. If other control commands are to be ignored by the typewriter, optional

CR detecting gating, similar to that shown in Fig. 5-11B or 5-12 can be added.

You can build this with a single 64 × 8 PROM or a pair of 32 × 8 PROMs with parallel outputs and selective enables. The two-IC route is sometimes cheaper since these ROMs come in smaller packages and are more widely available as surplus.

If we want all the Selectric functions, including bell, tab, backspace, and index, we can use the circuit of Fig. 3-6. It takes a ROM

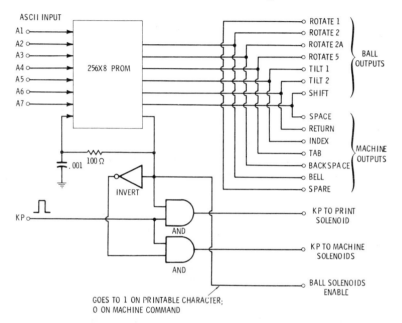

Fig. 3-6. Full-function ASCII to Selectric code converter uses larger PROM.

four times the size of the previous one but provides more functions and is a simpler circuit overall. This time, the eighth PROM output decides whether the received ASCII command is to be a printed character, a machine command, or an ignored machine command. This output reaches around to the PROM's *input* bit number 8 and automatically switches the code from one that the ball outputs can use to one that the machine outputs need, and vice versa. After a switching, the "8 to 8" feedback has to *hold* in the same address state —otherwise you have an oscillator.

The ball output codes are the same as in the simpler circuit, and their solenoids are disabled when a machine command is received. Useful machine commands are converted to a one-high code as needed. For instance, if an ASCII *horizontal tab* (HT) code is put in, the bit-8 feedback selects the machine command output words and disables the ball code outputs. It then puts out a 00010000 output that enables the TAB line only. An unwanted machine command, such as ESC, is put out as 00000000 and is ignored. The key-pressed command is routed to the printing solenoid when a character is to be typed, and energizes the selected machine solenoid for space, return, index, tab, backspace, and bell commands. More details on Selectric interface appear in Chapter 9.

DOT-MATRIX CHARACTER GENERATORS

The single most important factory-programmable ROM used in tvt systems is the *dot-matrix character generator*. This integrated circuit accepts an ASCII input code and some timing information and converts them into a pattern of dots suitable for tv displays, printers, and other systems in which characters are to be represented by dot groupings.

While the number of dots used could be almost anything from a 3×5 matrix on up to elaborate phototypesetting 17×19 arrays, Fig. 3-7 shows the four most common and most popular dot arrangements. These are based on a 35-dot matrix that is five dots wide and seven dots high and a 63-dot matrix that is seven dots wide and nine dots high. Both are available either as uppercase only or as full alphabet versions. The 5×7 uppercase-only system is the cheapest and easiest to use. It takes only six bits of character storage, has less internal circuitry, and allows a lower output video bandwidth. The main limitation of 5×7 systems is that lowercase alphabets are not

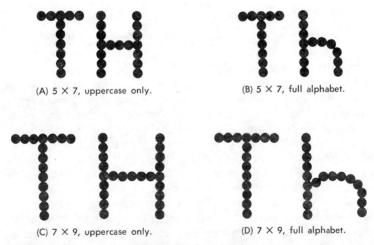

(A) 5 × 7, uppercase only.   (B) 5 × 7, full alphabet.

(C) 7 × 9, uppercase only.   (D) 7 × 9, full alphabet.

Fig. 3-7. Common dot-matrix formats.

overly attractive. The full alphabet 7 × 9 system takes seven ASCII inputs, has a more complex internal circuit, and needs more video bandwidth, often more than you can easily get out of an unmodified tv for long line-length uses.

Note that the dot matrix applies only to the characters. Extra dots or "undots" are placed between characters, and extra lines are put between character rows to give "daylight" between displayed characters.

When you are using lowercase characters, some sort of *descender* circuitry may be needed to handle the tail on a lowercase "g" and similar characters. The descender circuitry is often internal to the character generator and sometimes also gives us the options of underline, subscripts, and superscripts, such as N2, N2, N_2, and N^2.

Even if we wanted all the dots at once, the number of ROM package pins would be far too high. So, our character generator has to be arranged to give us certain dot groupings at one particular time. These groupings form only part of a complete character. Extra *timing* address inputs determine which part of the character is produced.

Fig. 3-8 shows the two basic types of character generators, the *column* style and the *row* style. *These two types are NOT interchangeable, and any dot-matrix system can be used with ONLY ONE of the two types.*

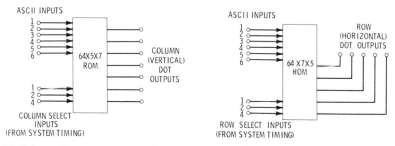

(A) Column character generator for strip printers, advertising signs, and special uses.

(B) Row character generator for tvt raster scan and other television-style scanned displays.

Fig. 3-8. These two dot-matrix ROM character generators are *not* interchangeable.

The *column* output character generator puts out one vertical column of character dots at a time, starting at the left end of the character and working its way across. This style is used in strip printers and other printing systems where the entire vertical portion of a character is to be put out at once. It is *not* suited for ordinary tvt raster scan use. In addition to the six or seven ASCII input code lines, three additional input lines called *column-select inputs* are supplied. These are tied to system timing and sequentially ask for successive columns of the dot matrix as the character is produced.

The *row* output character generator is used with ordinary raster scan tv systems, and anywhere else the character is to be put down from top to bottom. This type is far more common in tvt systems. The inputs to the row scan generator accept the six or seven ASCII character lines and the three "what row is it?" address lines that are tied into system timing.

Fig. 3-9 shows how we can convert the output row groupings into serial video by parallel loading the dot outputs into a shift register

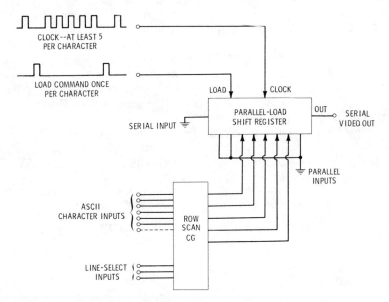

Fig. 3-9. Row-scan character generators usually need an external shift register to convert dot patterns into serial video.

and then marching them out one at a time in sequential order. A shift register is used rather than a data selector because of the speeds involved and the need for glitch-free, always-valid operation. The clocking rate of this register is typically 5 to 12 megahertz (MHz) and is usually an external TTL or CMOS package.

Once each character, a load command is used to transfer the output of the character generator into the shift register. This load command must take place after the character generator has settled down to a valid output. Following an input change, a delay of 400 to 1000 nanoseconds (ns) is usually involved. It is extremely important to set up system timing so that the dot output is stable and valid when the characters are transferred. More details on this appear in the next chapter. If input addresses and data are constantly changing, some sort of *holding latch* may be needed in front to hold the data constant long enough to get a valid output from the character generator.

Note that we have to get the *same* character back over and over again, at least seven to nine times. On the first scan of a tvt, the top row of a certain character is produced and converted to serial video. The scan line then goes on to the next character and the next and the next, putting down only the top row of dots. It continues to the end of the scan. On the next sequential scan, the character generator is indexed to put out the second row of dots, and the same sequence of characters must be returned to, in the same order, with the process repeated enough times to put down each part of every character in the row. If the main character store is a shift-register memory, an additional memory called a *buffer register,* capable of storing one line of characters, will be needed. If we use the more common and more popular random-access memory (more on this shortly), all we have to do is readdress the same characters. This is a much simpler process and takes practically nothing in the way of extra timing signals. The next chapter will give more details on this sequential addressing process.

WHICH CHARACTER GENERATOR?

Table 3-3 lists some commercially available character generators. To narrow your choice of circuit, first decide on whether you will be using row or column scan. Then pick the matrix format; finally, decide whether or not you want lowercase alphabet. Note that the lowercase will take a seventh memory bit in the character store and may not be compatible with printer outputs, particularly uppercase-only Teletypes such as an ASR-33. If you use the premium 7×9 matrix format, be sure to check the output video bandwidth (see Chapter 8) to make certain your display can handle the characters without smearing.

Some very old character generators use unusually high supply voltages and hard-to-drive input swings and may need dynamic clocking. These should be avoided, even if they are available very cheaply as surplus. Many of the character generators in Table 3-3 are being updated into single supply voltage n-channel devices. The General Instruments 2513 is one example, and more can be expected shortly. For tv typewriter use, the uppercase-only, 5×7 row scan, 2513-style device is often the best choice, with the Standard Microsystems 5004 being reserved for premium, full alphabet 7×9 systems.

Table 3-3. Some Commercially Available Character Generators

Manufacturer	Part	Matrix	Scan	Lower-case?	Package	Supply
American Microsystems	8773	5 × 7	Row	No	28 Pin	+5, −12
	8564	7 × 9	Row	No	28 Pin	+5, −12
	8771	9 × 7	Column	No	28 Pin	+5, −12
Electronic Arrays	3815	9 × 7	Column	Yes	28 Pin	+12, −12
	4001	9 × 7	Column	No	24 Pin	+12, −12
	4004	5 × 7	Row	Yes	24 Pin	+12, −12
	40105	7 × 5	Column	No	24 Pin	+12, −12
Fairchild	3257	7 × 5	Column	No	24 Pin	+5, −12
	3258	5 × 7	Row	No	16 Pin	+5, −12
	3260	7 × 9	Row	No	24 Pin	+5, −12
General Instruments	2240	7 × 5	Column	No	24 Pin	+5, −12
	2513N	5 × 7	Row	No	24 Pin	+5
	5184	9 × 9	Row	No	24 Pin	+5, −12
Monolithic Memories	6055	5 × 7	Row	No	18 Pin	+5
	6061	5 × 7	Row	Yes	24 Pin	+5
	6072	5 × 7	Row	Yes	24 Pin	+5
Mostek	2002	7 × 5	Column	No	28 Pin	+14, −14
	2302	7 × 5	Column	No	24 Pin	+5, −12
	2408	5 × 7	Row	No	28 Pin	+5, −12
National	5230	7 × 5	Column	No	24 Pin	+12, −12
	5240	5 × 7	Row	No	24 Pin	+12, −12
Nitron	6571	7 × 9	Row	Yes	24 Pin	+12, +5, −3
	6572	7 × 9	Row	Yes	24 Pin	+12, +5, −3
	6581	9 × 7	Column	Yes	24 Pin	+12, +5, −3
Nortec	4881	4 × 5	Both	No	40 Pin	+14, −14
Signetics	2513	5 × 7	Row	No	24 Pin	+5, −5, −12
	2516	7 × 5	Column	No	24 Pin	+5, −5, −12
	2526	7 × 9	Row	No	24 Pin	+5, −5, −12
Standard Microsystems	5004	7 × 11	Row	Yes	24 Pin	+5
Texas Instruments	2501	5 × 7	Row	No	24 Pin	+5, −12
	4103	7 × 5	Column	No	28 Pin	+5, −12

More details on character generators appear in the June 1974 issue of *Radio Electronics* magazine.

READ-WRITE MEMORY

The contents of read-write memory circuits can be changed rapidly at system timing rates. This makes them useful for storing characters, computer programs, update commands, and anything else we want to temporarily store and recover. Most read-write memory circuits are volatile, holding their information only as long as supply power remains present and so long as any timing restrictions are not ignored.

Read-write memories for tvt use can range from single-bit control and debouncing circuits up through thousand-word character stores to 16-k and 32-k microcomputer memory systems. Some of the more important memory types include the set-reset flip-flop, the word-storage latch, the shift register, the static random-access memory (RAM); the micropower RAM; and the dynamic RAM. Let's look at these in turn:

Set-Reset Flip-Flop

One of the simplest read-write storage systems is the *set-reset flip-flop*. It can store only one bit of information and may be built by using the NOR gates of Fig. 3-10A or the NAND gates of Fig. 3-10B. When *set*, the Q output reaches and stays in the 1 condition. When reset, the Q output returns and stays in the 0 state. A *complementary* or $\overline{Q}$ (not Q) output is also supplied—it is a 1 when Q is a 0, and

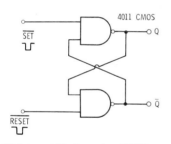

(A) Set-reset flip-flop using NAND gates.　　(B) Set-reset flip-flop using NOR gates.

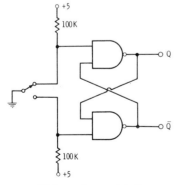

(C) Bounceless push button.　　(D) Hex contact conditioning.

Fig. 3-10. Set-reset flip-flops are the simplest type of read-write memory.

vice versa. If you simultaneously try to set and reset simple set-reset flip-flops, they go into a *disallowed* state, and their final state depends on the last input to be released.

Fig. 3-10C shows us how to use a set-reset flip-flop to eliminate the mechanical noise and bouncing of a spdt push button or mechanical contact. At the instant the first contact is made, the flip-flop jumps to the 1 state and stays there until the first instant after the switch is completely released, eliminating any bounce, noise, or chatter. Circuits of this type are absolutely essential anytime you want to enter data from a switch or mechanical contact into any digital system. Fig. 3-10D shows us a simple hex contact conditioner using one CMOS noninverting buffer.

Word-Storage Latch

Operation of a set-reset flip-flop is nearly instantaneous. If we tried to cascade several of them, we would get an unchecked wild race, for after changing the first one, the rest would follow domino style. It is much better to have digital circuits change only when you want them to and then do so on a one-stage-at-a-time orderly basis. To do this, we go to a *clocked flip-flop*, such as the D or JK flip-flops of Fig. 3-11.

With these devices, the D input or the J and K inputs set up what the flip-flop is to do, but the actual change is not carried out till a certain edge or level of the clock input takes place. With a D flip-flop we can clock in a 1 or clock in a 0, most often on the positive edge of

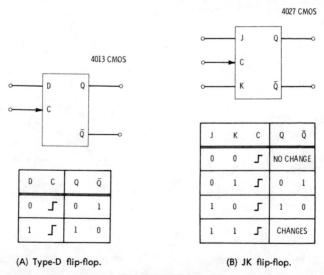

(A) Type-D flip-flop.   (B) JK flip-flop.

Fig. 3-11. Clocked flip-flops.

the clock. We can also divide by two with a D flop by cross coupling the $\bar{Q}$ output to the D input, making the logic block change states every clocking. With the JK flip-flop, we have the options of clocking in a 1, a 0 doing absolutely nothing (ignoring) or changing every state by binarily dividing. For convenience in use most JK and D flip-flops also have extra direct *set* and *reset* inputs; these operate immediately and are useful for clearing or initializing memory states.

Many more details on JK and D flip-flops appear in *TTL Cookbook* published by Howard W. Sams & Co., Inc.

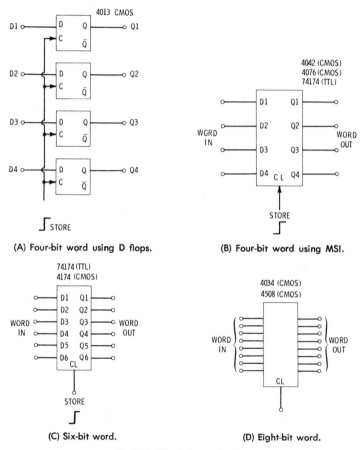

(A) Four-bit word using D flops.

(B) Four-bit word using MSI.

(C) Six-bit word.

(D) Eight-bit word.

Fig. 3-12. Word-storage latches.

One flip-flop can store only one bit at a time. If we use flip-flops in groups, we can store multiple bits all at once. In Fig. 3-12A, we use four D flops to store a four-bit word. Data are entered on the leading (positive) edge of the clock. Figs. 3-12B, C, and D show

how we can use larger MSI logic blocks to store words of four, six, and eight bits in length.

Often, a *word-storage latch* of this type is handy for "catching" an input signal on the way by and holding it until you can use it. For instance, a microcomputer may put out a word for only a microsecond or two, but your circuit may not get around to using the word for milliseconds or even seconds later. In this case, you catch the microcomputer output word with a storage latch and then keep it till you are certain you have used it. You then release the latch and ask the microcomputer for a new word through a *handshaking* signal.

Another important use for word storage is that of *resynchronizing* data and making sure it is valid. As an example, suppose your system changes words every microsecond, but that the previous block that is giving you inputs takes 900 ns or so to get around to giving you a valid output after *its* inputs change. This gives you only 100 ns or so of valid data and may change with temperature or supply voltage. Add a storage latch, and you can catch this output and hold it for the entire *next* microsecond. The output data will always be one microsecond late, but it will always be valid and locked to your system timing. A word-storage latch of this type may be needed between the memory and the character generator of a tv typewriter if very long line lengths are in use.

Shift Registers

We can cascade a stack of D flip-flops so that on each clocking they pass their contents one stage to the right. This is called a *shift register*, and Fig. 3-13 shows several examples.

Fig. 3-13A shows a four-stage register built out of D flip-flops. Each clocking passes data one stage to the right. In Fig. 3-13B, some enter-recirculate logic has been added to let us either send the data round and round or change selected bits at once. We can make the register any length we like by adding extra internal flip-flops.

In Fig. 3-13C, we use a MSI integrated circuit arranged as an 8-bit parallel-in serial-out, shift register. We have already seen how these are useful for converting dot-matrix dots to serial video; they are also handy for converting data from parallel to serial form. Fig. 3-13D is the opposite; this is a serial-in, parallel-out shift register useful for converting serial data into parallel form. More details on serial and parallel conversion appear in Chapter 7. Finally, Fig. 3-13E shows us a 1024-bit serial-in, serial-out register, useful for storing bulk data. Use several of these side by side if larger words are to be stored. For instance, to store 1024 ASCII characters, six of these could be used side by side. They can also be cascaded end to end for 1024, 2048, 4096, or more, bits per word.

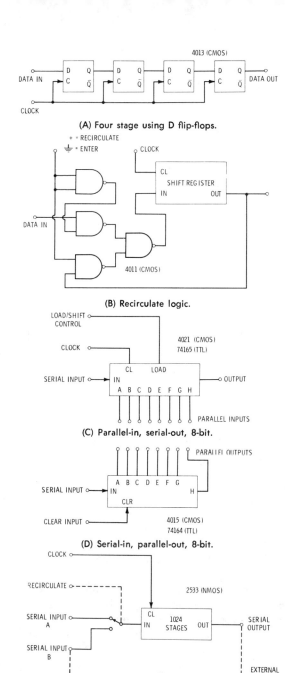

(A) Four stage using D flip-flops.

(B) Recirculate logic.

(C) Parallel-in, serial-out, 8-bit.

(D) Serial-in, parallel-out, 8-bit.

(E) Serial-in, serial-out, 1024-bit.

Fig. 3-13. Some shift-register memories.

There are lots of MOS-type long shift registers available. Other popular bit arrangements include the hex 32-bit and hex 40-bit shift registers, the 2518 and 2519. On the surface, shift registers would appear to be ideal for character and program storage in tv typewriter circuits. One of the earliest tvt's (see September 1973 issue of *Radio Electronics* magazine) made extensive use of shift-register storage, and similar registers are still used in many premium computer terminals.

Today, a far better approach to data storage is the static random-access memories described in the next section. While these long shift registers were the first truly low-cost semiconductor storage and are still useful for certain applications, they do have problems and the RAM techniques are often better.

Many of the early shift registers were dynamic devices in which you had to keep the data moving above some critical rate. Most early clocking circuits required a waveform that had to come from a fast, high-current, noisy clock driver, swinging 17 volts or more with very strict pulse width and spacing restrictions and having any pulse overshoot strictly forbidden. Some earlier multiplexed shift registers, particularly the 1402, 1403, and 1404, exhibited selective dropouts called *bit pattern sensitivity* that would change data if the particular IC did not happen to like the combination of clocking waveforms, supply voltage, temperature, and internal data that it had on hand.

Newer static n-channel shift registers have eliminated most of these problems, but they still have one key drawback: you cannot immediately get at the data you want. The memory must be clocked around once, and exactly once, to get back any bit. All the other bits are usually between you and the bit you are after. With the RAMs of the next section, you can selectively pick off any bit at any time, rather than waiting till it comes around. More importantly, you can be extremely sloppy about your timing and addressing between the times you are actually using the data. With a shift register, one missed timing pulse is a disaster. Two final limitations of shift registers as bulk storage devices are that they often cost more at system levels than RAMs do and that they are not directly microprocessor compatible.

Two areas where we can continue to see shift registers as important tvt parts are in *first-in, first-out* (FIFO) buffer memories, such as the Fairchild 3341 (64×4) and 33512 (40×9) and similar devices by AMI and Western Digital, and in the newly emerging charge-coupled device bulk storage systems, such as the Western Digital 1502E (40×9) and the Fairchild CCD450 (1024×9) and CCD460 ($128 \times 32 \times 4$) devices. A FIFO gives us a way to interface two systems having different data rates, while the CCD devices promise to eventually provide very low-cost and dense bulk storage.

More information on long MOS shift-register techniques appeared in the December 1974 issue of *Radio Electronics* magazine.

Random-Access Memory (RAM)

A *random-access memory,* or RAM, differs from a shift register in that we can get to any memory location any time we want. If we like, we can address the RAM shift-register style, working with the storage cells in sequential order. But we do not have to—we can get at any cell, at any time, in any order.

To do this, some external binary *address* lines are routed to internal decoder and selector circuits. When a memory cell is addressed, it is available either for *reading* as an output or for *writing* new information into it. Many RAMs tend to be only a single-bit wide to save on package pins, but 4- and 8-bit words are sometimes offered.

There are lots of RAMs available. *Bipolar* types using TTL technology are usually fast and expensive. They generally provide less-dense storage and fewer bits per can. Two examples are the 7489 arranged as 16 words of four bits each and the 74200 arranged as 256 words of one bit per word, or 256 × 1. Both cycle in under 50 ns.

MOS memories using PMOS, NMOS, and CMOS are also widely available. These are often slower and cheaper. They usually offer more bits per package; up to 4096 bits per package is common, and several 16,384-bit packages have just been introduced at this writing. Two early and essentially obsolete examples of MOS memory were the 1101, which was a fully static 256 × 1 device, and the 1103, which was a dynamic RAM organized as 1024 × 1 and which single-handedly toppled "King Core" from the computer world. The early 1101's ran extremely hot with weird supply voltages, while the early 1103's had incredibly complex clocking, refresh, and timing restrictions, besides being bit-pattern sensitive.

After several generations of much improved MOS memories, a device called the 2102 arrived and dropped enough in price to often be the best all-around choice for tvt character storage and most smaller microcomputer memory tasks as well. The 2102 is arranged as 1024 × 1. It is n-channel MOS, works on a single +5-V supply, and is fully compatible with TTL and CMOS logic on all pins. It is fully static, needing no clocks, refresh, charge pumps, memory-busy interlocks, sense amplifiers, or related garbage. Economy versions of the 2102 cycle in one microsecond, while premium jobs are available with 200 ns, or less, cycle time. Even the slowest 2102's are usually more than adequate for tvt use.

Best of all, at this writing, 2102's cost less than $3 in singles and as low as $1.20 in large quantities. While originally designed by Intel, sources today include TI, Intersil, AMD, National, Signetics, Fairchild, and Synertek.

Fig. 3-14 shows the connections to a 2102 memory. We see a data input pin, a data output pin, ten address lines, a write line, and an enable line. Actual pinouts are shown in Chapter 2. The data-in and data-out lines are not inverted, meaning that a 1 input is stored as a 1 and appears as a 1 at the output. Ten address lines select one of the 1024 storage cells by providing binary addresses ranging from 00000-00000, 00000-00001 through 11111-11110 and 11111-11111. We can mix up input address lines any way we want so long as all packages and all input address timing circuits agree on what address combination goes with what storage cell. Jumbling the memory address inputs sometimes helps the circuit layout and makes such things as bcd and other nonbinary addressing, feasible.

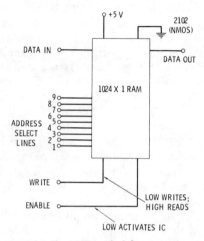

Fig. 3-14. The 2102 is ideal for many tvt uses.

The chip enable controls whether the memory will do anything. If the chip enable is high, the data-out line assumes a floating, high-impedance, tri-state mode, and the write input logic is disabled. If the chip enable is low, the IC operates normally. The *chip enable should stay grounded except in very special uses.* The memory will read if the write input is high and will write if the write input is low.

There is one important timing restriction on the write input—*input addresses must be stable when the write input is low.* To write into memory, apply input data and an input address. After the inputs are stable, bring the write input low for at least the minimum write time (this varies with the IC in use from 100 to 700 ns—see data sheet). Then release the write input, letting it go high before you change the address inputs or the data inputs. If you try to change addresses during the write process, certain memory locations may get "flashed" in the address decoding and could lose or alter data.

Incidentally, this write-only-when-stable rule applies not only to 2102's but to practically all RAM circuits. For normal 2102 read operation, make the write input *high* and the chip enable *low*.

Fig. 3-15 shows how to build a 1024 × 8 memory that is good for tvt character storage. Eight 2102's are simply put on the same pc card with their write, address, and enable lines in parallel, the latter usually grounded. All inputs and outputs go to separate pins, and this way we can read or write eight-bit words. In Fig. 3-15B, we have combined this circuit four times over to get a 4096 × 8 static memory suitable for a microprocessor main memory and big enough to hold a compiler for a higher-level language. Two new address lines are one of four decoded and routed to the chip selects of each quarter of the memory. One chip select is made low and the other

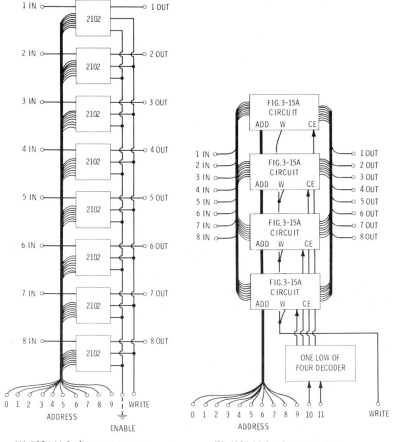

(A) 1024 × 8 character store memory.   (B) 4096 × 8 microcomputer memory.

Fig. 3-15. Larger 2102 memories.

three remain high; the tri-state outputs are shorted together as shown. A total of 32 ICs are needed.

When building either type of memory card, lots of 0.1-microfarad (μF) bypassing capacitors are recommended, along with wide supply and ground runs. The pc layout is usually simplest with a double-sided board and through-the-pins lead routing. Use plated-through boards and keep the through-the-pins routing on the component side if possible. A typical 1024 $\times$ 8 memory card is shown in Fig. 3-16. It uses a single-sided foil pattern.

(A) Memory card.

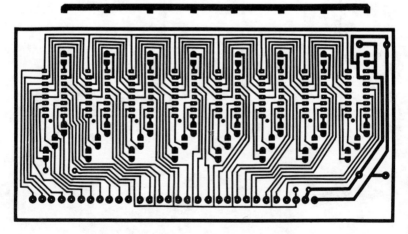

(B) Reduced printed-circuit pattern.

Courtesy Synergetics

Fig. 3-16. Typical 1024 $\times$ 8 memory card.

Reorganized 2102's

Sometimes shorter words of more bits per word may be desirable. For these applications, some manufacturers have reworked the 2102 into different organizations, including 128 eight-bit words and 256 four-bit words. The Motorola and AMI 6810 are typical 128×8 units in a 24-pin package. The Signetics 2606 and Intel 2112 are a 256×4 version in a 16-pin package. Since there are not enough pins to go around, these ICs share common input and output lines and must be used with a carefully managed bidirectional data bus system. The Intel 2101 is a 22-pin version of the same thing with separate input and output pins, while the 2111 is an 18-pin memory that still needs a bidirectional input/output system, but with eased i/o management. At this writing, the costs of these devices are somewhat higher than conventional 2102's.

Micropower Static RAMs

We can also build CMOS random-access memories similar to the 2102. CMOS has one major advantage—when the memory is not cycling, the amount of standby power needed is almost zero. This makes CMOS memories ideal for nonvolatile storage where a small battery can fill in for extremely long-term data holding, as well as safely handle routine power outages. CMOS memory cells tend to be physically larger than NMOS ones, and more process steps are often involved. So, CMOS memories will probably remain a somewhat more expensive route but a very attractive one when micropower memory is essential. Obvious applications include electronic checkbooks and remote data-acquisition systems.

Typical devices are the 64-bit Motorola 4505; 256-bit devices including the RCA 4061, Intersil 6523, and Motorola 4532 (the latter is arranged 64×4); 512-bit versions include the *Nortec* and AMI S2222, the Intel 5105 arranged as 1024×1, and the 5101 set up as 256×4.

Dynamic RAMs

A static RAM takes a full memory cell for data storage. We can get by with nothing but a capacitor as a storage device if we are willing to reshuffle, move around, or *refresh* the stored data more or less continuously. This is the principle behind the dynamic RAM. To gain cheap and dense storage, more elaborate system timing must be used. This involves the addition of clocking and system-level restrictions in the form of memory-busy times, refresh cycles, and clock lines, often combined with analog output sense amplifiers. Traditionally, any particular size RAM starts out as an impossible to use dynamic device, upgrades itself into a very difficult to use device, and then gets replaced with a hassle-free static IC the third time around.

Because of this, dynamic RAMs should be entirely avoided for all tvt and microcomputer usage. While there are a wide variety of as yet unstandardized 4096 × 1 dynamic RAMs on the market, including the Electronic Arrays 1504, Intel 2107, Standard Microsystems 4412, TI 4030, Mostek 4096, and the Motorola 6605, they presently cost much more than the equivalent storage using 2102's and are harder to get and harder to use. They do have the potential advantage of reducing package count by a ratio of 4:1 in very large memory systems where the 4096 × 1 format can be used, and they are ideal for larger computer memories.

At this writing 4k × 1 and 1k × 4 *static* 2102 style memories are just becoming available. The American Micro Devices 9130 and 9140 are typical.

More information on random-access memories appeared in the September 1974 issue of *Radio Electronics* magazine.

BUS ORGANIZATION

Any memory system has input data lines, output data lines, and address data lines. It is usually simplest to keep these lines completely separate. In this way, no timing commands are needed to separate the input, address, and output signals, and at no time can one interfere with the other. This is called an *isolated bus* or *separate i/o system.*

Instead of an isolated bus system, many microcomputers use *bidirectional data bus* arrangements to save on pins and interconnections. If something wants to transmit, its tri-state output is enabled. If something wants to receive, its input is enabled. The signals can go either way on the bus, but system timing has to make certain that only one source is transmitting and only the receivers for that source are responding to the transmitted information.

We can convert an isolated bus system into a bidirectional bus system by using *bus transceiver* integrated circuits as shown in Fig. 3-17. Transceivers are built into the 2111 and 2112 (they do not have enough pins to do otherwise) and may be externally added to regular 2102-type memories. In the case of a tv typewriter, it is usually desirable to keep the display and its memory source connected together; this eliminates dropouts when the bus is going downstream. Thus, the display electronics is best placed between the memory read outputs and the bus transceiver.

Address lines can also share the same data bus as the input and output data lines, but this leads to extremely difficult timing, particularly in 8-bit systems. More often, the address bus will remain sepa-

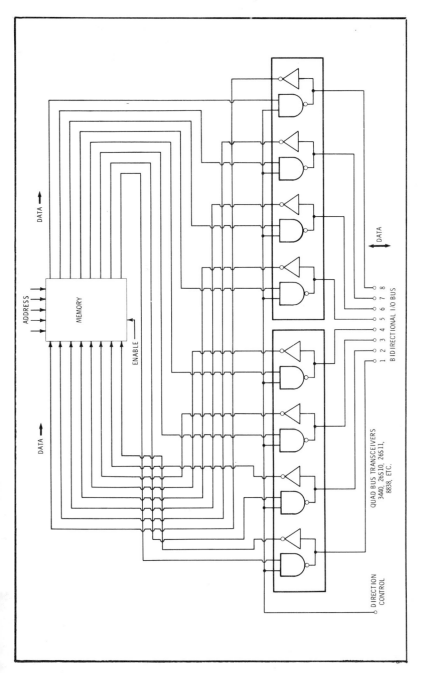

Fig. 3-17. Connecting a memory system to a bidirectional input-output bus.

rate but will be able to accept address commands from several sources. These sources could include the tv typewriter's live scan timing; a cursor address for update during retrace; and an optional, external, microcomputer control for rapid and wholesale screen changes. More details on this technique appear in Chapter 5.

CHAPTER 4

System Timing—Calculations and Circuits

The *system timing* of a tv typewriter or terminal system consists of circuitry that constantly looks at what is stored in the memory and converts it into properly placed groups of dots that, along with the sync and positioning, make up the video display. Most tv typewriter system timing can be built with a dozen or less conventional TTL or CMOS integrated circuits.

The basic decisions we make about the character format are called the *system timing constants*. Once these constraints have been established, we can go on to the actual timing circuits.

Fig. 4-1 shows a block diagram of a typical tv typewriter system. We have a main memory that stores as many characters as we want. This is usually organized as so many pages of so many characters per page. If we are interested only in uppercase characters, only six memory bits per word are needed. Seven and eight bits per word let us use lowercase characters, store and retransmit machine commands, directly handle 8 bit microprocessor words, or do extra things like protect portions of the display against changes or provide for color variations. If you are using shift registers as memory, the memory is usually permanently dedicated to display-refresh use. With random-access memories, through a *direct memory access* technique (see Chapter 5), we have the option of *sharing* the memory between a tv typewriter and an external computer, microprocessor, or data acquisition system. Thus, an internal memory reserved strictly for video refresh is not necessarily needed.

Hung on the output of the memory is a dot-matrix character generator and a video output circuit. The system timing controls how and when the addresses of the memory change, beside controlling the signals needed to keep the display happy. The system timing also controls the *cursor and update* circuits covered in the next chapter and provides for locking to outside-world signals.

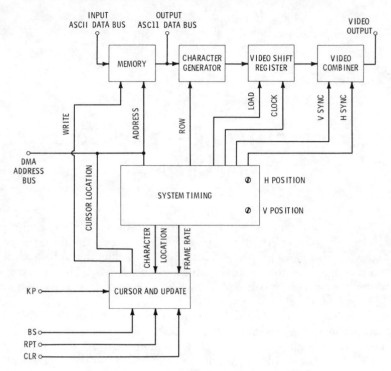

Fig. 4-1. System timing provides these control signals.

TIMING RESTRICTIONS

In a tv typewriter design, everything is connected to everything else, so very definite limits are set in the way of what you can and cannot do with character formats.

We often start with three definite system limitations—the size of each page of memory, the vertical scan rate, and the display video bandwidth—and work from these basic limitations until we have a viable system. For unmodified tv use, particularly when entering via the rf terminals, a 512-character page arranged as 16 lines of 32 characters each often turns out to be an optimum.

For practically every application, our vertical frame rate *must* be either 60 Hz or a pair of 60-Hz fields interlaced into a 30-Hz frame. The reason for this is that most tv sets are poorly regulated and poorly shielded. A vertical rate that differs even slightly from the 60-Hz power-line frequency will give us a weaving, breathing, or otherwise "seasick" display.

The size per page of the memory is a matter of how much we want to pay for it. Binary-sized memories such as 256, 512, 1024, 2048, and 4096 words usually turn out to have the simplest system timing. We can have as many pages as we like, but it is probably cheaper to store more than two pages on a cassette or other magnetic device.

The video bandwidth sets our main limitation to the number of characters we can have per page. Fig. 4-2 shows some of the con-

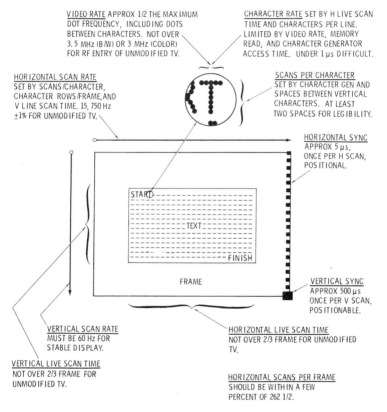

VIDEO RATE APPROX 1/2 THE MAXIMUM DOT FREQUENCY, INCLUDING DOTS BETWEEN CHARACTERS. NOT OVER 3.5 MHz (B/W) OR 3 MHz (COLOR) FOR RF ENTRY OF UNMODIFIED TV.

CHARACTER RATE SET BY H LIVE SCAN TIME AND CHARACTERS PER LINE. LIMITED BY VIDEO RATE, MEMORY READ, AND CHARACTER GENERATOR ACCESS TIME. UNDER 1 μs DIFFICULT.

HORIZONTAL SCAN RATE SET BY SCANS/CHARACTER, CHARACTER ROWS/FRAME, AND V LINE SCAN TIME. 15, 750 Hz ±1% FOR UNMODIFIED TV.

SCANS PER CHARACTER SET BY CHARACTER GEN AND SPACES BETWEEN VERTICAL CHARACTERS. AT LEAST TWO SPACES FOR LEGIBILITY.

HORIZONTAL SYNC APPROX 5 μs, ONCE PER H SCAN, POSITIONAL.

START------------
------TEXT------
------FINISH

FRAME

VERTICAL SYNC APPROX 500 μs ONCE PER V SCAN, POSITIONABLE.

VERTICAL SCAN RATE MUST BE 60 Hz FOR STABLE DISPLAY.

HORIZONTAL LIVE SCAN TIME NOT OVER 2/3 FRAME FOR UNMODIFIED TV.

VERTICAL LIVE SCAN TIME NOT OVER 2/3 FRAME FOR UNMODIFIED TV.

HORIZONTAL SCANS PER FRAME SHOULD BE WITHIN A FEW PERCENT OF 262 1/2.

Fig. 4-2. Some constraints on system timing.

straints on system timing. The highest practical bandwidth for rf entry of a quality, unmodified black-and-white tv set is only 3.5 MHz, and a color set can allow only 3.0 MHz. These limits are set because the video response must reject thoroughly a 4.5-MHz sound subcarrier and a 3.58-MHz color subcarrier. Most economy tv's have far less bandwidth than even these meager values. A bandwidth of 3.5 MHz roughly corresponds to a maximum character dot rate of 7 million character dots per second.

We can get more video bandwidth out of a television set by direct video entry and by "souping up" techniques such as additional peaking and higher video output stage currents (see Chapter 8). In a video monitor or a custom display, you can increase the system bandwidth as needed to math the video dot rate. Bandwidths of 10 to 12 MHz are not unusual for 80 character-per-line displays, particularly when higher-resolution (7 × 9) character generators are used.

Scanning Rates

If we are using a stock or slightly modified tv set, we should keep the horizontal scan rate near 15,750 Hz. If we must superimpose the display on an existing tv program, the horizontal rate must be exactly 15,750 Hz and properly locked to the external program source. If we are simply displaying data, hitting this figure within a percent or two is acceptable. Interlace, or two-fields-per-frame operation, is essential for video superposition, but for ordinary data displays, interlace is not needed and has no advantages. Without interlace, a 262-line or 264-line system may be used with corresponding horizontal scanning rates of 15,720 or 15,840 Hz.

Horizontal and vertical scanning *must* be locked together. In the vertical direction, the scan lines actually used to display characters are called the *live scan time,* and the remaining lines the *retrace and blanking* time. The total number of scan lines, multiplied by the 60-Hz vertical rate, will equal the horizontal scan rate.

How much blanking and retrace time do we have to allow? Most unmodified tv sets, particularly the economy jobs, have extreme overscan to improve the display linearity and minimize line-voltage effects. Beside being concerned with the extreme overscan, we are very much concerned about the corners of our message and have to be certain the rounded edges of the picture tube do not eliminate them.

It is not at all unreasonable to use ⅓ of the vertical time for vertical blanking and retrace, and ⅓ of the horizontal time for horizontal blanking and retrace. With custom displays and video monitors, we can shorten these times somewhat.

We center a vertical-sync pulse in the vertical retrace interval, and we center a much shorter horizontal-sync pulse in the horizontal retrace interval. These pulses can be moved with respect to system timing to provide for positioning. Positioning is almost essential on unmodified tv displays. One important design consideration that must be considered is that the positioning not affect the *shape* or *width* of the sync pulses.

For most tv typewriter uses, we need not provide the exact EIA sync used by commercial tv stations. Instead, we can approximate the pulses and the video we need, as in Fig. 4-3. Note that it is extremely important to keep the system timing horizontal- and vertical-sync pulses locked together so that one is an *exact* multiple of the other. Otherwise, the phase-locked loop horizontal-sync circuit in the tv will cause tearing and the character dot lines will blur into

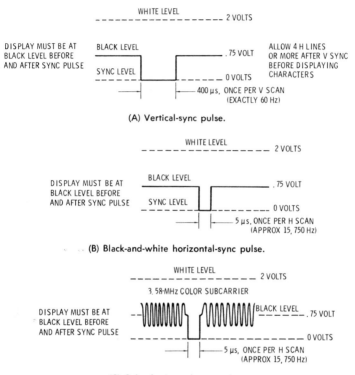

(A) Vertical-sync pulse.

(B) Black-and-white horizontal-sync pulse.

(C) Color horizontal-sync pulse.

Fig. 4-3. Recommended sync signals.

each other. Several blanked horizontal lines should be provided following the vertical-sync pulse. This gives the tv set a chance to catch up and adjust for the several horizontal-sync pulses it may have missed during the vertical interval. Otherwise, the first character row may be bent or displaced.

Raster Lines per Character

The minimum number of horizontal scans we need per character is set by the dot-matrix character generator we use. To this, we have to add spaces between vertical characters and possibly provide for a blinking cursor overline or underline. With a 5×7 dot-matrix system, the minimum we can get by with is eight raster lines per character, but this does not look very good and forces us to use a box-type cursor. Its obvious advantage is simple binary timing.

Ten raster scans per character seems to give a good appearance, gives three scan lines between character rows, and optionally lets us do either an overline or an underline cursor. With a 7×9 premium dot matrix, 11 or 12 lines per character works as well.

One possible combination is to use 16 lines of characters of 10 lines each, for 160 lines of active scan. We combine this with 102 lines of blanking and retrace, for a total of 262 noninterlaced lines and a horizontal scan rate of $60 \times 262 = 15,720$ Hz. This particular combination works well with an unmodified tv.

There are several ways we can get more character lines. If you have a display system that can retrace fast, 24 character lines of 10 scan lines per character will give 240 scan lines. But this would leave us with only 22 lines for retrace. With minimum retrace times, the height of the actual display has to be reduced inside the corners of the screen so that everything in the display is visible without any overscan.

Another possibility for more characters per screen is to use interlace and put down the odd-numbered dot lines on one field and the even-numbered ones on the next field. This will cram 32 character lines in the space of 16 noninterlaced lines. Characters done this way will be rather squat, might have noticeable flicker, and might push the spot size limits of some tv systems.

On the first field, raster lines 1, 3, 5, 7, and 9 of the character matrix are put down. On the following scan, 2, 4, 6, 8, and 10 are placed, interwoven with the dots previously put down. The half lines at the top and bottom of the frame occur during retrace and blanking and will not affect the presentation.

Combining all these techniques would give an absolute limit somewhere around 48 character lines per display. Yet another approach is to use tv systems of higher resolution than the usual 525 lines. The problem with these higher-resolution systems is that if they increase the horizontal frequency, they will dramatically increase the video output rate, which is already a system limit.

Horizontal-Rate Timing

The number of characters per horizontal line, the dots per character, and the active scan time set the output video dot rate. If we are not careful, the dot rate can get unrealistically high, particularly for rf entry of an unmodified tv. For instance, suppose we are using a premium 7×9 dot-matrix character, 80 characters per line, and

⅔ of a horizontal line for active scan time. Regardless of whether we are using 262, 262½, or 264 horizontal lines per frame, we will have something around 63 microseconds (μs) per scan line. Two thirds of this is around 42 μs, which leaves us with half a microsecond or so per character. If we have seven dots per character and two *undots* between characters, we have to get nine dots in half a microsecond, or eighteen million dots per second peak rate output as video. The relationship between video bandwidth and dot rate is subtle and takes some complicated math, but if you assume that the video bandwidth you need is one-half the dot rate, you will not be far wrong. For this example, this means that you need around 9 MHz of video bandwidth, a figure that seems unreasonably high for direct rf entry into an unmodified tv set, particularly a color one. Because of these simple mathematics, *it will be very hard to get acceptable performance of an rf entry in an unmodified tv if you use long line lengths and premium character generators.*

Instead, let's look at a more reasonable line length for unmodified tv use. What happens with 32 characters per line in a 5 × 7 dot matrix? Since 32 characters in 42 μs is 1.3 μs per character, this time gives us lots of "daylight" for memory access and character-generator settling times. It also lets us use ripple delay rather than synchronous counters in our timing chain and might get us by with lowest-performance memory parts. Now, if we use five dots and two undots in 1.3 μs, we have seven dot positions in 1.3 μs, or an equivalent rate of 5.4 megadots per second. The equivalent video bandwidth for good contrast is around 2.7 MHz, a value that is compatible with direct rf entry of even a color tv set.

These short line lengths primarily apply to low-cost circuits driving unmodified tv sets. Usually, if you can use direct video and modify the circuit, or if you build your own display, black and white bandwidths ranging from 6 to 10 MHz should not be unduly difficult to reach.

Another absolute limit to the video bandwidth is the character rate we can get out of the memory and character generator. It may take 600 ns to get a stable output from the memory after an address change, and another 400 ns to get a stable dot pattern after this from the character generator. Usually we can *delay* the *output* timing to take up much of this time, but the absolute limit to what you can do with delay techniques is set by the *difference* between the minimum and maximum memory settling time, or by the *difference* between the minimum and maximum character-generator settling times. Exceeding these values, even with perfectly delayed timing, will give a torn display, missing dots, or wrong characters. If you have a microsecond or more per character, things will be simple and easy. With half a microsecond or less, you will have troubles, and you may have to go to double memory and double character generators that take turns giving an output.

The essential system timing calculations are shown in Fig. 4-4.

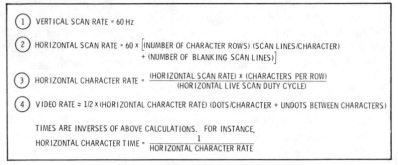

Fig. 4-4. Basic system timing calculations.

TIMING CIRCUITS

The system timing has to set up a frame with positionable sync signals for the tv. On the live scan part of each horizontal line, we have to address the memory, changing the memory addresses at the character rate. As each character appears at the memory output, it is routed to a character generator along with line address commands to get the right dot-pattern output. This pattern output in turn is loaded into a shift register and then clocked out to provide serial video.

Note that we have to provide the *same* horizontal character sequence over and over again for the seven or more raster lines it takes to produce all the dots of a certain character. With older shift-register memories, this meant that a new *buffer* shift register, one line long, was needed. With modern RAMs, we get the same results with a simple and essentially free readdressing scheme.

The timing has to always address the proper memory locations until the end of the vertical live scan is reached. While all this is happening, we have to provide for sync and positioning, and have to generate suitable timing signals for the *cursor and update* circuits of the next chapter. We have to provide for *blanking* of repeated or unwanted outputs, and we probably will be locking all of this to an external tv or 60-Hz power line reference.

Normally, we begin with some frequency *system clock*. Most often this is at the character rate and usually around 1 MHz. From here, we multiply up in frequency for the video-rate high-frequency timing and divide down for the *frame-rate* timing that addresses the memory, character generator, sync, positioning, and update circuitry.

With random-access memory systems, we are free to address any memory location in any sequence we want. As long as we have the right locations when we actually need data, it does not matter what gets addressed in what sequence at other times. Thus, there is usually no need to stop addressing during retrace or other blanked output times, unless we really want to. This is an extremely important advantage of RAM memory circuits, and it can very much simplify system timing.

Frequency References

The *system clock* is some master frequency reference from which everything else is derived. This is either the *video rate* or the *character rate*. The video rate is several megahertz, while the character rate is typically one megahertz. Character-rate master timing is easier to do with phase-locked loop circuits and gives more control of memory and character-generator access delay times.

A simple astable multivibrator, ring oscillator, or other "quick and dirty" signal source is not recommended for master system timing, because it is critical that the display have a 60-Hz vertical rate for a stable presentation. The frequencies usually needed are well beyond what you can do with a 555 or other reasonably stable timing circuit. This leaves us with two alternatives. Either we can use a very stable timing source, or we can use a *phase-locked loop* (PLL) circuit that locks the presentation to an outside reference. Two obvious references to use would be the 60-Hz power line or the horizontal rate from an external tv signal that we wish to lock to.

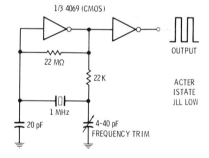

Fig. 4-5. Crystal oscillator is a stable signal source.

A simple crystal oscillator is shown in Fig. 4-5. It does generate a very stable output in a simple circuit but may require an expensive crystal (often having an oddball frequency such as 1.006 or 1.008 MHz) and cannot be directly gated (because of the crystal Q) without some external circuitry.

A phase-locked loop circuit using a 4046 (CMOS) phase-locked integrated circuit is shown in Fig. 4-6 and provides a reasonable way

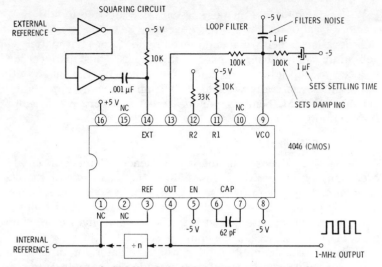

Fig. 4-6. Phase-locked loop locks system timing to external reference.

to lock to almost anything we like. Input frequencies at pins 3 and 14 are compared, and their difference is stored and integrated in a *loop filter* that controls the frequency of a *voltage-controlled oscillator* (vco). The vco output is divided down by system timing to form one of the references, thus locking everything to the outside signal.

We lock this circuit to the power line by using the circuit of Fig. 4-7 or to an external tv source with the Fig. 4-8 circuit.

In Fig. 4-7, the PLL output is divided down to 60 Hz with a divider chain that provides all the intermediate frequencies needed

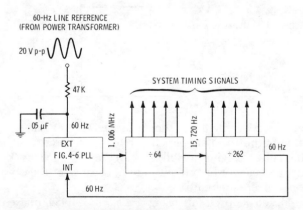

Fig. 4-7. Phase-locked loop locked to power line.

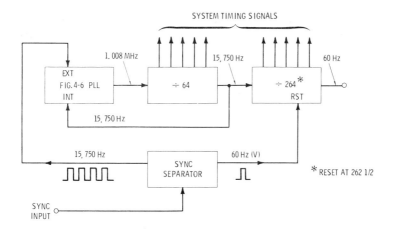

Fig. 4-8. Phase-locked loop locked to external tv sync for video titling or superposition.

for system timing. This 60 Hz is compared with a reference from the power transformer, thus locking all the system timing, and the frame rate in particular, to the power line. In Fig. 4-8, the sync from an external video source is split to extract horizontal- and vertical-sync signals. The horizontal is compared against a divided-down horizontal reference from the phase-locked loop, thus locking the start of each horizontal line to the external line beginnings. Vertical sync is used to reset a counter that is never allowed to reach maximum count, ending up with two properly interlaced 262½-line frames per 60-Hz fields that combine for a 30-Hz frame. The Fairchild 3262B is an IC useful in splitting horizontal and vertical sync.

This particular 4046 phase-lock loop circuit operates up to only 1.5 MHz or so. It is important to have a fast rise and fall time input for the reference, and the external reference should preferably be leading-edge coupled as shown. The 0.1-μF capacitor (Fig. 4-6) provides a glitch filter, since the vco input has a very high impedance, and any nearby strong logic signals can produce a glitch or offset in a character row, which is very annoying in a display. With the horizontal dividers shown, we usually work with a 1:1 ratio of live scan in the horizontal direction to blanking and retrace time.

Simple Line Lock

Can we come up with a simpler way to lock the timing to the power line? The *gated oscillator line-lock* circuit of Fig. 4-9 offers one interesting possibility and eliminates the need for horizontal blanking as well.

The two inverters in the upper left form a gated oscillator that runs at a frequency near 1 MHz. In a 32-character-per-line system, it is only allowed to run for 32 counts, and then it shuts down and is held off by the voltage-controlled delay made up of the other two inverters. Thus, we get 32 clock pulses per horizontal scan. These pulses arrive in *bursts,* and the spacing between bursts determines the blanking and retrace time. Without feedback from the rest of the circuit, the oscillator and delay are set to produce a horizontal frequency of 15,720 Hz. This is divided by 262 to obtain a 60-Hz vertical rate. The 60-Hz vertical rate in turn clocks a D flip-flop set up

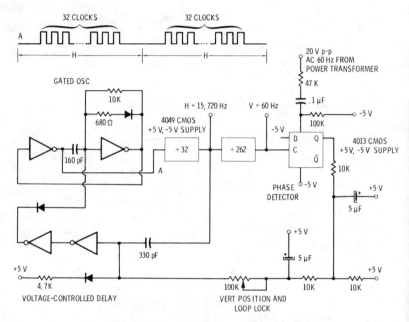

Fig. 4-9. Economy line lock circuit uses gated oscillator.

as a phase detector. The D flip-flop is set by the power line, so the time per cycle during which the Q output remains negative is set by the phase difference between the vertical timing and the power line. Any phase error is filtered by the loop filter and routed via the vertical position control to the delay circuit. Errors between system timing and the power line modulate the spacing between the 32 clock pulse bursts, adding more dead time if the circuit frequency is high and removing space if the frequency is low.

Most of the circuit is built with four inverters and one flip-flop. Besides simplifying the blanking and the video rate timing, this circuit self-conditions the power-line reference so that squaring is not needed, and automatically provides a "free" vertical-position delay output, since loop phase adjustment will also set the vertical position. A suitable delayed position signal appears at the $\overline{Q}$ output of the flip-flop.

Interlace

Full interlace operation is neither needed nor desirable for most tvt applications. The only exception to this is when the tvt circuitry must be locked to existing video for titling or other superposition. A traditional interlace scheme is shown in Fig. 4-10. Here, we start with a reference of twice the horizontal frequency and divide by an even number (2) to get the horizontal rate and by an odd number (525) to get the vertical rate. This locks the two signals together but lets the vertical sweep alternate its beginnings—once at the start of a horizontal line and once in the middle and then repeating. Any similar technique that gets the same effect can probably be used.

Fig. 4-10. Traditional interlace generator.

Ram-Address Timing

Fig. 4-11 shows how we use the intermediate outputs of our timing-chain counters to drive a random-access memory character store and a dot-matrix character generator. We first go to a horizontal or H counter that times out 32 or 64 binary address waveforms for the

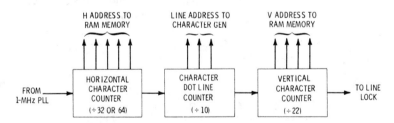

Fig. 4-11. This counter arrangement automatically gets the same characters out of a RAM for each successive row of a dot-matrix character.

horizontal RAM characters, doing so once each horizontal line. The horizontal line-rate output of this counter goes to a character or C counter that tells the character generator ROM what line of dots to put out. This is usually a divide-by-ten or a divide-by-eleven. You can sometimes save on blanking circuitry by using a divide-by-eight and setting up the circuit to inhibit (ignore) two or three input clockings when in the 000 position.

Note that the horizontal RAM addresses continually change for every character scan line. This automatically, and at zero cost, returns each horizontal character, over and over again, as needed to put down a whole character. Note that shift-register memories would need a line buffer for the same effect.

The output of the character counter goes to a vertical address or V counter (often a divide-by-16) that is binarily decoded into vertical addresses to tell the RAM which line of characters to put out. The output of this counter usually generates a vertical blanking signal and a reference signal for vertical position, sync, and line lock as well.

With random-access main memory, it does not matter how often and when any particular character is addressed, so long as we get that character out when we really want it. Thus, we are free to address the memory any way we like during blanking and retrace times. This is a dramatic simplification over shift-register techniques where the memory must be turned over once, and only once, per frame.

The H outputs should change together or very nearly so. This means you should use synchronous counters or very fast ripple counters, or allow enough extra "daylight" in the character-generation time to allow the lines to settle. The vertical character-rate outputs usually have a lot of retrace time in which to settle and are not at all critical.

Video-Rate Timing

The *video-rate timing* decides when the output of a character generator gets loaded into a serial video shift register and how fast the register contents will get clocked out as video. Since all this happens once for each addressed horizontal character, video-rate timing is much faster than the RAM-address timing and more critical in terms of rise and fall times and pulse widths.

One circuit appears in Fig. 4-12. It is simply a free-running astable that is synchronized by a load command when and if the load command arrives. The load command is derived from the phase-locked loop or the line-lock circuit of Fig. 4-9. The load command automatically puts out bit 8 of the shift register, which is hard-wire programmed as a blank. The astable clocking then shifts out bits 7, 6, 5, 4, and 3 in sequential order, which are character dots previously provided by the dot-matrix ROM character generator. If we get more clocking pulses before the next load command, hard-wired blanks on bits 2, 1, and the serial input are put out as logic 0's or as a black screen. Note that if the load commands stop arriving, this circuit automatically puts out blanks. The frequency of the astable is set by the capacitance and resistance values, and the frequency determines the spacing between characters.

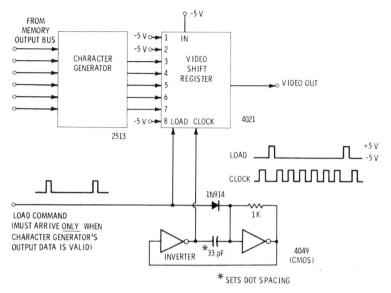

Fig. 4-12. Video-rate timing.

One extremely important detail to observe on the video-rate timing is to *make absolutely certain that the load command arrives when the character generator output is valid.* Usually, one whole clock-cycle delay is used in order to be absolutely certain of this validity.

Fig. 4-13 shows a typical video-output timing cycle. We see that the address changes to the input of the RAM happen roughly at a 1-microsecond interval. Assuming we are using either fast ripple counters or synchronous counters for addressing, these addresses are stable and valid practically all the time. (If they are not, they have to also be taken into the account that follows.)

The RAM memory takes a while to put out valid data. This will range from 100 to 700 ns, depending on the type of RAM you are using. So sometimes we get bad data out and sometimes we get good data out. This mixture of good and bad data is routed to the character generator. It, too, takes a while to put out good data, but obviously it cannot even begin to work until it gets valid data. A typical amount of time in which to get good output data is 500 ns. Thus, *most of the time, the output of the character generator will be garbage.* So, it is extremely important to load the character generator output only when the data is known to be good and when all worst-case delays have been accounted for.

In very high-speed systems, there might not be enough "daylight" to go around, and you could never get valid data out. More typically, the valid data-output times could be short enough to be time or

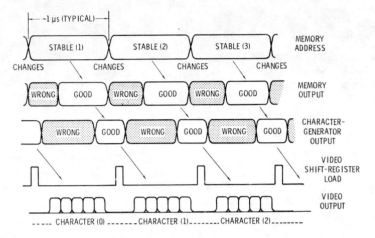

Fig. 4-13. Memory and character-generator access time delays must be carefully allowed for by video output timing.

temperature dependent. Three ways around this problem are to put a resynchronizing latch between memory and character generator, to use extra fast memory and character generator components, or, in extreme cases, to use pairs of memory and character generators and take turns using them on alternate characters.

BLANKING

We can eliminate character presentations from unwanted portions of the screen with *blanking techniques*. A blanking technique is any scheme to prevent the characters from getting out as video. Blanking is obviously important during horizontal and vertical retrace times, as well as on horizontal lines between character rows. Fig. 4-14 shows several blanking techniques. Technique 1 enters ASCII space commands 100000 into memory and displays them as regular characters. Note that a cleared or all-0's memory is an "@" and not a blank. Technique 2 disables the memory outputs and floats a space command on the character generator inputs. Technique 3 addresses a blank portion of the character generator, most often the top line in response to a 000 code. This is particularly handy for introducing the blanking between character rows, and is done by holding the character generator in the 000 state for these times. Technique 4 disables the character generator outputs. With a CMOS shift register, pulling the outputs low gives blanks, and pulling them high gives a white screen. With a TTL register, blanking cannot be obtained this way. Technique 5 stops load commands from reaching the shift register, so it clocks out blanks initially obtained from its own serial

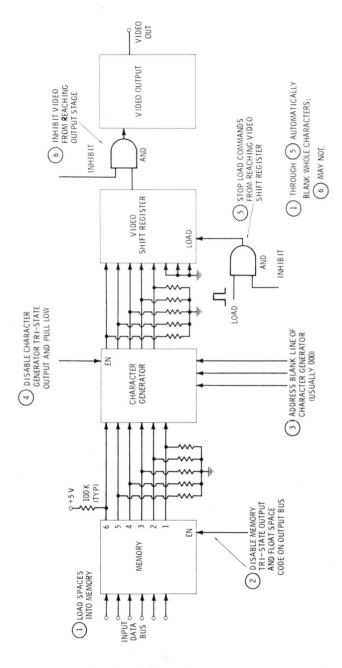

Fig. 4-14. Blanking techniques.

101

input. Finally, technique 6 simply stops the characters from reaching the video combiner or output stage. Any combination of methods that is handy and works may be used to blank unwanted display sections. Many times a good policy is to spread the blanking out among several techniques—this eliminates the need for a "blanking tree" full of extra logic. Also, it is usually simpler to set things up so that they are *normally* blanked and then unblanked only when you want a character, rather than vice versa.

While techniques 1 through 5 automatically eliminate *whole* characters, technique 6 will not do so unless you are extremely careful about timing delays and widths.

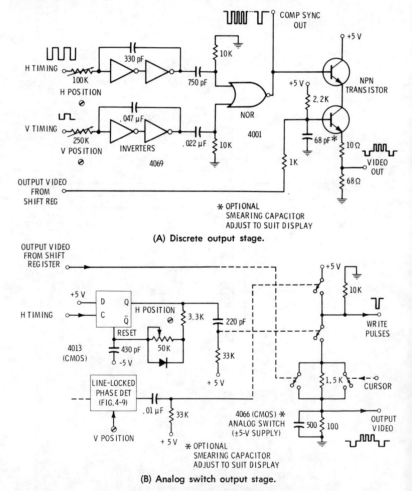

(A) Discrete output stage.

(B) Analog switch output stage.

Fig. 4-15. Sync, position, and video output circuits.

SYNC, POSITION, AND VIDEO COMBINATION

Fig. 4-15 shows some circuits that will combine the positioning circuit and the sync and video circuits. Fig. 4-15A is an older circuit that works with almost any tvt system. Horizontal and vertical timing outputs are shortened to suitable pulse widths (5 microseconds horizontal and 400 microseconds vertical), logically NOR-combined, and then routed to a video output transistor. In circuits of this type, it is very important that the positioning controls do not change the *shape* or *width* of the sync pulse. The key to this is a fast rise and fall waveform after the positioning delay. The sync transistor is on and saturated *except* when either sync pulse is desired—then it turns off and the 68-ohm resistor pulls the video output to ground, assuring us that the output sync tips are exactly at ground. The transistor must have a low storage time.

Video from the shift register is smeared slightly with the 68-pF capacitor (see Chapter 8—the optimum capacitor value just closes the inside of a "W") and is routed to a second series transistor. A video 1 gives around 2 volts of output, a 0 gives around half a volt (and a sync-signal ground), all with roughly a 70-ohm impedance level.

A simpler circuit, shown in Fig. 4-15B, uses the free vertical position control from the economy line lock circuit of Fig. 4-9. Horizontal delay is done with a D flip-flop that resets itself for a specified time delay after clocking. This approach gives sharp rise and fall times and uses the other half of the phase-detector IC. Output signals are combined in a quad analog switch, the CMOS 4066. Either sync pulse opens the connection to +5 V and grounds the output. The vertical-sync pulse also is put out separately as a write output for write-during-vertical-retrace update circuits. Video is used to pull the output between half a volt for a 0 and two volts for a 1, while an optional cursor input gives us a white character, box, or underline. Cursor timing must be suitably lined up as needed.

CHAPTER 5

Cursor and Update Circuits

A *cursor* is a blinking indication that decides which character gets changed next. It remembers this character for the internal *update* or change circuitry and also shows it to the operator. Circuits associated with the cursor take care of actually changing the memory contents and allowing for the character-to-character cursor movements.

The *essential* things a cursor has to do are:

* Show the operator the next character to be entered.
* Update and enter a new character when it arrives.
* Advance one character *after* an update or advance one line at the end of a line.
* Be able to return to an upper left-hand home position.
* Be able to return to the beginning of the next line.
* Be able to erase the entire memory, filling it with spaces.

Cursors will sometimes also do these *optional* things:

* Retransmit screen contents.
* Backspace.
* Repeat a character or a motion.
* Rapidly move in any direction, either with manual or software control.
* Scroll upwards or change pages at the end of a page.
* Automatically erase to the end of a line or the end of a frame whenever an update is to begin.
* Protect certain parts of the display so that they cannot be changed.
* Add or remove characters and lines for editing.

* Emphasize certain parts of the display through blinking, half brightness, reverse field, or color changes.
* Turn itself off and on.

The specific type of cursor circuit we can use is very much tied into the memory we chose for our system. With shift register and some charge-coupled device memories, we can get a particular character once, and only once, in an unchangeable sequence during a display frame. We *have* to use or change this character the instant it becomes available, either recirculating it into the shift register or entering a new character.

With random-access memories, we *can* do the same thing. More important, we can easily change a character any time we like, simply by addressing it. For instance, we can address the character continuously for the entire vertical retrace interval, changing it if we like. Or, with slightly fancier circuitry, we can say to our microprocessor or whatever is giving us characters: "Here is the entire memory. Put whatever you want wherever you want and then give it back." So, it turns out that RAM systems are far more flexible in how they change the characters, although the shift-register systems do allow a few special types of actions like scrolling to be done slightly easier.

The important thing when using RAMs is not to have a "shift-register mentality." While we *can* update a RAM shift-register style, this has to be done fast and at a variable time through the display. It is usually much better to use a slower, more available, and fixed time slot for update. This is especially true with microprocessors, for an update during the vertical retrace time can take a leisurely few milliseconds, compared to a fraction of a microsecond needed when the character is flying by as video.

There are two basic types of cursors. These are the *character-rate cursor* and the *frame-rate cursor*. Character-rate cursors are extremely fast, letting us change the entire screen contents in a fraction of a second. They usually take complex external circuits and software for control. Frame-rate cursors take $\frac{1}{30}$ or $\frac{1}{60}$ of a second for a single character update. These are generally much simpler and much more versatile. While frame-rate cursors are much faster than typing or Teletype rates, it can take up to sixty seconds for an entire screen update or readout.

FRAME-RATE CURSORS

Frame-rate cursors take either one or two frames to change a single character. This rate is much faster than anyone can type and three to six times faster than most Teletype systems. In *single-frame update* systems, the character is entered or retransmitted, and the cursor is advanced after update but before the next frame. In *double-frame* systems, the character is entered or transmitted on one frame, and the cursor is moved on the *next* frame. Some double-frame circuits actually take three frames total, the first to synchronize the update command to the frame-rate timing, the second to enter the character, and the third to adjust the cursor. But the same frame can be used to adjust the cursor as well as synchronize the *next* update command, so updates can take place on a once-every-other-frame rate.

No matter how many frames it takes, there is always a three-step process involved. First, the update command must be synchronized to the frame-rate timing, to make sure the character gets entered only once and in the right position. Second, the character must actually be entered. Third, the cursor must be moved to a new location.

Two types of cursor systems are the traditional *count and compare,* or *C and C,* cursor and the *McFadden,* or dynamic, cursor.

COUNT AND COMPARE CURSOR

Fig. 5-1 shows a traditional count and compare cursor. Two cursor counters, called the horizontal counter and the vertical counter, are

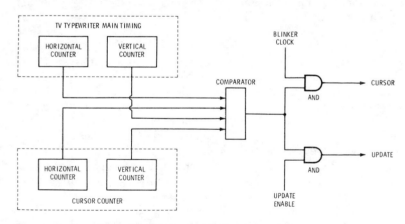

Fig. 5-1. Count and compare cursor system.

cascaded. Their total number of possible counts equals the number of available character slots. Taken together, the outputs of these two counters are a digital word that describes the line and row of the next character to get entered or retransmitted. This static digital word is compared to the constantly changing system timing that is addressing the memory locations or marching the ASCII commands out of a shift register.

Whenever the words are equal, both the cursor and system timing are at the same character, and a 1 output is provided by the comparator. This coincidence output is combined with a blinker as a display indication and is combined with an update command to do the actual entry or retransmission of a character. The blinking output by itself will generate a box type of cursor that makes the entire character white, since the same coincidence repeats over and over again for the seven or more lines it takes to put down a dot-matrix character. Additional logic is easily added to change the box cursor into a single blinking upperline or overline if this is preferred. Often the single blinking line is better for large-size displays (ordinary tv sets, etc.) of few characters, while the flashing box is preferable for small displays of many characters.

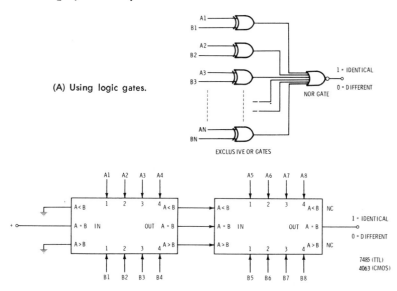

(A) Using logic gates.

(B) Using magnitude comparator integrated circuits.

Fig. 5-2. Comparing two digital words.

Fig. 5-2 shows how we can compare two digital words to see if they are identical. Fig. 5-2A shows the basic logic. Each pair of bits (one from each word) is exclusive-ORed, producing a 0 output if the bits are identical and a 1 output if the bits are different. The outputs of all the exclusive OR gates are then run to a NOR gate having one input for each pair of bits being tested. If the words are different, one or more inputs to the NOR gate will be positive, and a 0 is produced. If all the inputs to the NOR gate are low, all the bit pairs are identical, and a 1 is put out, indicating a coincidence.

In Fig. 5-2B, integrated circuits called *magnitude comparators* are used to test four bit pairs at a time. These ICs may be cascaded to compare addresses of any length. A 512-character system needs three magnitude comparators to handle the nine bits used. The TTL 7485 and the CMOS 4063 are typical magnitude-comparator integrated circuits.

If we do not change the input to the cursor counter with the C and C system, it continuously puts out the same address, on the same character. Whenever a write or a retransmit command arrives, the character will get updated. To move the cursor around, we add or subtract counts from the counter or fully or partially reset the system.

Fig. 5-3 shows how we pick up the three basic cursor motions. A pulse on the SPACE input advances the counter one count, moving us

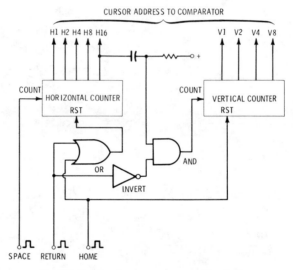

Fig. 5-3. Count-and-compare cursor motion logic.

to the next character. At the end of a horizontal line, a carry is produced to the vertical counter, so a space at the end of the line will move us to the beginning of the next line. The HOME input resets both the horizontal and vertical counters to zero, moving us to the upper left-hand corner. The RETURN input clears only the horizontal counter, while adding one count to the vertical counter. This gives us a combined line feed and carriage return. Note that the output of the horizontal counter is capacitor-coupled to the vertical counter and that the return command is longer than the time constant of this coupling. This ensures that one, and only one, count is routed to the vertical counter during a carriage return. If we direct-coupled H16 to the vertical counter, H16 would be high for characters 16 through 31 and low for characters 0 through 15, and the carriage return would work properly on the right-hand half of the screen but would return to its *own* line start for returns from left of screen center.

Fancier cursor motions are easily obtained with additional logic. By using a parallel-loading counter system, cursor addresses can be directly and immediately addressed from an outside microprocessor system. By using up/down counters, space can become a backspace, and repeat actions are easily introduced. All of the output bits can be ANDED together to spot the end of frame character location. This logic can be used to scroll the display or to automatically change memory pages. Erase-to-end-of-line logic or end-of-frame logic is also easily added.

The count and compare system is an obvious way to go and is a good system for high speeds, very long line lengths, and situations where extensive remote control is needed. Its main disadvantages are that it takes a lot of complex integrated circuits, has a complex pc board layout, and, in the case of TTL, uses lots of supply current.

McFADDEN CURSOR

The McFadden cursor is far simpler than the C and C system and uses fewer and cheaper integrated circuits. It is a little more difficult to understand and follow. Essentially, the McFadden system is completely the reverse of the C and C system. The McFadden cursor counters run *continuously* and are *stopped* briefly only when a location is to be changed.

Fig. 5-4 shows the McFadden cursor system. A single binary ripple up-only counter keeps track of character locations. The CMOS 4040 is ideal for many systems. Simple gating before the cursor counter

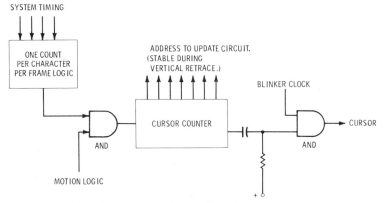

Fig. 5-4. McFadden cursor needs no up/down counters or comparators.

provides one count per character per frame. With a 512-character system, 32 pulses are generated on the top line of each row of characters, resulting in 512 pulses per frame. Each pulse corresponds to both the location of a character and the dot-matrix line on that character where we want to put either an underline or an overline.

During normal operation, these 512 counts are routed continuously to our cursor counter, which has a capacity of 512 counts before it overflows. We monitor the $2^9 = 512$ output and generate a brief cursor pulse every time this output falls to zero. Note that the 2^9 output will go around exactly once per frame and that it will always drop and produce a cursor underline at some location.

What location is it? We do not know yet, but unless we interfere with the count process, the count at the end of the frame stays the same. Even more important, the character position where the 2^9 output drops stays the same. It is unique and may generate a cursor directly, without needing any comparator logic.

Supposing at the end of a frame, we throw in an *extra* count pulse. What happens? Since there is now one more count in the cursor counter than before, it reaches its maximum count *one earlier* than it did before, and so it apparently *backs up* one character.

Supposing we *hold back* one of the normal 512 timing counts so that only 511 arrive on a given frame. What happens now? The counter starts off one count behind where it was before, so it overflows *one count later* than it used to, which moves us ahead one space. If we reset the counter, being extra careful to release the reset precisely at the end of a frame, our counter goes to count 0000 . . . 0, which means it will overflow on its *maximum* count, moving the cursor to the lower right-hand corner. If we reset and then hold back one more normal timing count, one gets added to the maximum count, moving us to the upper left-hand home position. So, we can backspace by adding a pulse, go forward by withholding a pulse, and move to home by resetting and then withholding a pulse.

Note that the cursor counter is stationary during the entire vertical retrace interval. *The contents of the McFadden cursor counter will be the* complement *of the cursor address during vertical retrace.*

All that remains for the essential cursor motions is a combined carriage return and line feed. This is a bit trickier to understand but is just as simply done as the other motions. To return, we have to hold back some number of count pulses, but just enough to move us to the end of the line we are on and then one more to move to the beginning of the next line. Depending on where we are, this can range from 1 to 32 counts.

The 2^5 output of the counter provides a useful signal for combined line feed and carriage return. Note that this 2^5 output overflows, dropping from + to ground, precisely at the end of a cursor line. From our main timing, we can also get a signal that ends at the end of the system timing line. If we set a flip-flop with the 2^5 output and reset it with the system line timing, the flip-flop will be set for exactly the time needed to subtract just enough pulses to move us to the end of the line we started on, no matter where we started. Holding back one more count then moves us to the beginning of the next line.

So, for carriage return, set a flip-flop with the 2^5 output and reset it at the end of the line, holding back all normal cursor counts in between. Then hold back one more pulse and the return is complete.

Note that we will always hold back one count on the next frame, regardless of whether we are entering a character, homing the counter, or returning to the beginning of the next line. If we want to, we can make things unanimous by throwing in a *double* extra count for backspace and then holding back one count there also. This moves us back two and then ahead one.

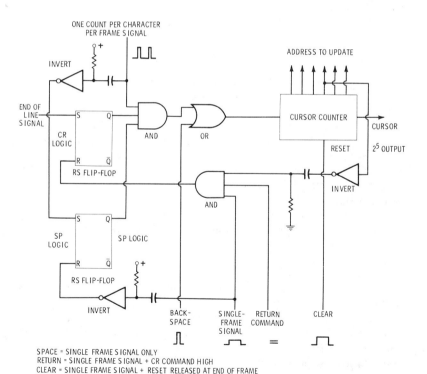

Fig. 5-5. McFadden cursor motion logic.

SPACE = SINGLE FRAME SIGNAL ONLY
RETURN = SINGLE FRAME SIGNAL + CR COMMAND HIGH
CLEAR = SINGLE FRAME SIGNAL + RESET RELEASED AT END OF FRAME
BACK SPACE = SINGLE PULSE DURING VERTICAL RETRACE

Fig. 5-5 shows more details on the basic cursor motion circuitry. Note that the need for individual up/down counters and the complex word-comparison circuitry are eliminated. As a bonus, with 512-character systems, if a 12-stage counter like a CMOS 4040 is used, we also get a 2^{12} output that is around 7.5 Hz and is useful as an absolutely free blinker, repeat, and retransmission signal.

Note once again that the parallel contents of the McFadden cursor counter will be the complement of the character addressed during the vertical retrace time. This feature is extremely handy for direct memory access, for vertical interval writing systems, and for end-of-frame logic.

On fast systems with lots of characters, the ripple delay time of the binary counter can be a problem. This problem can be solved by pretriggering ahead of the system timing, using fast logic, re-synchronizing the ripple output to the next available fast system clock pulse, or using any of a number of other techniques. With RAM systems, using the updating during vertical retrace greatly minimizes this ripple delay problem. If CMOS is used, at least a 10-V supply is recommended in most systems, or the premium 50-MHz SOS (silicon-on-sapphire) CMOS devices should be chosen.

DIRECT MEMORY ACCESS TECHNIQUES

If we permanently connect all the memory address lines of our memory to the system timing, we are pretty much limited to when, how, and where we update. On the other hand, if we break loose the memory address lines so that we are free to connect them to a number of different address sources, we end up with a far more useful and flexible system. When the memory address lines are flexible and available for use, we say we have a *direct memory access*, or DMA, system. Note that DMA is far and away the easiest to use on static RAM memory systems. Dynamic RAM, shift register, and particularly dynamic shift-register memory components will place very definite "memory busy" and "minimum refresh" timing restrictions on direct access.

Direct memory access has many unique advantages. The most important is that you can now use the display memory as a micro-computer or microprocessor memory as well, letting one storage system do double duty. A second advantage is that we are now free to control when and how to interrogate or change the memory contents. This means we can get character-rate loading or reading of memory without difficult external buffering and timing. More importantly, it means we can take our time about writing a character into memory. Instead of a critical 400-ns write pulse staggered 200 ns from any timing change, you can use a half-millisecond write pulse, perhaps even derived from the vertical-sync signal. Direct memory access lets the outside circuitry do the timing and commanding, rather than trying to match the internal tv typewriter timing. If we restrict the available DMA time to the vertical retrace time of the display, lots of time is available for DMA use, but the display will still be continuous and the actual update sequences invisible.

Fig. 5-6 shows a DMA circuit with several interesting features. We could, in theory, bring out all the memory address lines to a giant n-pole, three-throw selector switch. In the first switch position, the normal tv typewriter timing would exercise the memory in the usual way for sequential video output. In the second switch position, a frame-rate cursor addresses one location in memory for update or readout. In the third switch position, an external microprocessor or computer could take over the memory completely and do whatever it wanted to it. When it was finished, it would return the switch to position 1 for display.

Giant selector switches are rarely needed in digital circuits. Instead, we use the *bus organization* technique in which we use *tri-state* drivers to gain access to the memory lines. A tri-state driver has three output states, a low-impedance 0 state, a low-impedance 1 state, and a floating or invisible high-impedance state. So, we can short together the outputs of as many tri-state drivers as we like, without harm, provided we *enable* only one set of outputs at a time. Suitable tri-state drivers are the TTL 74125 or the CMOS 4502.

In Fig. 5-6, we have used inverting tristate drivers for the tv typewriter timing and for external minicomputer control. We could also use a third set of drivers for access by a frame-rate cursor. But, since the frame-rate cursor rise and fall time is not very critical (we have the entire vertical interval to use), we can continuously "float" the frame-rate cursor addresses onto the memory address lines with high-values resistors. If we enable neither the tvt timing nor the external timing, the frame-rate cursor addresses appear on the memory bus. If we enable either of the other address sources, the low-impedance output of the drivers swamps the cursor address and takes over. The memory addresses from the McFadden cursor get complemented with respect to the other timing sources. Since they were complements to start with, everything gets addressed in the right location.

A floating background technique like this works only when there is no time when we would not want *some* address on the memory bus, when we are using high-impedance MOS memories that do not load address lines, and finally, when the memory is small enough and the system well-behaved enough that noise problems do not become excessive with relatively high-impedance sources on the address bus. We do have to be certain never to enable both driver systems at

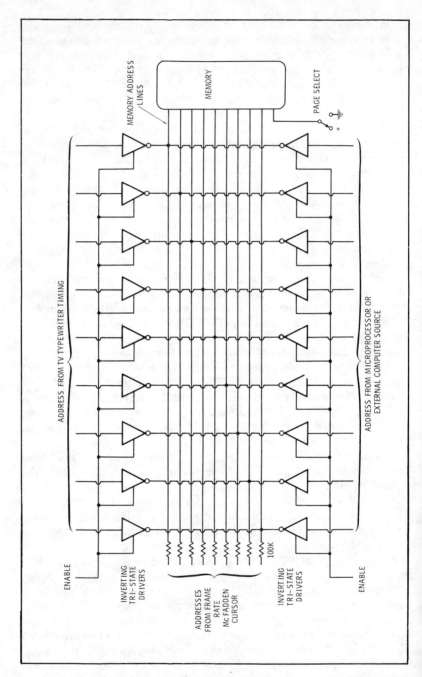

Fig. 5-6. Direct memory access using tri-state gates.

once. One approach is to let the tvt timing turn itself on during live scan and off during retrace. The external computer control driver is normally off and controlled externally. Whenever it turns on, it locks out the tvt drivers, gaining dominant access to the memory.

Character-rate update is best handled by reading out or loading an entire frame at a time. This way, the frame-rate cursor can simply be reset, rather than parallel-loaded to a new address.

A MICROPROCESSOR CURSOR

Fig. 5-7 shows another approach to providing external, high-speed control of a tv typewriter system. In this example, the memory of an existing microprocessor is used for character storage and refresh. The system lends itself to long line lengths and premium systems with uppercase and lowercase characters, particularly when extensive editing is needed.

Instead of a main memory in the tv typewriter portion of the display, only enough memory for two lines of characters is provided, usually as shift registers. While the microprocessor is filling the even-row memory, the odd-row memory is reading out to the character generator and video output circuitry, and vice versa. If we have an 11-line dot matrix (nine for a premium character and two spaces), the microprocessor can spend the entire eleven lines loading one line's worth of characters. This slower speed is much more compatible with many microprocessor cycle times than the submicrosecond video rate. Cursor motions are handled directly with microprocessor software.

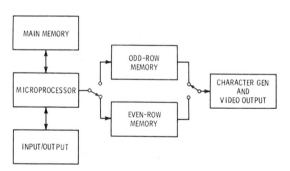

Fig. 5-7. A microprocessor-controlled cursor.

A DOUBLE CURSOR

Adding a second cursor system that is pretty much independent of the first has several advantages when fancy editing is needed. For instance, if a portion of the screen is to be transmitted, the first cursor can indicate the start, and the final one the ending. Double-cursor techniques also simplify line deletion and addition, word changes, justification for phototypesetting, and other format tasks. Double cursors are obviously much more complex than single ones, and their design varies extensively with application.

A STORED CURSOR SYSTEM

Dedicating one bit of the memory word to cursor storage offers yet another approach to cursor design. For instance, we could use a memory of eight bit words, reserving seven of them for uppercase and lowercase ASCII characters and saving the last bit of each word for cursor storage. One possibility would be to clear the cursor bits to 0 at the beginning of a screen load, except for a timing 1 that happens just *before* the first character location. Our cursor looks for a 1 to 0 transition on the eighth memory bit. This transition may be used to blink the cursor or to enter a new character. When a new character is entered, its *own* cursor position is made a 1, automatically advancing the 1 to 0 transition to the next character down the line. As the screen fills, the cursor memory also fills with 1's, automatically advancing. Line feed can be based on repeated writing of 1's till a line timing signal comes up. Backspace and other fancier cursor motions might be considerably more difficult to do. This technique offers an interesting and not yet fully explored option for tvt design.

THE "UNCURSOR"—CAPTIVE TVT'S

In cases where the tvt circuitry is to be intimately and permanently associated with a microprocessor system, the dedicated cursor can sometimes be eliminated entirely, and character motions, entry, retransmission, etc., can be done with software.

This can lead to an ultra low-cost tvt, possibly eliminating the internal tvt memory and update circuits as well as the cursor circuitry. In a microcomputer system, the same technique can give you a "super front panel" that lets you view *all* the memory contents of the entire computer a page at a time under command. A similar approach works well with ultrasophisticated tvt systems in which extensive word processing—line justification, sorting and rearrangement, deletion of text, and so on—is needed.

Fig. 5-8 shows one possibility. Here a microprocessor chip has four (or more) pages of memory associated with it. The microprocessor addresses its memory through tri-state drivers set up so that drivers are disabled whenever the microprocessor is in its HALT or

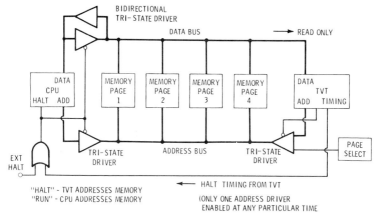

BIDIRECTIONAL
TRI-STATE DRIVER

DATA BUS

READ ONLY

| DATA CPU | MEMORY PAGE 1 | MEMORY PAGE 2 | MEMORY PAGE 3 | MEMORY PAGE 4 | DATA TVT |
| HALT   ADD | | | | | ADD   TIMING |

EXT HALT

TRI-STATE DRIVER

ADDRESS BUS

TRI-STATE DRIVER

PAGE SELECT

HALT TIMING FROM TVT

"HALT" - TVT ADDRESSES MEMORY
"RUN" - CPU ADDRESSES MEMORY

(ONLY ONE ADDRESS DRIVER
ENABLED AT ANY PARTICULAR TIME)

Fig. 5-8. Captive "cursorless" tvt forms microprocessor "super front panel" and needs no internal cursor, memory, or update circuitry.

STOP mode. This is easily done with many current microprocessor systems.

Whenever the microprocessor halts, the tvt timing and addressing are enabled, and the selected page of memory is interrogated. A tvt circuit, set up as 64 characters of 16 lines each, interrogates $1 K \times 8$ of memory at one time. Pages or portions of larger pages are selected with thumbwheel switches or other coding.

Since the tvt and the microprocessor are sharing memory addressing, it is of utmost importance that they take turns addressing, never attempting to both control memory at the same time. If we are not careful about how the memory is shared, either large holes will appear in the tvt display during computer operation, or else the tvt display will be continuous but the compute time (throughput) will take forever. There are several good ways we can trade off the memory access.

Generally, it is better to *let the tvt timing dominate*. Although a computer program can usually be started and stopped as needed without introducing serious problems, the scanning requirements of the tvt are very exact. One simple approach is to compute only during the vertical retrace time. In this way, the tvt is continuous, but the computer throughput is only ⅓ of normal, increasing program times by a factor of three. This is simple, but probably unacceptable for all but the shortest programs.

If we run the tvt on alternate frames, blanking on one field and displaying on the second, the display brightness will go down by 50%, but the presentation should still remain relatively flicker free with a 30-hertz refresh rate. This technique increases the throughput to ⅔, which only increases the compute time by 50%. If we also let the computer run during horizontal retrace and on the unused lines between characters, we can get the throughput up to ⅚ or so of normal, an almost negligible increase of only 20%. Another obvious and simple route is to display the tvt presentation only between actual computations.

If the central processing unit (CPU) and tvt are to share memory on a continuous basis, you have to be certain the CPU software programming does not contain any "timer loops," in which a fixed number of clock cycles are counted out in order to get a specified output *time*. Since the tvt can take over in the middle of such a loop, the output times can be erratic, although the number of counted clock cycles will remain constant and under software control.

When the tvt is used as a "super front panel" to interrogate an eight-bit machine, the first seven bits may be displayed as uppercase and lowercase characters, while the eighth bit can be used as a cursor, a blinking, a brightness change, or a color shift. In this way, the *entire* memory can be displayed and read as needed, using a "modified ASCII" rather than an octal or hex notation. Alternately, a small read-only memory and a data selector can be used to give us HEX-ASCII conversion. This flashes the upper hex character, the lower, then a blank. The result is a direct tvt readout of hex computer memory storage.

The captive, or "uncursor," approach is handy and simple whenever you are already using a microprocessor or whenever you need ultraexotic tvt manipulations. At this writing, the dedicated cursor circuits of earlier portions of this chapter are much cheaper and much simpler to use than a CPU-RAM-ROM system for ordinary stand-alone, nonexotic tvt uses.

UPDATING

The actual update circuitry also depends on which type of cursor you are using and how much external control is to be provided. With character-rate update systems, there is not too much in common from system to system. But, with the more usual frame-rate update, there are several common features most systems share.

One often-used circuit is a one-and-only-one or *single-frame generator* that takes a keypressed command and generates an output gate that lasts for precisely one frame and locks into system timing. Fig. 5-9 shows a typical circuit. The first flip-flop is set with the leading edge of a properly delayed and debounced keypressed command, or it is strobed by the output of a UART serial-parallel converter. This first flip-flop absorbs the time difference between the arrival of the key-pressed command and the beginning of the next frame. The second flip-flop Q output goes high the instant a positive edge on

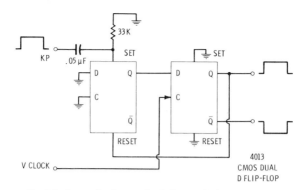

Fig. 5-9. One-and-only-one circuit for single-frame update.

the V clock arrives, almost always a 60-Hz clock signal. This output reaches around and resets the first flip-flop, enabling it to go back to ground on the next clocking. The result is a positive-going gate that lasts for one frame at the Q output and for one frame at its complement, the $\overline{Q}$ output. Internal storage circuitry of a UART can sometimes be used as part of the one-and-only-one configuration.

Writing a character is usually done by switching a shift-register memory from *recirculate* to *enter* or by switching a RAM from *read* to *write*. Our write pulse has to obey certain rules:

1. The cursor address must be valid for the entire write time.
2. The memory addresses must not be allowed to change immediately before, during, or immediately after the write pulse.
3. Writing must take place only once and only when wanted.
4. The write pulse and the "daylight" on either side of it must meet minimum requirements spelled out on the memory data sheet.

Usually, we continuously generate write pulses in their proper timing slot to meet these requirements, and then we restrict them from reaching the memory with a "write enable" logic tree such as the one in Fig. 5-10.

Our write signal can be a narrow pulse that arrives with the character-rate timing for shift registers or RAM memories. Typical would be a 500-ns pulse that begins 200 ns after the character address is stable. With RAM systems that have DMA, such as the one in Fig. 5-6, our write pulse can be a wide and convenient signal that arrives during vertical retrace. The vertical-sync signal is an ideal source.

This write pulse is ANDed with a single-frame output, so that a single write pulse is generated following a keypressed command. This single write pulse can be further inhibited by a PAGE-ENABLE input, by a MACHINE-COMMAND input if we do *not* wish to display

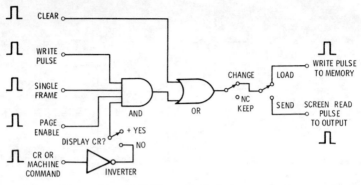

Fig. 5-10. Write-enable logic tree.

carriage-return commands, or by any other local or remote logic that wants to keep the write pulse from arriving. The valid write pulse is then ORed with a *clear* command that lets us generate a much longer write pulse that is used for clearing the entire memory. The combined output is routed to a KEEP-CHANGE switch and then to a SEND-LOAD switch. If both switches are in the correct position, and if all other logic is valid, a single write pulse is routed to the memory and one character gets updated.

The trailing edge of the single-frame output is often used to advance the cursor, following our three-step process of synchronizing the character available command to the system timing, entering the character, and then adjusting the cursor.

By inhibiting the write pulse with logic or by placing the KEEP-CHANGE switch in the KEEP position, we can use the same sequence to move only the cursor without changing the memory contents.

REPEAT ACTIONS

Fig. 5-11 shows how we can add a *repeat* capability to our single-frame update circuit. A low-frequency *blinker clock*, often 7.5 Hz, is routed to the clock input of the first flip-flop, and the D input is routed to a signal that is high when repeat action is needed and low whenever normal character entry action is desired. Repeat is handy for rapid cursor motions and for readout of existing screen contents, as well as for special effects. With the circuit shown, the repeat clock should be limited to 30 Hz or less.

CONTROL DETECTION

Somehow we have to be able to separate the commands that control our display from the characters actually displayed. This is

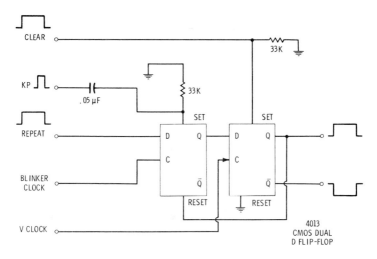

Fig. 5-11. Single-frame update circuit with repeat and clear.

called *control detection* or *machine-command separation*. The complexity of the separation process very much depends on how many different control functions you need.

For instance, in the basic display system, space is already an internal character, and backspace is often a local command useable even in a *change* or load condition. The only needed control command is a combined carriage return and line feed. Ideally, this should be coded as a "CR" or an "LF" ASCII command. Most of the fancier terminal systems use "LF" as a combined carriage return and line feed, an 001-1011 code.

If a line feed is the *only* control command that we will ever need, sometimes we can say that *any* control command will do the job. The limitation of this, of course, is that nothing else in the system is allowed to use a control command for anything. This does have one big disadvantage—any errors that look like machine commands tear up the display rather violently. Fig. 5-11A shows us how we can use a NOR gate to pick off any control command.

More often, we need extra control commands elsewhere in our system. This is particularly true in Teletype systems where two distinct commands, CR and LF, are needed to return the carriage to a new line and where other commands, such as ESC, CAN, BEL, etc., might see use. Fig. 5-12 shows simple logic that only detects two commands: the CR command, which is used to return the display; and the CAN, or cancel, command, which is used to clear the display or home it. In order to get by with two simple gate packages, we have cheated just a bit—rarely used machine-command EM will also

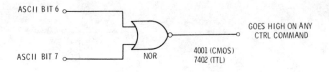

(A) Simple control detector.

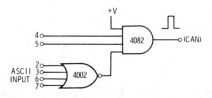

(B) Return and clear detector.

Fig. 5-12. Simple machine command detectors.

get read as a cancel, but all other machine commands will get ignored by the detection process.

Fig. 5-13 shows a full-blown control decoder that individually and exclusively extracts all 32 control commands. Two 1-of-16 decoders are combined with bit 5-6-7 logic to do this. Control outputs that are used are routed to the appropriate places in the system.

One problem that crops up often when using tv typewriters and Teletypes together is setting up and recognizing the different control commands after they are on the screen. If a tv typewriter is set up to not display an LF, it essentially swallows every line feed it receives. For instance, if you receive a message and then retransmit it, there are no LF commands left to get retransmitted.

There are several ways out of this bind. The most practical is to be able to display the machine commands without swallowing them. To do this, you use at least a seven-bit memory instead of the usual six, and you do *not* inhibit the writing of a J during a carriage return. All machine commands will get written on the screen as "J" for line feed, "M" for carriage return, and so on. Optionally, the seventh bit can alter the display to distinguish these commands, either by flashing, reverse field, different color, reduced brightness, etc. During program writing, debug, editing, and Teletype interactions, you keep

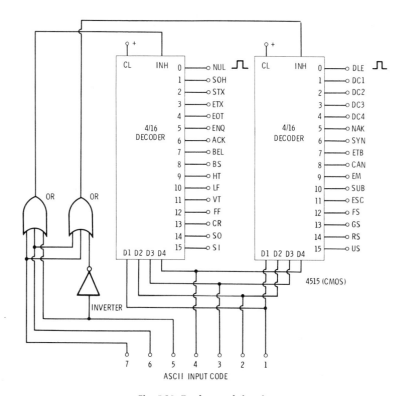

Fig. 5-13. Total control decoder.

displaying the machine commands. When the tv typewriter is finally to be used only as an output device, these commands can be blanked.

CLEARING

We "erase," or clear, the memory by writing ASCII blanks in each and every memory location. The rules for clearing are somewhat different than those for writing a single character:

1. Each and every memory location must be addressed during clear.
2. An ASCII input space command 100000 must be provided during the clear process.
3. The cursor must be reset to home immediately after clear.
4. The input space command 100000 must last till clearing is complete. This can be much longer than the input clear command, since clearing may not be complete till the end of a frame.

Usually, we can simply force our write logic into the write position (as is done with the clear input in Fig. 5-11) and continuously change addresses during the writing process. Some memory locations may get "flashed" during the address changes, but with most memory systems, everything will end up with an ASCII space in it eventually. The ASCII space command can be obtained from a keyboard that inherently puts out spaces between key pressings, or from one that is forced into this mode by an external clear command. Note that the space command must last till the end of the clearing frame. This could be 30 or more milliseconds after the clear command goes away. Other ways of getting a space command are to use tri-state inputs and float a space command onto the lines with high-value resistors, use the receiver latch of a UART (Chapter 7), or use input latches or true-complement 1-0 logic to do the same thing. Note that an all-0's input condition will get you a screen full of "@" symbols rather than a blank screen.

If CAN (cancel) is used as a machine command to provide clearing, it will fill the screen full of Xs instead of blanks. This is actually handy for cassette playback since playback errors are quite obvious, and since all the Xs get erased eventually.

SCREEN-READ CIRCUITS

We can retransmit the contents of a stored program in a tv typewriter simply by hanging another device, such as a UART parallel-to-serial converter (more on this in Chapter 7), on the output bus, as shown in Fig. 5-14. The normal write pulses are diverted with a switch to load the UART instead of changing the memory contents. Another alternative is to use a latch whenever a parallel output word is needed.

With shift-register memories, the output word is usually only briefly available and is combined with a short write pulse, often a fraction of a microsecond long. In these systems, an output latch *may* be needed to catch the word and hold it long enough to be used. With RAM memories using direct memory access and vertical-interval writing, we have a much longer time during which the word is available, and simple buffering, such as the input latch internal to a UART, is all that is needed to catch the word.

The output rate varies with application. If the output word is to be sent over a phone line or stored on an ordinary audio cassette recorder, or is to be Teletype compatible, we usually use a character output rate of 100 words per minute, equal to 10 characters per second. For a faster readout, most frame-update circuits can be run at a 30- or 60-character-per-second rate. With direct memory access under microprocessor control, the readout can be virtually any rate

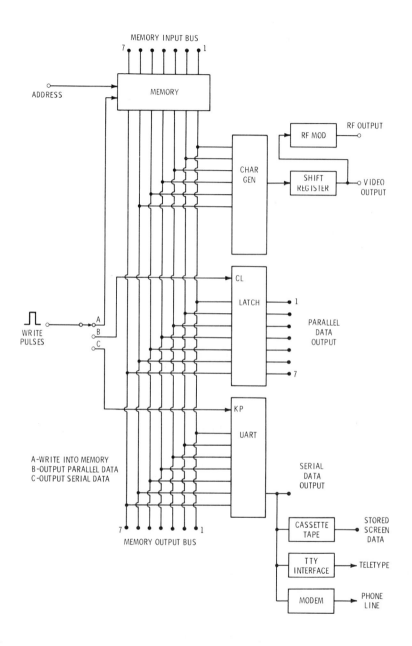

MEMORY INPUT BUS

ADDRESS

WRITE PULSES

A—WRITE INTO MEMORY
B—OUTPUT PARALLEL DATA
C—OUTPUT SERIAL DATA

MEMORY OUTPUT BUS

MEMORY

CHAR GEN

RF MOD — RF OUTPUT

SHIFT REGISTER — VIDEO OUTPUT

CL

LATCH

PARALLEL DATA OUTPUT

KP

UART

SERIAL DATA OUTPUT

CASSETTE TAPE — STORED SCREEN DATA

TTY INTERFACE → TELETYPE

MODEM → PHONE LINE

Fig. 5-14. Screen-read techniques.

125

up to the minimum read times of the memories themselves. This can range up to several million characters per second.

One important thing to remember when using a cassette interface is to record slightly slower than system-limit rates, so that playback on a machine with fresh batteries will not overrun the system. For instance, a 7.5-Hz repeat rate is a good choice for a normal 100-wpm Teletype system, as it allows considerable recorder speed variation (with the proper circuitry attached) without overrunning the Teletype. With a 60-character-per-second system, a 45-Hz retransmission rate is a good choice. At a 7.5-Hz readout rate, a full 512-character screen readout will take 68 seconds, while a 45-Hz system will take 11 seconds. These times can be virtually minimized by filling one page while another is being viewed and by creative use of carriage returns ignoring everything after the last *used* character on a line and ignoring unused lines.

It is usually best to screen read an entire frame at a time, for this lets you simply reset the cursor to its home position rather than have

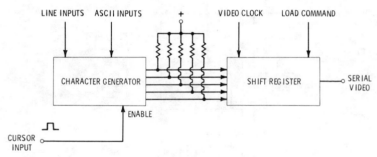

(A) Entry at character-generator enable—one character delay.

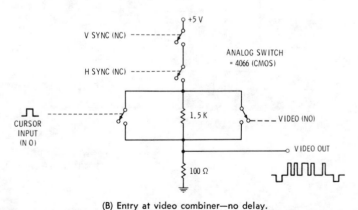

(B) Entry at video combiner—no delay.

Fig. 5-15. Adding the winking cursor to output video.

to keep track of cursor positions with external logic. Note that when you display the carriage returns, the readout for each line must stop at the carriage return; otherwise, spaces get added to the beginning of the next line, and the format gets jumbled. If carriage returns and machine commands are not displayed, each line should be read in its entirety to pick up an automatic carriage return at end of line. With displayed commands, the screen read should stop on the carriage return command of each line. This can be done either manually or by feeding the carriage return readout back into the tv typewriter.

OUTPUT OPTIONS

Fig. 5-15 shows us two ways we can enter the flashing cursor into the video output. In Fig. 5-15A, we disable the character generator output and pull the output up to get a white box, underline, or overline. This pull-up is free with TTL and takes the high-value resistors

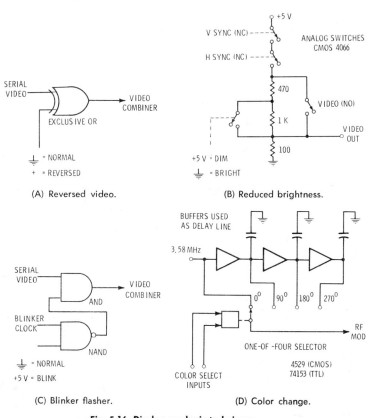

(A) Reversed video.

(B) Reduced brightness.

(C) Blinker flasher.

(D) Color change.

Fig. 5-16. Display emphasis techniques.

shown with CMOS. Alternatively, we can directly produce a white screen at the video output as shown in Fig. 5-15B. Note that the character generator entry will provide a *one-character delay* before the enable gets loaded and the cursor is produced, while the direct video method provides an immediate output. It is obviously of major importance that the cursor blinking line indicate the same character that can be written for that cursor position.

There are several "bells and whistles" games you can play with the

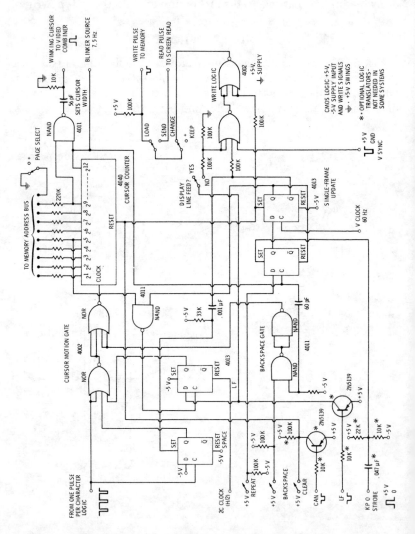

Fig. 5-17. Complete McFadden cursor and update schematic.

video output, particularly if you are using a seven- or eight-bit memory. Fig. 5-16 shows some possibilities.

In Fig. 5-16A, we exclusive OR the video output whenever we want to provide a controlled inversion that gives us a black character on a white background. In Fig. 5-16B, we reduce the gain on selected characters or words for partial brightness. In Fig. 5-16C, a blinker is added to flash certain characters. In Fig. 5-16D, we use the seventh and eighth bits of the memory to select one of four output colors on a color display. This is done by suitably phase-shifting a color sub-carrier oscillator. More details on this in Chapter 8.

Emphasis techniques like these may be used to distinguish control characters from alphanumerics or used anywhere else we want to outline, identify, or call attention to a portion of a display.

We can use similar logic to alter the cursor actions by means of the memory output. For instance, an eighth bit of memory could be used to protect certain portions of text, preventing them from being changed by the operator. Alternatively, feedback of this type can be used to automatically line feed when the LF command is reached on each line, thus speeding up the screen-read process and preventing format errors.

A COMPLETE CURSOR SYSTEM

Fig. 5-17 summarizes many of the techniques of this chapter. Here we have shown a complete CMOS logic McFadden cursor and update system for a 512-character-per-page tvt system using RAM memory, DMA, and writing and retransmission during vertical interval.

CHAPTER 6

Keyboards and Encoders

A *keyboard* of some sort is the usual way of entering manual data into a tv typewriter system. Most keyboards consist of two distinct parts, the *keyswitches* and the *encoder*. The keyswitches are often single-contact spst normally open switches; the encoder converts the single-contact switch closures into a complete ASCII code. The output code is most often in parallel form (all the bits at once), but it is easily converted to serial form (one bit at a time in sequence) with the circuits of the next chapter. A properly designed encoder also eliminates the effects of switch bounce and noise, and minimizes or eliminates the effects of more than one key being pressed down at once. It also gives us a *"keypressed"* or *strobe* output and optionally gives us a *parity*, or error-testing, output bit.

The encoder also lets us use one key for more than one purpose. This is usually done with an extra SHIFT and a CONTROL key that suitably change the code. This is often called a *tri-mode* system where one key can do up to three different tasks. For instance, one key in its normal position would be a semicolon (;); shifted, it would become a plus (+); and changed to CTRL or a machine command, it would turn into escape (ESC), a command often used in time-sharing computer systems to change languages. In fancier *quad-mode* systems, a fourth character or command per key can be obtained, but usually CTRL will dominate SHIFT and give us up to three codes per switch.

Our seven-bit ASCII code is repeated in Table 6-1. To this basic code, we usually either add an eighth bit that is always a 1 or add a *parity* bit that makes all the 1's in the particular word an *even* number. The choice of even parity makes DEL (delete) a 1111-1111 code, useful for rubbing out a paper tape.

Table 6-1. The Standard ASCII Code Generated by Most Keyboards

							BIT NUMBERS →	0 0 0	0 0 1	0 1 0	0 1 1	1 0 0	1 0 1	1 1 0	1 1 1
b_7	b_6	b_5	b_4	b_3	b_2	b_1	COLUMN → ROW ↓	0	1	2	3	4	5	6	7
			0	0	0	0	0	NUL	DLE	SP	0	@	P	`	p
			0	0	0	1	1	SOH	DC1	!	1	A	Q	a	q
			0	0	1	0	2	STX	DC2	‖	2	B	R	b	r
			0	0	1	1	3	ETX	DC3	#	3	C	S	c	s
			0	1	0	0	4	EOT	DC4	$	4	D	T	d	t
			0	1	0	1	5	ENQ	NAK	%	5	E	U	e	u
			0	1	1	0	6	ACK	SYN	&	6	F	V	f	v
			0	1	1	1	7	BEL	ETB	'	7	G	W	g	w
			1	0	0	0	8	BS	CAN	(	8	H	X	h	x
			1	0	0	1	9	HT	EM	)	9	I	Y	i	y
			1	0	1	0	10	LF	SUB	*	:	J	Z	j	z
			1	0	1	1	11	VT	ESC	+	;	K	[	k	{
			1	1	0	0	12	FF	FS	,	<	L	\	l	¦
			1	1	0	1	13	CR	GS	–	=	M	]	m	}
			1	1	1	0	14	SO	RS	.	>	N	∧	n	~
			1	1	1	1	15	SI	US	/	?	O	—	o	DEL

A simple ASCII keyboard appears in Fig. 6-1. It is nothing but seven (optionally eight) slide switches and a bounceless push button. The switches are set to the desired character, and pushing the button enters the character. The two inverters make a set-reset flip-flop that changes state on the first instant the switch closes and eliminates any switch bounce and noise. While this is a simple, cheap, and almost essential tool for debugging and testing, the device is difficult to learn and impossible to use at any rate of speed.

KEYBOARD DESIGN FACTORS

Most of today's keyboards use single-contact switches followed by an electronic encoder. Self-encoding or multiple-contact switches have not proved either cheap or reliable. Similarly, most useful key-

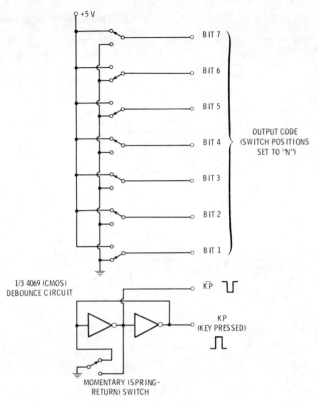

Fig. 6-1. Manual ASCII code generator is useful for tests but very slow.

board systems use a positive key area and positive key travel, preferably with some form of *tactile feedback,* click, snap action, or other way of reassuring the user that the key has been entered and entered only once. "Fingers through the holes" keyboards of zero travel seem to fly in the face of too much tradition and user experience. So far, they have turned out totally unacceptable, even in pocket calculators, let alone for alphanumeric uses, despite their potentially low cost.

Let's look at some of the major keyboard design factors in which we will be interested for most tv typewriter uses:

Style

There are two basic types of key arrangements that we can consider, the linear, or calculator, style and the common typewriter, or "Qwerty," style.

Fig. 6-2 shows one possible calculator style arrangement. The advantages of the calculator style are low cost and small size. Mod-

Fig. 6-2. Calculator-style keyboard layout.

erately short-travel keys with integral legends can be used, placed on ½-inch centers instead of the ¾-inch standard spacing of the Qwerty layouts. In addition, the *numeric* keypad type of entry is much faster, and nontypists are less error-prone with this type than with the Qwerty arrangement. You can use the calculator-style keyboard wherever low cost and a nontypist user get together. Important applications are educational terminals, deaf communication aides, cable tv answer-back applications, and so forth.

Note that color, keyshapes, and logical grouping combine to make this an easy-to-use system. The numeric keypad should have the distinctive shape that it has on most calculators and should stand out from nearby keys. Similarly, the alphabet should be symmetrically arranged, isolated and a contrasting color to nearby keys. Other advantages of the calculator arrangement are that multiple switching arrays can be used instead of individually mounted switches and that callouts are low in cost and relatively easy to change.

As long as the user can touch-type, the typing or Qwerty arrangement is obviously better suited for long-text messages and has more appeal than when the tv typewriter system is imitating premium terminal devices. Two popular key arrangements are the ANSI keyboard of Fig. 6-3 and the Data Communications (ASR-33) keyboard of Fig. 6-4. The American National Standards Institute (ANSI) keyboard usually offers a choice of uppercase only or uppercase and

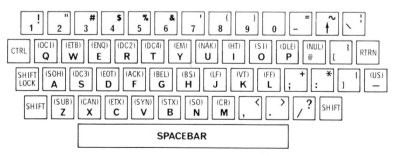

Fig. 6-3. ANSI keyboard arrangement.

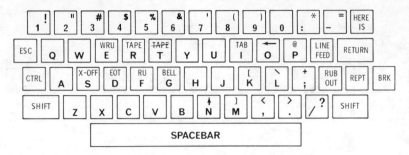

Fig. 6-4. Communication or ASR-33 keyboard.

lowercase combined, while the Data Communications style usually offers uppercase only, along with some control functions that work well with punched tape systems.

Keyswitches on the typewriter-type keyboard normally have longer travel than those on calculator keyboards, typically 0.167 inch compared with 0.050 or less in the calculator versions. A separate double-shot-molded keytop is usually provided. Double-shot molding lets the character go all the way through the keytop so that it cannot be altered or rubbed away with heavy use. These are available in a wide variety of callouts, but special characters or functions tend to be expensive in small quantities. Keytops must be matched to the particular brand of switch in use, as there is no standard keytop shank. Typical tangs include the IBM bar, the cruciform tang, the modified cruciform tang, and box-type tangs of several sizes. The usual sources of keytops include Mechanical Enterprises, ITT Thermotech, Cherry Electrical, Keytronic, Emconite, and Leo Tanaka. Standard keytops in reasonably large quantities usually cost a nickle each; custom callouts require a die costing $50 to $250. In small quantities, custom callouts can be done by an engrave and fill method that sharply reduces any setup charges.

Usually, a full-length space bar is provided that has a torsion wire *equalizer* under it to provide a uniform action regardless of where along its length it is pressed.

Qwerty keyboards are almost always designed with keys on ¾-inch centers. The row-to-row key offset is staggered. Staggering half a key per row is simple and provides a more nearly rectangular panel cutout, particularly if 1½-width keycaps are used for shift and return. Some premium keyboards use a "four-phase" staggering that was demanded by the mechanical keyboards of early typewriters but has no clear-cut advantage over the simpler arrangement. The four-phase arrangement is shown in Figs. 6-3 and 6-4.

Keytops must be dished inward slightly to properly home the fingers during typing. For economy systems, the keytops are all the same height and parallel to the pc board on which they are mounted. A stepped keyboard effect can be approximated with keyswitches that have stems bent on a 12° angle. Alternatively, a "sculptured" keyboard effect (IBM style) is obtained by changing the height of the upper and lower rows of keycaps. Keyboards are almost always sloped on a 12° angle for easier typing. In fancier systems, additional keypads are added to the right and left of the Qwerty layout for elaborate cursor movement, calculator-style numeric entry, and advanced editing commands.

Fig. 6-5 shows three less-common keyboard arrangements also based on the Qwerty typing system. Fig. 6-5A is a Baudot keyboard.

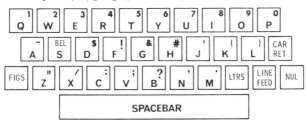

(A) Baudot (obsolete).

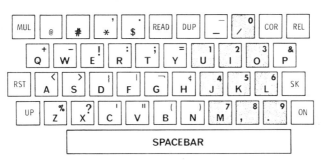

(B) Keypunch (obsolete).

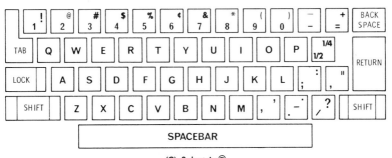

(C) Selectric.®

Fig. 6-5. These other keyboard arrangements are not directly ASCII compatible.

This is an obsolete five-level typing arrangement still used by some hams and deaf communications people. A case memory forces each key into double duty, typing letters in the LTRS case, and figures and punctuation in the FIGS case. Fig. 6-5B is a punched-card keyboard that is fast becoming obsolete and is being replaced with the ANSI layout. Finally, Fig. 6-5C is the standard Selectric electric typewriter layout used with office typewriters. Note that many of the keypairs are not directly compatible with the ASCII code and not easily interfaced with a simple ASCII encoder.

Switching

We have three basic types of switches available for keyboard use. These are the *mechanical switch, the elastomeric switch,* and *exotic switching technologies.*

The mechanical switch (Fig. 6-6) gives us a metal on metal contact. Typical examples are a gold-plated wire between two gold contacts, a gold-plated vee-bar contact, a stainless steel snap-disc and contact, a spring and wire arrangement, or something similar. If properly designed, high-reliability mechanical switching should combine both a wiping and a cross-point contacting, should have

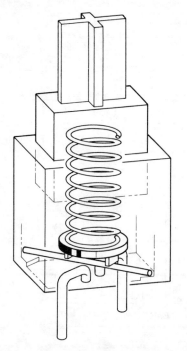

Fig. 6-6. Mechanical keyswitch.

Courtesy Mechanical Enterprises

some sort of positive action and tactile feedback to indicate *after* contact has been made, should have some protection against long-term corrosion and degradation, and should minimize keybounce and noise.

One low-cost series of mechanical contact switches is the T5 manufactured by Mechanical Enterprises. Competitive devices are available from Cherry Electrical, Oak, Stackpole, Microswitch, Texas Instruments, Bomar, Amp, Datanetics and others.

Elastomeric techniques use a piece of flexible conductive plastic or foam. One type of elastomeric material has to be physically moved against a contact and has a constant, relatively low resistance. A second type is pressure sensitive and dramatically lowers its resistance under pressure. Sources of suitable materials include Emerson and Cuming, Dynacon Industries, Pressex International, Chomerics, Technit, and Custom Materials. Light-duty, short-term keyboards have even been built out of the protective foam shipped with many MOS integrated circuits.

The on resistance of elastomeric contacts usually is several hundred to several thousand ohms. The progressive make action minimizes switch bounce. These fairly high-resistance values are usually compatible with ASCII encoder circuits, particularly those using MOS or CMOS circuitry.

Several problems limit the widespread use of elastomeric contacts. First and foremost is the problem of getting acceptable key travel and tactile feedback. A mushy, ill-defined response is rather easy to get, and foam systems have a response that is distinctly different from mechanical spring-return switching systems. A second major problem is long-term degradation. This is particularly true of high-conductivity foams that are loaded with silver particles, where fingerprints and overstressing effects can permanently and dramatically raise the resistance. A related degradation effect is surface contamination or corrosion of the mechanical contacts that the elastomer is supposed to be contacting.

There are lots of exotic switching techniques. Many premium computer-terminal keyboards use reed switches that are magnet operated. These have very long life, low bounce, and excellent tactile snap action. They are also very expensive, and you end up with a fairly thick keyboard. Another premium technique uses a *Hall* effect semiconductor switching device. As a magnet in the keyswitch moves toward the semiconductor chip, a snap action occurs. Both inductive and capacitive key array elements have been offered in the past, driven by oscillators and monitored by sense amplifiers, but their usage is not widespread, and their small-quantity costs are unreal.

Other exotics include nonelectronic keyboard encoding. One system blocks conductivity in tubes of mercury. Teletype keyboards set up a mechanical code with a group of bars and contacts that is then serially scanned with a mechanical commutator to get a direct serial code output. Mechanically encoded bars that block or pass several beams of light have also been offered.

Rollover and Lockout

A way to prevent wrong codes from happening when more than one key is down is absolutely essential. Three possible techniques for the prevention of wrong codes are *n-key lockout, two-key rollover,* and *n-key rollover.*

In n-key lockout, any key that is down generates a strobe or a keypressed command. Any extra keys pressed do not generate additional keypressed signals and are ignored. This is the simplest and cheapest system. While it prevents the wrong character from being entered, it can miss entire characters, since one key must be released before the next one is pressed.

In two-key rollover, any key that is down generates a strobe or a keypressed command. A second keypressed command activates logic that delays a new keypressed command until the first key is *released.* No wrong codes are produced, and no keys are missed as long as only two or fewer keys are down at any instant. Two-key rollover is reasonably easy to build into an encoder and should be included in all but "bare bones" designs.

In n-key rollover, the instant a key is depressed, its code is stored. Any number of keys can be down for any length of time. The output codes will change each time a new key is pressed. The n-key rollover takes a special output latch and may need external buffering. Worst of all, though, most current n-key rollover systems need a diode in series with each and every key to eliminate "phantom key" effects in scanning arrangements. For the overwhelming majority of applications, true n-key rollover is a useless luxury with no advantage over conventional two-key rollover circuits.

Error Minimization

Most mechanical switching systems generate noise and contact bounce during their initial contact. During this initial contact time, the wrong code could get generated, and the same or wrong codes could be sent out many times in a row as the keypressed or strobe output stutters. To beat this problem, a *debouncing* circuit is an essential part of any keyboard system. Most debouncing systems delay the keypressed or stobe command for a few milliseconds, long enough to be certain that the switch is settled and the output code is solid. Good debouncing circuits will also provide a sharp rise and fall time on the strobe output and will shorten the output so that it goes away long before the key is released.

An optional parity bit can also minimize system errors. The parity generation circuitry often makes the total number of 1's in the output word an even number. After transmission, parity is retested, and if there is an odd number of 1's in the word, one or three or five or seven errors have occurred during transmission. Parity cannot fix the mistake by itself, but it can tell you that an error has happened. You can then ask for a retransmission.

Parity also cannot spot an even number of mistakes. But the odds of two errors at once are usually far lower than the odds of a single mistake, so parity is a genuinely useful error indicator. Parity normally is not used in local tv typewriter systems. It is most often used when you are transmitting data over long distances, particularly over an ordinary phone line. If a keyboard does not generate parity by itself, single integrated-circuit parity generator/checkers are available. Typical are the CMOS 4531 and the TTL 74180. The serial interface circuitry of Chapter 7 usually includes built-in parity.

There are also more elaborate error-detecting systems that use more bits and can actually fix their own mistakes. These are most often used with blocks of data in magnetic recording applications, and are only called for when data integrity is of utmost importance.

Lowercase

One very important keyboard design factor is whether or not you are going to produce and use lowercase alphabets. Many tv typewriter and most Teletype systems can handle only uppercase characters. This is also true of most economy dot-matrix read-only-memory character generators. On the other hand, systems that are doing typesetting or are writing form letters must have both cases available.

In an uppercase-only system, the keyboard generates the capital letters and numbers without shifting. A shift either does nothing or generates punctuation symbols on certain keys.

In a two-case system, the unshifted key makes the small letters, and the shifted key gives you a capital, just as on an office typewriter.

Note that a two-case keyboard cannot be used directly on an uppercase-only system without generating a lot of wrong codes. If we simply use the bottom six bits of the ASCII code, a small *Q* is the same as an *1*, not the same as a large *Q*. This problem is straightened out with the simple logic of Fig. 6-7, which *must* be added to any two-case keyboard if it is to operate in a single-case system.

ENCODER CIRCUITS

The basic thing our encoder has to do is change the single-contact switch closure into a seven- or eight-bit parallel ASCII code. Along

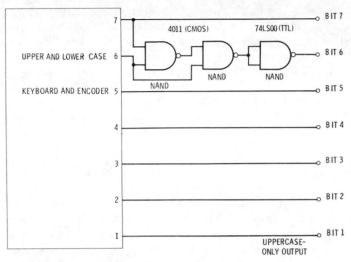

Fig. 6-7. A keyboard system that generates lowercase alphabet codes cannot be used in an uppercase-only circuit without this additional logic.

with this, it should provide for debounce, shifting, machine command or "CTRL" shifts, and some sort of lockout or rollover. There are four popular types of encoder circuits. These are, in order of cost and complexity, the *static,* the *scanning,* the *scanning and converting,* and the *scanning and converting with latch.*

Static Encoder

In a static encoder, conventional digital logic is used to directly generate a desirable code. We might try to build a simple "brute force" static encoder using nothing but resistors and diodes as shown in Fig. 6-8. Each key routes positive supply voltage to each output that has a diode connected to the key. In the keypressed method, there is a diode from each and every key, so that any key that is down gives us a positive output voltage. The N-key lockout is inherent in this circuit.

This is obviously a crude circuit that will take far too many parts, for several hundred diodes will be needed to encode the 50 or 60 keys we normally use.

The key to simplifying this circuit is to arrange the keys in an 8×8 matrix array, rather than in the linear 64×1 we just used. This reduces the keyboard-to-encoder interconnections from 65 to 16, and drops down our six-line encoding to a pair of three-line encodings that are shared by common keys, a much simpler circuit.

Fig. 6-9 shows us a minimum, uppercase-only matrix array static encoder. The circuit has three current sources logically tied to bits

1, 2, and 3, and three current sinks logically tied to bits 4, 5, and 6. Between the current sources and the key array is a three-line to eight-line diode encoder, and between the key matrix and the current sinks is an eight-line to three-line diode decoder. Pressing any key allows some combination of current sinks and sources to activate, generating an output code.

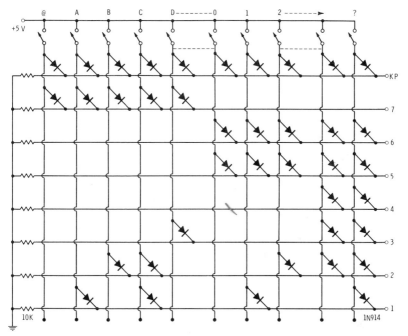

Fig. 6-8. "Brute-force" static ASCII encoder.

For uppercase-only systems, bit seven is the inverse of bit six. Both bits six and seven may be pulled to ground for control-key operation. For a very simple shift command, bit 5 may be forced to ground. This is simple and cheap but has the disadvantages of making the period, comma, equals, and question mark keytops upside down from standard systems. Also, half the letter keys will shift to an incorrect code if the shift is inadvertently pressed while typing capital letters.

For keypressed detection a common current source is sensed above the others. Routing current through any key activates the keypressed output. A storage capacitor, as shown, gives us a simple leading-edge delay and debounce. For many systems, additional circuits are added to improve the rise time of this command and shorten it to a narrow pulse that goes away well before key release.

The static encoder is simple, cheap, and easy to understand. It needs a single supply voltage and draws little current. It does have several obvious limitations, though.

The first of these is that the logic at the input must be able to both source and sink current. While pnp transistors combined with RTL integrated circuits can easily do this, the circuit cannot be built with

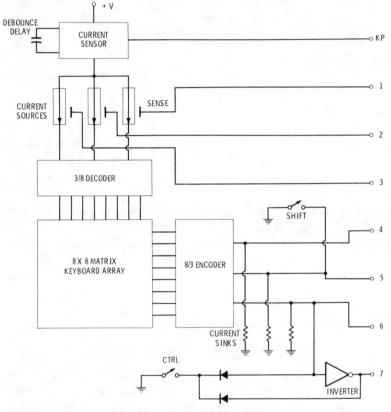

Fig. 6-9. Matrix static ASCII encoder.

ordinary TTL gates, and CMOS versions of the circuit take many input resistors and possibly will need voltage translation. A second disadvantage is that this circuit, built in "semidiscrete" form, takes 40 to 50 parts. But since we are talking penny parts instead of dollar parts, the static encoder circuit usually turns out to be the cheapest. Other limitations are that two-key rollover is hard to introduce and, since the keys are directly generating the output, we are very much limited in the callouts and options available to each key and how it is wired to the matrix.

Ordinary RTL gates, such as the 789 hex inverter or the 724 quad gate, work well with this type of circuit. Two fancier ICs that might be used are the Harris HD0165 keyboard encoder and the 4532 CMOS priority encoder. The HD0165 can handle the bottom four bits and keypressed and can give us a *partial* two-key rollover. Watch the strange supply pinouts if you use this device. The 4532 generates three code bits and an undelayed keypressed command.

Scanning Keyboard

A scanning keyboard (Fig. 6-10) also uses a key matrix. Each key is continuously interrogated in *time* sequence through an oscillator and decoder/selector circuit. The scanning process is continuous,

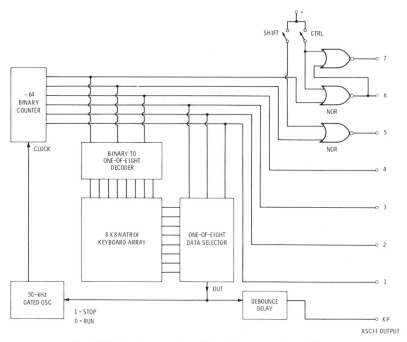

Fig. 6-10. Scanning encoder offers inherent two-key rollover.

spending around 20 μs on each key. If no key is pressed, scanning continues indefinitely. If a key is pressed, the scanning stops, and the counter state for that key gets output. The scanning keyboard inherently provides two-key rollover and simplifies the debounce circuitry needed.

In operation, a gated oscillator, running around 50 kHz, cycles a 6-bit counter. The top three bits are decoded to a 1-of-8 sequence that sequentially activates one key column at a time. The bottom three bits of the counter drive a 1-of-8 data selector that interrogates one key row at a time. When a key is pressed, the column active state is detected by the row data selector and rounted back to shut down the oscillator, thus holding that particular code, which appears as an output. A delay on the hold command provides us with a key-pressed output.

If a second key is pressed, nothing immediately happens. The keyboard stays locked in the position it is being held in by the first key. When this key is released, scanning starts up again, goes to the second key closure, and then stops again. Any number of keys can be pressed in overlapping sequence so long as only two keys are down at any particular instant.

Between keypressings, the output code is a jumble of all the characters, changing at the clock rate. Circuitry downstream must ignore these outputs when no keypressed command exists.

One sticky design detail of a scanning keyboard is that the column-output *active* level must very much dominate the column-output *passive* level. Otherwise, when a second key is pressed, it can present too heavy a load on the valid, active-column line and either restart the scanning or produce an invalid output code. Note that two keys in the same row will short two columns together if they are simultaneously down.

Scanning keyboards can be built with a single supply and usually with fewer but more-expensive parts than static keyboards. They, too, are restricted in the key-to-encoder wiring and the available key-top pairings. CMOS scanning keyboards have the potential for micropower operation and, in general, are handy for battery-powered terminals and remote-control operation. The CMOS 4051 is particularly attractive for this use.

Scanning Keyboard With Memory

We can add an output read-only memory to our scanning keyboard and pick up several additional features. The read-only memory (Fig. 6-11) takes the output word from the keyboard and changes it into any code combination we want. Usually we have a choice of three combinations set by the SHIFT and CTRL keys in a tri-mode system, or a choice of four combinations in a premium quad-mode system.

This does several good things for us. Instead of having to arrange our key matrix A - B - C - D . . . , we can now arrange it A - S - D - F . . . , dramatically simplifying the encoder-to-keyboard wiring on a Qwerty arrangement. SHIFT and CTRL can now selectively affect certain keys. This prevents false codes when a letter is accidentally shifted in an uppercase-only system. We nicely eliminate the upside-down keys on comma, period, question, and equals. Optionally, in

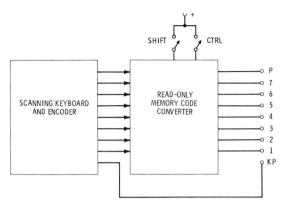

Fig. 6-11. Scanning encoder with conversion ROM offers wide choice of keytop pairs and simplifies keyboard to encoder wiring.

two-case systems we can use a single key for a period and another single key for a comma, just as in ordinary typewriter systems. And, we can locate our CTRL commands just about anywhere we like.

The Standard Microsystems and General Instruments 2376 single-chip MOS keyboard encoder is a typical example of a scanning keyboard with memory. It encodes up to 88 keys and provides both uppercase and lowercase outputs. Fig. 6-12 shows how to pick just uppercase or both uppercase and lowercase outputs from the 2376 *without* needing the add-on logic of Fig. 6-7.

Two supply voltages of +5 V and −12 V are needed, and the outputs are compatible with most logic families. Outputs are not tristate, and this may be a limitation in some bus-oriented input systems.

Scanning Keyboard With Latch and Memory

Fig. 6-13 shows us a premium encoder technique. If we add an output latch to our scanning encoder with memory, we can eliminate

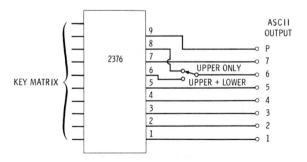

Fig. 6-12. The 2376 keyboard encoder IC offers a choice of case options.

the changing outputs during no-key scanning. We can also *potentially* provide true n-key rollover by letting the scanning operate continuously and then loading the output latch only at the instant a key is pressed. Since the leading edge of key action is all that counts, it does not matter how long the key is down and it can overlap as many keys as you want. Output codes get entered in sequence. One hangup is that if you press three keys in just the wrong location on the matrix at once, you can get a "ghost" key or "phantom" key with the resultant sneak path. One way around this problem is to place a diode in series with each key. This, of course, is expensive and complex. Most keyboard encoders that claim n-key rollover will, in fact, provide this action only when extra (and expensive) deghosting is provided for.

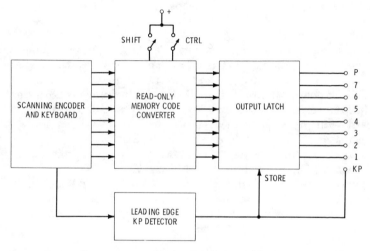

Fig. 6-13. Premium scanning, converting, and latching ASCII keyboard eliminates wrong output codes between keys. For true N-key rollover, "antiphantom key" circuitry must be added.

EXTRA KEYBOARD FEATURES

Several add-on features outside the basic code and key matrix may often be used. The first of these is a feature that combines all local, momentary and slide switches onto the keyboard, even if they are not going to provide an ASCII coded output. Clear and repeat are two obvious examples, while backspace and cursor motion keys are other possibilities. Keeping the backspace key local lets you back up on a page that otherwise is able to load characters.

Note that nonencoded keys usually can be used only locally, for there is no way to transmit them as serial data, unless they also "force feed" the keyboard into generating special machine commands. Usually the simplest interconnection of these nonencoded keys will result if you connect them to the positive supply through a keyswitch for a 1 output when activated.

Another potentially handy feature is a space output during the clear command. Somewhere in the tv typewriter system, we have to be able to clear the screen. In simpler systems, this is easiest to do at the keyboard itself.

With a static keyboard, we can design our code and key locations to inherently put out a space when no key is pressed. In scanning keyboards, the clear switch should short the scan matrix in the space position. Since a tv typewriter can take as much as one whole frame to complete the clearing after the clear command has been released, some way of keeping the output in the clear state for a few milliseconds *after* clear is essential. This is free in a static keyboard designed for clear output and can be provided by a storage capacitor when clear is shorting our matrix. In systems using UARTs, the output latch of the UART can be used to hold the clear command for us.

MOUNTING AND INTERCONNECT TECHNIQUES

Using a single printed-circuit board to mount all the keys and the encoder and the key-to-key interconnections is usually a good idea, but there are several cost and performance factors here that we should look at.

The first is mechanical rigidity. The keyboard *must* be absolutely solid. An ordinary pc board by itself usually is far too flexible. Ways around this problem are to provide a rigid frame around the pc board, to mount the pc board to a chassis *at least at twelve places,* to "honeycomb" the pc board to another circuit board or panel with threaded spacers, or to solder reinforcing strips to the rear of the pc board at right angles for a box-style construction.

Similarly, the entire case holding the keyboard should not scoot around when it is used, should be stable and comfortable, and should support the keyboard at a convenient use angle, perhaps somewhere around 12°.

A second problem is cost. The Qwerty-style keyboards take a large pc board and if the obvious two-sided-plate-through board route is used, the pc board can be extremely expensive. For lower cost, we can sometimes use a much cheaper single-sided board (foil side down) and make the reinforcing strips serve as jumpers. If we reinforce with double-sided pc strips, we get one conductor per side without needing any layout or etching. This simplification works very well with the 2376 encoder IC, since only two strips and no jumpers are needed on the keyboard proper.

Another route is to use solderable-through-the-insulation magnet wire (Beldsol, etc.) for the extra connections as needed, still sticking with a single-sided board layout. With continuous runs, only a few pieces of wire are actually used and the cost is far less than with a double-sided board. This also lets you *field-program* a keyboard array, allowing you to customize extra keys to your particular job without any special setup charges and to easily make changes later on. Newly available wiring pencils make this an easy, cheap, and attractive job.

Many keyswitches have critical hole sizes and positions. Usually these have to be precision located and drilled.

NONSTANDARD CODES

Any of these keyboard systems can be used to generate virtually any parallel code you want, simply by rearranging the key matrix to suit the code you want or by changing the codes in the read-only memory. Almost always, oddball codes will take nonstandard or hard-to-get keycaps, and the cost of a custom circuit board may be prohibitive in small quantities, unless you are using a field-programmable keyboard. Usually, it is far more practical to build a standard ASCII keyboard and encoder and then add an output programmable read-only memory.

Conversions to Selectric, Baudot, EBCDIC, and thte APL subset of ASCII are easily done this way, although specific differences be-

Table 6-2. Correspondence Between Baudot and Lower Five ASCII Bits

Baudot	ASCII	Baudot	ASCII
Blank	Space	T - 5	P
E - 3	A	Z - ‖	Q
Line Feed	B	L -)	R
A - —	C	W - 2	S
Space	D	H - #	T
S - '	E	Y - 6	U
I - 8	F	P - 0	V
U - 7	G	Q - 1	W
Car. Ret.	H	O - 9	X
D - WRU	I	B - ?	Y
R - 4	J	G - &	Z
J - BEL	K	Figures	;
N - ,	L	M - .	<
F - $	M	X - /	=
C - :	N	V - ;	>
K - (	O	Letters	?

tween each code's characteristics may take some outside circuitry and redefinitions. Examples of this are the figures-letters memory flip-flop needed in Baudot and the fact that space is an internal character in ASCII and an external command in Selectric. You can easily program suitable ROMs yourself. As surplus, they are priced as low as $2. Many standard or semistandard code conversion chips are available from National Semiconductor, Fairchild, AMI, Texas Instruments, and others.

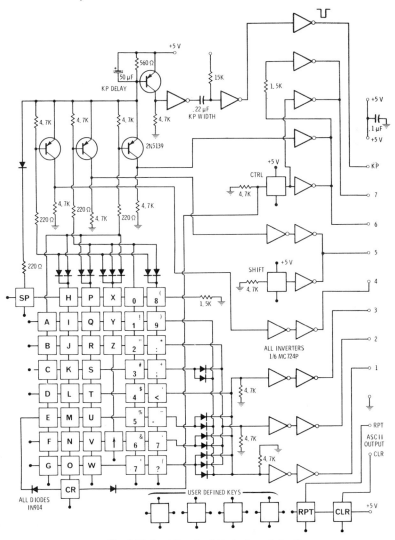

Fig. 6-14. Semidiscrete static keyboard circuit.

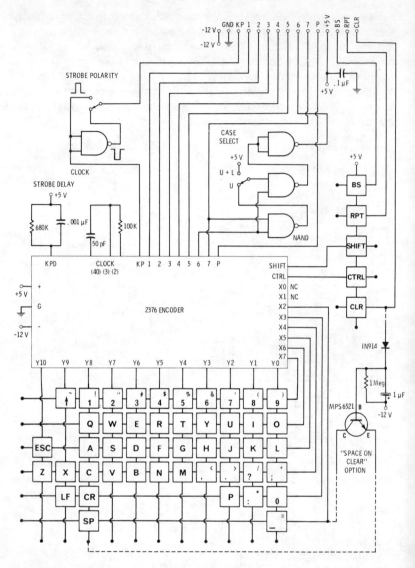

Fig. 6-15. Scanning keyboard with memory offers 2-key rollover, choice of strobe polarity, and "space on clear."

If we are willing to rewire a keyboard and have the keycaps available, we can use an ASCII encoder to generate Baudot simply by ignoring the top bits and using the bottom five properly redefined. Table 6-2 shows the correspondence between these two codes.

Fig. 6-16. Typewriter-style keyboard using MOS encoder.

KEYBOARD DESIGN EXAMPLES

Fig. 6-14 shows a static Qwerty keyboard based on a circuit that originally appeared in the April 1974 issue of *Popular Electronics* magazine. The version shown here has been updated to 53 keys. It provides a space output between keypressings and has a short, delayed, keypressed strobe and n-key lockout. Mechanical Enterprises LFW-CT switches are used along with companion two-shot keycaps.

Fig. 6-15 and 6-16 give details on a Qwerty keyboard with two-key rollover and choices of letter case, strobe polarity, clear and repeat keys, and a space output during clear. It takes +5-V −12-V supply voltages. Datanetics Series 60 keyswitches are used.

Fig. 6-17 shows the printed-circuit layout for a field-programmable, calculator-style keyboard.

Keyboard manufacturers include Microswitch, Oak, Keytronic, Cherry Electrical, Stackpole, Southwest Bomar, Texas Instruments, Mits, and others.

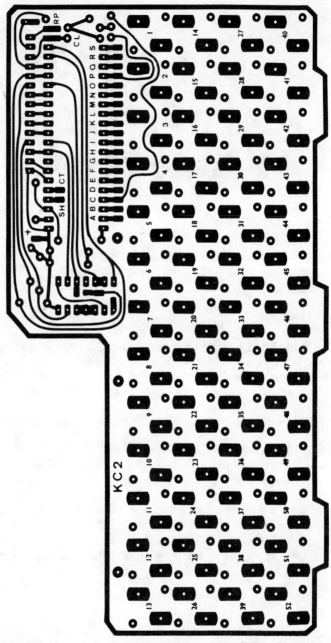

Courtesy Synergetics

Fig. 6-17. PC layout for user defined, field programmable calculator style keyboard.

CHAPTER 7

Serial Interface

Most tv typewriter circuits need to have all their ASCII character and command bits simultaneously available in parallel form. This is also true of most electronic keyboard encoders and the bidirectional data buses of many minicomputers and microprocessors. In simple systems, we can connect all these parallel sources and loads together, as needed, without any further interface circuitry.

Sometimes, it is far more useful or convenient to have the bits march by in *serial* form, one by one. While serial form is much slower, it has one big advantage—only a single wire or communications channel is needed, instead of multiple signal lines. Another benefit of serial form is that it can be made slow enough to communicate over ordinary phone lines, cassette tapes, radio channels, or electromechanical Teletype systems. Some of the places where we would like to use serial transmission are:

* *Remote keyboards,* where a single-pair interconnection could be used instead of expensive multiple-conductor cable.
* *Teletypes,* where the bits have to be converted to signals based on current or no current in a wire loop.
* *Industry-standard interfaces,* such as the RS232-C, the newer RS422, and the GPIB; this allows signals to travel relatively long distances.
* *Cassette recorders,* where we can store and exchange characters and programs with properly designed single-channel, speed-tolerant circuitry.
* *Radio transmission,* where only two tones on a single transmitted frequency are often used. This is typical of ham radio teletype-writter (rtty) communications.
* *Modems,* or modulator-*demodulators,* that let us exchange data over the telephone line, either one way or both ways at once.

The circuits that get us from parallel to serial and back again are called *serial interface*. Usually, there are two distinct parts to the interface problem. The first is to convert from parallel to serial (or vice versa) at *logic level*, staying compatible with CMOS or TTL integrated circuits. This is often done in an industry-standard, single integrated circuit called a UART, short for *Universal Asynchronous Receiver Transmitter*. A UART will simply and cheaply perform the conversion and back again along with providing all the necessary housekeeping bits, control signals, and noise immunity provisions.

The second portion of the conversion process gets us from logic levels to whatever form of signal the serial part of the system uses—such as dc currents for teletypes, bipolar signals for standard interface, and carefully selected tones suitable for cassette recording or transmission over a radio channel or a phone line. We will be taking a detailed look at most of these techniques later in the chapter.

HOW FAST?

There are two basic types of serial transmission we can use, *synchronous* and *asynchronous*.

In synchronous transmission, all the data words are locked into system timing. We know the exact time position of each piece of data. If some time is to go by during which nothing useful is to be done, do-nothing words called *nulls* are provided. Timing signals must somehow be supplied to each end of a synchronous serial data system so that we can tell when each word is to start. This usually means a separate timing channel or track or some sort of elaborate timing recovery circuit. Synchronous systems are usually fast and complex, but they are rarely used in most tv typewriter applications.

With asynchronous transmission, the data words are not locked into system timing and can arrive with almost any spacing between words. To tell the beginning and end of a word, we have to add some new bit groupings, called *start* and *stop* bits, to the data. We do not have to provide any other locking signal between the source and destination of the data. Asynchronous data are commonly used in tvt systems.

Both ends of a serial transmission system have to *exactly* agree on a system speed, usually called the *baud rate*. The baud rate is simply how many bits per second are going to be transmitted, including any start and stop bits. Table 7-1 shows some common baud rates. The most popular of these include 110, 300, 600, and 1200 bits per second. The 1200-baud rate is usually the fastest that can be handled by the phone company without fully dedicated lines. In systems where special lines can be provided, faster synchronous standard baud rates of 2400, 4800, and 9600 bits per second may be used.

Table 7-1. Standard Serial Communications Speeds

Baud Rate	Type	Teletype Compatible?	DDD Phone Compatible?	Frame Update Compatible?	Time to Load 512 Characters
110 BPS	Asynchronous	Yes	Two Way	Yes	51.2 Seconds
300 BPS	Asynchronous	No	Two Way	Yes	18.7 Seconds
600 BPS	Asynchronous	No	One Way	Often	9.3 Seconds
1200 BPS	Asynchronous	No	One Way	No	4.6 Seconds
2400 BPS	Synchronous	No	No	No	2.3 Seconds
4800 BPS	Synchronous	No	No	No	1.2 Seconds
9600 BPS	Synchronous	No	No	No	0.6 Seconds

Should the baud-rate change between transmission and reception, such as when two recorders are used or when the batteries on one recorder weaken, the receiving end of the system has to be able to immediately adjust itself to the new *effective baud rate* if errors are to be avoided.

The 110-baud rate is compatible with the ASR-33 eight-bit Teletype code and corresponds to a 100-word-per-minute typing rate. While this is the fastest that most teletypewriter systems can be driven and is easily handled by two-way 103-style phone modems, it takes painfully long to fill a tvt screen. Even with a 512-character screen, it takes almost a minute to load or retransmit the screen.

The 300-baud rate is equal to 30 characters per second, or 300 words per minute, and has been proposed as a hobbyist interchange standard. This rate is the fastest normally used by a two-frame update cursor system. It is also a rate easily handled by a cassette recorder and by many two-way, or *full-duplex,* modem systems. About 18.6 seconds are needed to load or dump a 512-character screen. These frame-update and retransmission rates can be minimized by use of a "virtual" update, in which one page is viewed while the other is updated, and by creative use of carriage-return commands so that the carriage returns after the last character of each line, rather than going on to the end of the line.

600 baud can usually be handled by a single-frame tvt update system, where rapid loading on screen reading is needed. Baud rates above 600 usually require more in the way of circuit design, and are usually limited to one-way modem transmission, premium recording techniques, and a direct memory access type of update in the tv typewriter.

A 110-BAUD STANDARD

The 110-baud, 100-word-per-minute code is an industry standard for slow data exchange. It is compatible with the Model 33 and

Model 35 Teletype systems and with other teleprinters using an 8-level code. The code takes 100 ms to send a character. The next character can follow immediately or can be sent any time later. Fig. 7-1 shows this standard.

The original Teletype notation still carries over to this code. A *mark* is a digital 1, a *shorted* line, or a completed connection. A *space* is a digital 0, an *open* line, or a broken connection. Between words, the Teletype line or digital output is constantly putting out 1's or marks and is *marking time*. One of the reasons this was originally done was so that any *break* in communications would be immediately known.

There are 11 bits to the code. Each bit is an identical 9.09 ms long, for a total code time of 100 ms per word. Each word begins with a *start bit*. The start bit is always a 0 and tells the receiving circuitry that a new character is to begin. The start bit is essential, since some ASCII characters will begin with one or more 1's and there is no way to tell a marking time 1 from an ASCII character 1.

The ASCII bits follow in sequential order, starting with bit 1 or the *least significant* bit. After the seven character bits, an eighth bit is sent either as a 1 or as a parity check bit for the rest of the word. At least two *stop bits* must follow the word. The stop bits are 1's or marks, and any number of additional marking 1's can follow between characters. The stop bits give the receiving circuitry a chance to shut itself down and await a new word.

The receiver can be electronic, in the case of a UART, or electromechanical, in the case of a Teletype. Between words, the receiver just waits. Since the data transmission is asynchronous, the receiver has no way of knowing ahead of time when a new word is to arrive, so it has to wait for a new start bit before it can do anything. The arrival of this bit activates the receiver, which then goes through a sequential procedure that sorts out the bits, puts them in parallel form, and outputs them.

With a UART, sequential time intervals of 9.09 ms each are electronically generated, and the center of each interval window is tested against the incoming code to see whether a 1 or a 0 is received. These ones and zeros are accumulated in a shift register, error-tested, and put out as a parallel word at the end of the interval. The stop bits are used to reset and shut off the circuitry.

With an electromechanical Teletype, the break in the line current caused by the stop bit releases a one-turn clutch on a mechanical scanning commutator that goes around once in 100 ms. It sequentially routes the incoming code to a group of scanning solenoid magnets. These set up the code in parallel form, and at the end of the word, the scanner resets and the code is typed or put out on paper tape.

TOLERANCES

It is extremely important that both the transmitter and the receiver clock out bits at the same 9.09-ms rate and that nothing happens in the channel to speed up or slow down the bits. There are many possible sources of error. If the bit positions jitter around or are differentially delayed by any tone keying, filtering, or channel response, we get a *bit-position error.* Bit-position errors put individual bits ahead or behind of where they actually belong. One source of bit-position error in a two-tone modem or cassette system occurs when one tone is delayed more than the other in any filtering circuit. This is called the *group-delay distortion* problem.

If the basic transmission and reception rates differ so that the bits get ahead or behind of where they are supposed to be, we have a *bit-rate error.* Note that bit-position errors apply to individual bits, while bit-rate errors are progressive, making each sequential bit decision that more difficult to detect without error. We get a bit-rate error if there is an absolute timing difference between transmitter and receiver. Cassette recording systems introduce a potential bit-rate error if the record and playback rates differ. This can easily happen with cheaper units, which are susceptible to speed variations with battery voltage, and it is almost inevitable if the recording is made on one machine and is played back on a second. Recording bit-rate errors are correctable if the recording signals are designed to include speed information and if the receiver is capable of using this information to speed up or slow down, as needed, to eliminate this error source.

How accurate do we have to be? This is easy to calculate. Assume temporarily that there are zero bit-position errors in the channel and that we are using an electronic receiver that very narrowly samples for valid data. The last data bit we are interested in is the parity bit. The center of the parity bit is 8½ bits removed from the beginning of the start bit, a delay of 77.26 ms. The receiver delay is also supposed to be 77.26 ms. If our sampling is narrow enough, we can be just under half a bit slow or fast and still be able to read the parity bit without error. This corresponds to a time error of 4.53 ms either way, or slightly over 5%.

But, this figure leaves no room for bit-position errors and does not give slower electromechanical circuits enough time width to reliably respond to the incoming data. As a practical rule, *the receiver and transmitter bit times must match to well within ±1%.* It is absolutely essential to hold things this close for low-error communications.

A 300-baud asynchronous timing system is very similar to that shown in Fig. 7-1 and uses the same 11-bit code of equally spaced bits. The only difference is that the per-bit time is 3.33 ms corre-

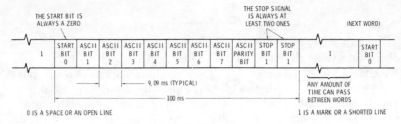

THE START BIT IS
ALWAYS A ZERO

THE STOP SIGNAL
IS ALWAYS AT
LEAST TWO ONES

(NEXT WORD)

| 1 | START BIT 0 | ASCII BIT 1 | ASCII BIT 2 | ASCII BIT 3 | ASCII BIT 4 | ASCII BIT 5 | ASCII BIT 6 | ASCII BIT 7 | ASCII PARITY BIT | STOP BIT 1 | STOP BIT 1 | 1 | START BIT 0 |

9.09 ms (TYPICAL)

100 ms

ANY AMOUNT OF
TIME CAN PASS
BETWEEN WORDS

0 IS A SPACE OR AN OPEN LINE

1 IS A MARK OR A SHORTED LINE

Fig. 7-1. A 110-baud, 100-word-per-minute code.

sponding to a 300-Hz clock rate. Optionally, only a single stop bit may be used. This rate is compatible with cassettes and tv type-writers and may be used for full-duplex (two-way) operation in most modem circuits, but it is too fast for Teletype use.

USING UARTS

Parallel-to-serial conversion and back again can obviously be done with CMOS or TTL circuits. Basically, you parallel-load a shift register and serially clock out data or serially clock in data to a shift register, and then you latch its parallel outputs when the data is valid. By the time you add all the error-testing circuitry, housekeeping bits, synchronization, and so on, the circuits tend to get specialized and complex.

Instead of this route, you can use an industry-standard MOS integrated circuit called a UART, for virtually any serial-to-parallel conversion and return process. Several pin-compatible UARTs appear in Chart 7-1. These are general-purpose, programmable devices that let you select the number of start and stop bits, the word length, type of parity, and so on to suit your particular system. Dedicated UART-like devices are also available for use with specific microprocessors. The Intel 8201 and the Motorola 6850 are typical of these.

The standard UART comes in a 40-pin package and has supply voltages of +5 V routed to pin No. 1, −12 V to pin No. 2, and ground to pin No. 3. The later versions of these devices are n-channel types that need no −12-V supply, and that pin is left unconnected. The General Instruments AY-5-1014 is one of these.

Chart 7-1. Pin-Compatible UARTs

S1883	(American Microsystems)
AY-5-1012	(General Instruments)
2536	(Signetics)
COM 2502	(Standard Microsystems)
TMS 6012	(Texas Instruments)
TR 1602	(Western Digital)

The low-number pins (1–20) are the receive portion of the UART, while the high-number pins (21–40) are the transmit portion. Except for common word length and parity programming, the two halves of the circuit are separate, although they are often used as a send-receive pair.

Both the receiver and transmitter portions of the circuit need a clock. The clock frequency is usually 16 times the baud rate. This high frequency lets the UART do such things as sample the center of each data interval and recheck for valid start signals. For instance, a 110-baud circuit needs a clock of 1760 Hz, while a 300-baud circuit uses a 4800-Hz clock, and so on.

The clock signals can be derived from a CMOS or 555 astable oscillator, but it is far better to digitally derive clock frequencies from tvt system timing, a baud-rate generator, or another stable source. Remember, these clock signals must be held to well within 1% and ideally should not have any adjustments. If our tvt has a 15,840-Hz horizontal rate, we can divide this by nine to get exactly 1760 for a 110-baud system. With a 15,720-Hz rate, we get 1746.6 Hz, a figure a bit low, but still useful and less than 1% under.

The receiver and transmitter clock inputs are on separate pins. They are often tied to a common clock source in simple send-receive circuits. One important exception is when a UART is used as part of a speed-tolerant cassette interface. In this case, the *receiver* clock frequency is derived from the tape during playback. While it is nominally the same as the transmitter frequency, its exact value is set by speed information recovered from the recorder. This can be used to eliminate much of the bit-rate error that would normally result from a change in tape speed from time to time or from machine to machine.

Fig. 7-2 shows the connections for transmission of the 11-unit code of Fig. 7-1. The input ASCII code goes on pins 26 through 33, with the least significant bit on pin 26. A 16× clock goes into pin 40, and a KP send command goes to pin 23. The positive edge of this send command starts transmission, but the input data must be valid for the entire time the command is low. Normally, this is a narrow pulse a few milliseconds wide, derived from a keypressed command on a keyboard. Serial output data appears on pin 25.

Pins 34 through 39 program the UART for different bit lengths and codes. Pin 34 is an enable that normally remains high. Pin 35 provides a parity bit if it is grounded and omits one if it is high. Pin 36 picks the number of stop bits. Ground gives you one, and high gives you two. Pins 37 and 38 together decide how many *data* bits are to be sent, ranging from 5 to 8. Grounding both of them provides for 5 data bits, useful for Baudot rtty transmission. The connection shown gives us a seven-bit data word. Note that if you use the

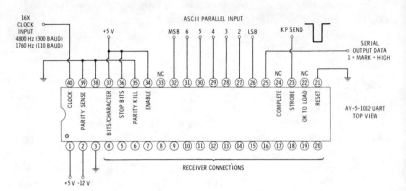

Fig. 7-2. UART circuit to transmit code of Fig. 7-1.

parity bit, it *adds to* the number of data words. The code of Fig. 7-1 uses one start bit, seven data bits, one parity bit, and one stop bit, for an 11-unit code. Pin 39 picks even or odd parity, with ground giving odd parity. An optional reset input is provided on pin 21. It is normally grounded. Bringing it high resets the UART. If it is not reset, the first word transmitted after power is applied can be wrong.

The UART transmitter is *double buffered*. This means that you can load a new character as soon as the one already inside *begins* its transmission. Two optional outputs are provided. Pin 22 tells you when it is all right to provide a new character by going high. Pin 24 tells you that a character has been completely sent when it goes high.

There are two ways you can use a UART transmitter, either in the *unconditional* mode or in the *handshaking* mode. In the unconditional mode, any time a character arrives, it gets sent. This is the simplest mode, but you have to make absolutely certain that characters do not arrive spaced or grouped too closely together. While pairs of inputs can be closely spaced in much the same way that two-key rollover works in a keyboard, you have to be absolutely certain that the long-term average is never exceeded by the word rate of the UART. This means a 100-ms character spacing for a 110-baud system, and around one third of that for a 300-baud system. In the handshaking mode, the UART decides when it wants to receive a new character, using the pin 22 and 24 outputs. The circuits driving the UART are set up to provide characters only when they are asked for them. For most tvt uses, unconditional UART transmission is simpler and easier to use.

Fig. 7-3 shows the UART receiver circuit, again set up for the code of Fig. 7-1. The receiver logic has elaborate noise-elimination provisions, made possible by the 16 times higher clock frequency. Whenever a start bit is purportedly received, that bit is retested later and

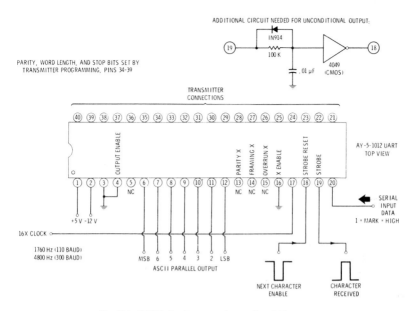

ADDITIONAL CIRCUIT NEEDED FOR UNCONDITIONAL OUTPUT:

PARITY, WORD LENGTH, AND STOP BITS SET BY
TRANSMITTER PROGRAMMING, PINS 34-39

1N914
100 K
4049
(CMOS)
.01 µF

TRANSMITTER
CONNECTIONS

OUTPUT ENABLE

PARITY X
FRAMING X
OVERRUN X
X ENABLE
STROBE RESET
STROBE

AY-5-1012 UART
TOP VIEW

NC

NC NC NC

SERIAL
INPUT
DATA
1 = MARK = HIGH

+5 V -12 V

16X CLOCK

1760 Hz (110 BAUD)
4800 Hz (300 BAUD)

MSB 6 5 4 3 2 LSB
ASCII PARALLEL OUTPUT

NEXT CHARACTER
ENABLE

CHARACTER
RECEIVED

Fig. 7-3. UART circuit to receive code of Fig. 7-1.

verified to prevent a random noise pulse from generating an unwanted character output. All data bits are narrowly sampled in the
middle of their possible time slots, allowing bit-position and bit-rate
errors to exist without error.

The same inputs (pins 34 through 39) that programmed the transmitter word length and format are used to identically program the
receiver portion of the UART. Although the receiver and transmitter
can be used in totally different circuits and at different baud rates,
they have to operate with a common format, set by these pins.

The receiver needs its own clock of 16 times its baud rate, applied
to pin 17. In send-receive systems, we can often tie the receiver and
transmitter clocks together. In speed-tolerant cassette interface circuits, the receive clock is reconstructed from speed information recovered from the recorder to eliminate bit-rate errors.

The serial input is routed to pin 20 and converted to the equivalent seven-bit parallel ASCII output on pins 6 through 12, with the
least significant bit on pin 12. When the output is valid, a strobe on
pin 19 goes high as an output.

*This output strobe must be reset before a new character can be
output.* If we are operating in a handshaking mode, the tvt circuitry
accepting the character sends back an acknowledgement or comple-
tion signal that momentarily drives pin 18 low. If we are using an
unconditional output mode, we have to somehow delay the pin-19

161

strobe output, invert it, and reapply it to the pin-18 strobe reset input. Fig. 7-3 shows us one way to do this with an RC network and a CMOS inverter. Many UART receiver problems are caused by failing to rest the strobe after each character.

Some UARTS do output a brief 3 μs or so pulse if the strobe is not reset when a new character arrives. Watch this detail very carefully.

Several additional outputs are available for use in fancier systems. Parity, framing, and overrun errors produce high outputs on pins 13 through 15, respectively. These can be used to ask for a repeat, to stop a loading, or to put in a question mark to indicate a transmission error. All receiver UART outputs are tri-state and may be floated in systems where the UART outputs must share a common or a bidirectional data bus. Making pin 4 positive *disables* the ASCII outputs, while making pin 16 positive *disables* the error outputs.

Besides its usual use as a two-way serial-to-parallel converter, there are other useful circuit tricks you can do with a UART. For instance, by connecting the parallel outputs of the receiver back to the parallel inputs of the transmitter, you can change baud rates. This is handy in speeding up slow data for use on a fast channel and in correcting speed errors on cassette systems.

Loading an ASCII space into a UART reciver is one way to hold a clear command long enough for tvt clearing to complete.

If the UART is to accept data from several sources, you can either tri-state combine the sources onto a single input bus, or use an input eight-pole double-throw selector switch to pick one of two input channels. This is common in tvt service, where the keyboard forms one channel and the screen retransmission output bus forms the other. Either 4502 hex tri-state drivers or 4019 four-pole selectors are suitable CMOS devices to use. In general, tri-state lines combined onto a common bus are much preferred to selectors, but few keyboard encoders have inherent tri-state output, and the output bus on the tvt often has to continuously drive the display if we want to view the retransmission process.

TELETYPE INTERFACE

There are two common types of Teletype systems in use today. Older machines use a 5-bit code. Typical examples are the Teletype Model 28, the Creed Model 75, and various Kleinschmidt models. While these devices are commercially obsolete, they still see usage in ham rtty and some deaf communications systems. Their reasonable price and availability make them attractive for home-computer hard copy as well, although the available character presentation is extremely limited. These older machines all use the obsolete Baudot code of Chapter 1 and are not directly ASCII and tvt compatible, unless conversion ROMs and figures-letters logic are added to them. More details involved in using these machines will be shown in Chapter 9. We will note in passing that a UART may be used in the Baudot code by applying the code to pins 26 through 30, with the least significant bit on pin 26, and by making pin 35 high and grounding pins 37 and 38. Older UARTs will generate two stop bits, while more recent ones (such as the TR1602B) will automatically generate the needed 1.42 stop bits in this mode.

The second common type is the computer and time-sharing standard Teletype, such as the Teletype Models 33 and 35, particularly the ASR-33. These models use a standard 8-bit ASCII code and follow the format of Fig. 7-1. They are directly compatible with tvt system coding.

Either type of system is based on breaking current in a dc loop. This current is often either 20 or 60 milliamperes (mA). Transmission occurs when a mechanically coded commutator generates an output code by once-around breaking the current as often as needed.

Reception reverses the process. A momentary break, representing the start bit, releases a once-around commutator that distributes the code breaks to magnets that set up a pattern for printing when the scan is complete.

Fig. 7-4 shows the interface for a Model 33 Teletype. For optimum use, the Teletype is internally programmed to a 20-mA current loop

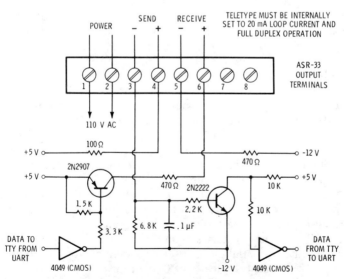

Fig 7-4. UART-Teletype (ASR-33) interface.

and full-duplex operation. This is done by following the Teletype maintenance manual. Full-duplex operation means that the keyboard and printer are not connected to each other. The keyboard can send and the printer can receive, both at the same time.

The transmitter interface provides a 20-mA current for a mark or a 1, and an open circuit for a space or a 0. The receiver senses a closed contact for a mark or a 1, and an open contact for a space or a 0. Extra inverters are added, as shown, to make the codes correspond, so that a 1 from the UART is read as a 1 by the Teletype. Be sure to observe the line polarities shown. The transistors can be almost any medium-power, reasonable-gain devices. More information on Teletype interface appears in the Intel MCS-8 user's manual.

Similar current/no-current interface loops can be used with older Teletype systems. However, some of these machines need substantially higher currents and are notorious as transient and ground-noise generators. With these older machines, total isolation through the use of small, high-speed reed relays or the use of optoisolator circuits is strongly recommended.

With any Teletype system, the transmit baud rate of the UART must match the needs of the Teletype to within 1%. In the case of the ASR-33, a 110-baud rate is needed, resulting in a 16× UART clock of 1760 Hz.

INDUSTRIAL INTERFACE

There are presently quite a few "standard" interfaces used to get between commercial modems, printers, test equipment, computers, and anywhere else you need a reasonably distant, noise-free interface. Three of the most common include the RS232, the RS422, and the general-purpose interface bus (GPIB). Fig. 7-5 shows what is involved in the way of signal levels and interface techniques.

The RS232-C is an old Electronic Industries Association (EIA) standard that predates IC techniques and is somewhat unwieldy. It is widely used in commercial modem circuits and for most large-scale computer serial interfaces. The signal is bipolar, with a logic 0 being defined as +3 to +9 V or more, and a logic 1 being defined as −3 to −9 V or more. Capacitors on the drivers limit rise times to 30 V per microsecond or less to minimize ringing and transient effects. Capacitors on the receivers limit the response as needed to reject noise but pass the highest-transmitted baud rate. The 1488 and 1489 integrated circuits form a typical interface pair.

The RS422 is a newer EIA standard that uses balanced transmission lines and differential current sensing to eliminate any common-mode noise. A current, typically of 6 to 12 mA, in one direction defines a 1, while the reversed current defines a 0. The balanced line

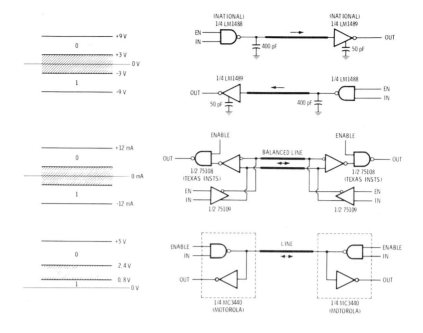

Fig. 7-5. Industrial interfaces for cable interconnections.

may be either unidirectional or bidirectional, depending on how the receiver enables are used. In any bidirectional or party line system, it is extremely important to enable only one driver at a time. The 75108 and 75109 are typical balanced-line drivers and receivers.

The general-purpose interface bus, or GPIB, uses TTL-compatible levels but combines them with a terminated line, high drive capability, and receivers with hysteresis for good noise immunity. The GPIB is most often used in parallel form to interface test and measurement equipment with computers and calculators. It can also be used as an effective serial interface that takes no special power supplies. The 3440 and 26S11 are quad-bus transceivers useful for GPIB service. This has recently become an IEEE standard.

More information on EIA standards is available from the Electronic Industries Association; 2001 Eye Street, NW; Washington, DC 20006.

CASSETTE INTERFACE—THE BIT BOFFER SYSTEM

Magnetic storage in the form of tape drive, disc files, and floppy discs has long been a standard, but expensive, way of storing bulk serial data for computer use. An obvious and low-cost substitute for this would seem to be the ordinary audio cassette recorder. Besides providing bulk storage, the cassette can replace paper tape and punched cards, and can handle programs as well. One big advantage of cassettes is the potentially low cost of duplication, distribution, and exchange of programs.

If we are free to build our own cassette mechanism or to extensively modify an existing one, we can include such features as automatic tape search, read-after-write verification, rapid location of a block of data, and so on. In this way, we can incorporate many features found on far more expensive floppy disc, tape, and disc-file systems. Commercial sources of these *cassette operating systems* include Phi-Deck and Processor Technology.

On the other hand, if we are to use unmodified home audio cassette recorders along with simple and inexpensive interface circuits, we have to set our sights somewhat lower, aiming only for a system that duplicates what has traditionally been done with paper tape.

Cassette recorders, particularly the low-cost varieties, present several serious design problems when they are used to store 1's and 0's. Speed variation is the first major problem. Even with a quality machine, speed will vary by a percent or more. With the lower-cost units, aging batteries and the machine-to-machine variations in record and playback can cause a total speed variation that far exceeds the bit-rate error allowed in the serial ASCII code of Fig. 7-1. We can compensate for these speed variations by recording a signal on the tape that provides us with both data 1's and 0's, *and* some speed information to indicate the rate of travel of the tape. This speed information can be used to speed up or slow down the UART receiver clock, keeping it in pace with the changing data rate and eliminating bit-rate errors. Naturally, for cassette compatibility we want to use only a single track for both data and speed information.

Most cassette recorders have an automatic record-level control. If this level-control circuit is to work with us rather than against us, we have to further restrict our signal to one having a constant amplitude. This suggests a frequency-modulated or frequency-shift keyed signal for recording. Using some frequency for a 0 and doubling that frequency for a 1 has a big advantage in that the clock or speed information is also easily recovered. This is one example of a *self-clocking,* or *clock-recoverable,* code.

Another very serious limitation of audio recorders is that they simply do not record and play back the same way a digital recorder does. The intrinsic response of an audio head doubles as the frequency doubles. This is the same as mathematically taking the derivative, or *slope,* of the signals. Taking the derivative happens *twice*—once during the record and once during playback. Digital recorders eliminate the recording derivative by saturating the tape, and they cancel the playback derivative by using a sense amplifier and set-reset flip-flop to integrate the output.

The audio people try to compensate for this double differentiation with low-frequency emphasizing networks. This works nicely on single-frequency sine waves (whose second derivative is a sine wave anyway). But, on a square wave (whose second derivative is a messy pair of double impulses), these compensation networks introduce *group delay distortion,* ringing, and other transient and smearing effects. *Thus, on a cheap recorder, inputing square waves is a no-no.* Furthermore, if we switch a sine wave off and on at the wrong time (or worse yet, with a dc offset or at a random time), we put in the same thing as a square wave's leading edge and still make a mess of the recording and playback process. So, *the best possible signal you can record on a low-cost recorder is a sine wave whose frequency is changed coherently either on the zero crossings or slightly before.*

<table>
<tr><td rowspan="6">Fig. 7-6. Tone standards for the bit
boffer system.</td><td>110 BAUD:</td></tr>
<tr><td>1 = 16 HALF CYCLES OF 880 Hz
0 = 8 HALF CYCLES OF 440 Hz</td></tr>
<tr><td>300 BAUD:</td></tr>
<tr><td>1 = 16 HALF CYCLES OF 2400 Hz
0 = 8 HALF CYCLES OF 1200 Hz</td></tr>
<tr><td>600 BAUD:</td></tr>
<tr><td>1 = 16 HALF CYCLES OF 4800 Hz
0 = 8 HALF CYCLES OF 2400 Hz</td></tr>
</table>

These requirements for a self-clocking, constant-amplitude, sine wave zero-switched, single-channel signal very much limit what we can do in the way of low-cost cassette storage. One very low cost and very flexible system that can use any old audio cassette recorder is called the *bit boffer* system. Its 300-baud version has been proposed as a standard hobbyist serial tape interchange. Important advantages of the bit boffer system are: it is highly speed tolerant; it is totally software independent; it is very simple and cheap; it works with ASCII characters, microcomputer op-code, or even Baudot; and it interfaces directly with standard UART serial interfaces.

Figs. 7-6 and 7-7 show us the standards for the bit boffer systems. For the 300-baud version, we record 16 half sine waves of 2400 hertz for a mark, or a digital 1, and record 8 half sine waves of 1200 hertz for a space, or digital 0. Figs. 7-8 through 7-12 show us a typical bit boffer, its block diagram, receiver schematic, transmitter schematic, and timing waveforms. The bit boffer system works with any serial interface has separate receiver and transmitter 16× clocks. This includes all UARTs and most microcomputer-dedicated serial interface systems.

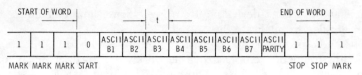

(A) ASCII character format.

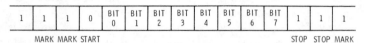

(B) Machine code (8-bit) format.

BASE RATE	110 BAUD	300 BAUD	600 BAUD
TRANSMIT TIME "t"	9.09 MS ±1%	3.33 MS ±1%	1.67 MS ±1%
RECEIVE TIME (WITHOUT ADJUSTMENT)	9.09 MS ±20%	3.33 MS ±20%	1.67 MS ±20%
RECOMMENDED BLOCK LENGTH	512 CHARACTERS	512 CHARACTERS	512 CHARACTERS
WORD TIME	100 MS	36.67 MS	18.33 MS
RECOMMENDED MAX WORD RATE (ALLOWS FOR OVERPLAY)	7.5 CHAR / SECOND	22 CHAR / SECOND	44 CHAR/SECOND

(C) Timing standards.

Fig. 7-7. Bit boffer format and time standards.

The transmitter portion (Fig. 7-10) starts with a 64× reference. For a 300-baud system, this can be a 19,200-hertz reference; a "300-baud, 64× clock" or a "1200-baud, 16× clock" from system timing, or one of the baud-rate generators of Chapter 2. This reference is divided by four and routed to the UART transmitter clock. It is selectively divided by two or by one, depending on the UART transmitter's serial output, and routed to a sine-wave synthesizer that generates either a 1200-hertz or a 2400-hertz sine wave. The synthesizer starts with a four-stage walking ring counter, followed by a Bessel active filter. A 1-V peak-to-peak sine wave, available for recording, is routed to the recorder's AUX input. Feedback from the sine-wave synthesizer to the divide-by-four automatically synchronizes everything so that the sine waves automatically switch just before a zero crossing each time the serial data changes from 1 to 0 or back again.

Our receiver (Fig. 7-11) starts with a filter and limiter. This minimizes the effects of hum and bias variations and gives us a square

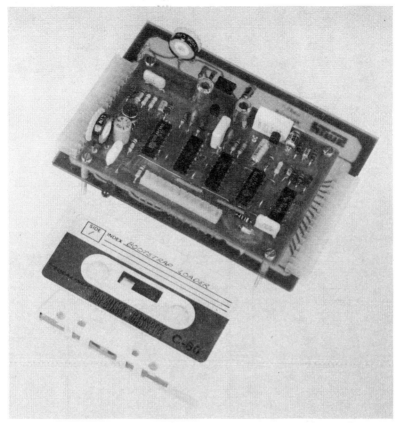

Fig. 7-8. Bit boffer cassette interface plugs into a UART test adapter.

wave whose zero crossings correspond to the recorded sine wave and appear at test point "C." The leading and trailing edges of the square wave are converted to narrow positive pulses with the exclusive OR circuit, and we get a stream of narrow pulses appearing at test point "D." One pulse occurs at each zero crossing.

The transistor, capacitor, and baud-rate control form a retriggerable monostable. This monostable is adjusted so that point E goes positive *three quarters* of the way through a low-frequency half cycle. Thus, point E produces a string of eight pulses for a 0 and no pulses for a 1. Our final flip-flop recovers the 1-0 data. The leading edge of waveform E is shortened and combined with the clock pulses to provide a composite UART clock output. Thus, our UART receiver gets sixteen clock pulses for a 1 and sixteen clock pulses for a 0. In the case of a 1, all pulses come from the tape signal. For a 0,

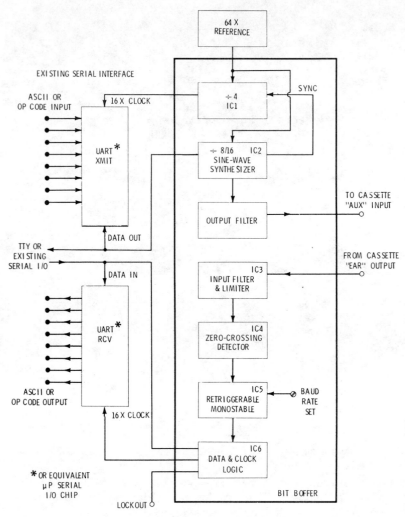

Fig. 7-9. Block diagram of the bit boffer.

half of the pulses come from the tape, and the other eight from the monostable. The spacing between these will change slightly as the speed changes, but the UART does not care, and this is what gives us the speed tolerance.

The outputs consist of a receiver 16× clock and a receiver data line. These are routed to the UART receiver for serial-to-parallel conversion. An optional lock input can be used to hold the receiver data in the mark, or 1, state during leader, search, and rewind times. This is useful to prevent entry of garbage into the system.

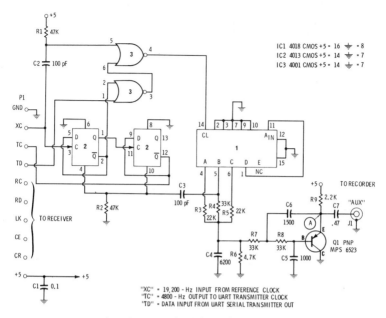

"XC" = 19,200 - Hz INPUT FROM REFERENCE CLOCK
"TC" = 4800 - Hz OUTPUT TO UART TRANSMITTER CLOCK
"TD" = DATA INPUT FROM UART SERIAL TRANSMITTER OUT

Fig. 7-10. A 300-baud bit boffer transmitter.

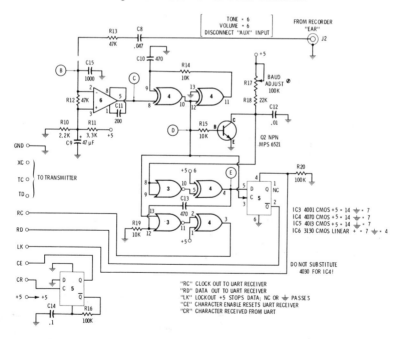

"RC" CLOCK OUT TO UART RECEIVER
"RD" DATA OUT TO UART RECEIVER
"LK" LOCKOUT +5 STOPS DATA; NC OR ⏚ PASSES
"CE" CHARACTER ENABLE RESETS UART RECEIVER
"CR" CHARACTER RECEIVED FROM UART

Fig. 7-11. A 300-baud bit boffer receiver.

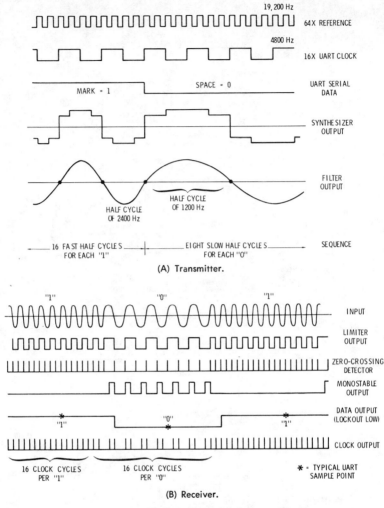

(A) Transmitter.

(B) Receiver.

Fig. 7-12. Key timing waveforms.

You can tune and test the system by using a scope *eye diagram.* To do this, sync the scope on "D" and view on "C." The waveform at E is adjusted to center on the right eye. Or, you can use the simple tuning indicator of Fig. 7-13, setting your baud-rate control to the center of the lamp's off portion.

It is very important to use quality tape whose amplitude response is specified to one-decibel variation or less. Radio Shack Supertape is one good source. You should also test your tape for dropouts before you use it. Your tuning indicator, or better yet your scope's eye diagram, will tell you the optimum settings of your recorder. Usually, you enter via the AUX input and use the automatic level control. You exit by way of the EAR output, usually setting the tone and volume to "6" on a scale of ten. Some recorders get unhappy if you leave the AUX input connected during playback. If yours is one of them, disconnect before playback.

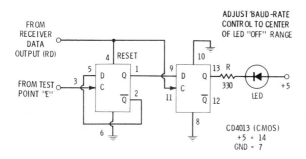

Fig. 7-13. Tuning indicator schematic.

The bit boffer error rate seems good enough for most hobbyist interchange use. You can further decrease the error rate for fully professional use with any of a number of good methods. First and foremost is careful adjustment of your baud-rate control by using the tuning indicator or scope eye diagram. Other add-ons would include a clock recovery phase-locked loop, data integration, use of UART parity error flags, total control decoding downstream, etc.

Your tvt can be used with a screen read to format data for dense recording, usually into blocks of 512 or 1024 characters. Groups of marks, or 1's, similar to rubouts on a paper tape, should precede and follow the data.

Two minor problems you may have to watch for are overspeeding and nonconstant clock rates. Overspeeding is caused by recording on a slow machine and playing back on a fast one so that the final data arrives faster than your tvt or Teletype. This problem is eliminated by holding the character rate down to something less than the "wide open" speed of a 300-baud system. That way if things speed up a little, they are still within acceptance range. Some peripherals, particularly mechanical Teletypes, demand absolutely constant baud rates. To beat this problem, simply connect your UART parallel data outputs back to the parallel data inputs and retransmit at a constant speed.

More details on the bit boffer system appear in the March 1976 *Byte* magazine.

RADIO DATA LINKS

One of the more common methods of sending serial digital data over a radio channel is to use a two-frequency, *frequency-shift keyed* method in which one frequency represents a digital 1 and the other a digital 0.

Ham rtty provides a typical example. At the audio baseband, two tones are used, defined as 2125 Hz for a mark, or 1; and 2975 Hz for a space or 0. These tones represent the fifth and seventh harmonics of 425 Hz.

These tones may be digitally generated in the same way that the modem tones of the next section are produced, or they may be generated by a voltage-controlled oscillator such as a 555, 8038, or a 566. These frequency-shifted tones are used to frequency-modulate an rf carrier. Alternatively, the carrier itself can remain at its normal frequency for a mark and can be shifted down 850 Hz (the difference between 2125 and 2975) for a 0, with the audio difference being picked up by mistuning the receiver by 2125 Hz.

Fig. 7-14 shows us a typical receiver demodulator circuit. The carrier is received and detected by an fm receiver, adjusted to put

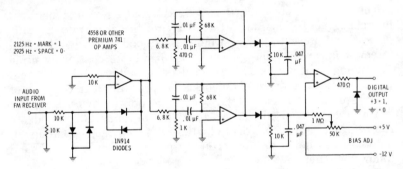

Fig. 7-14. Audio processor for rtty receiver.

out audio tones of 2125 and 2925 Hz. These tones are limited and routed to two bandpass filters, one set to the upper frequency and one set to the lower frequency. The outputs are amplitude-detected and compared, resulting in a 1 output for a frequency of 2125 and a 0 output for 2975. This output may be routed to a UART for serial-to-parallel conversion. Normally a 7.42 unit code of 60 or 100 words per minute, using Baudot encoding, is used for ham rtty. This format appears in more detail in Chapter 9.

Any radio carrier system must follow the rules and regulations for the particular frequencies used. Normally, the best performance of a frequency-shift keyed system results when the generated frequencies are sine waves and are switched, transient free, at their zero crossing. Receiver filters should delay both sets of frequencies identically, to prevent 1's from getting ahead of 0's or vice versa; therefore creating times when neither a 1 nor a 0, or both of them together, are simultaneously present. As with any serial interface, input and output code formats and baud rates must very definitely closely agree.

MODEMS

Modems, or modulator-demodulators, are devices used to get tones or tone groups onto the telephone line and off again in order to send and receive digital data. Two common ways of coupling modems to the phone line are to use small speakers to *acoustically couple* the tones to a standard handset, or to *directly connect* them to the phone line through a suitable protective network or data-access arrangement. Acoustical coupling can be used anywhere on an unmodified telephone, but there are problems with frequency response, microphonics, and second-harmonic distortion caused by the carbon transmitter. Direct coupling gives better control and better performance, but it has to meet certain telephone company regulations and interconnect restrictions. Also, it needs a physical connection to the phone line and needs its own *duplexer,* or means of separating transmitted and received data.

There are several basic ways to use modems. *Simplex* transmission goes one way only. Simplex with a *back channel* goes one way only, but provides for some low-frequency communications, often limited to 4 baud or less, in the other direction. This can provide for handshaking, message acknowledgement, etc., but it is far too slow to return data. *Half-duplex* systems can send or receive data, but not simultaneously. Either the transmitter must be off or in a mark condition while data are being received, or the receiver must be disabled while data are being sent. In *full-duplex* systems, data can be sent both ways, independently, and at the same time.

There are at least three basic types of modem systems that are useful over ordinary telephone lines, based on the Bell 103, 202, and 400 series systems. You can rent these from the phone company or others, buy them outright from modem firms, or design your own with the guidelines given in this chapter. Most of the commercial modems use RS232-C interface standards and may include such logic and switching functions as automatic answer and hang up, carrier detect, and other housekeeping signals.

The 400 systems are based on the touch-tone ringing frequencies. They accept contacts as inputs and are limited in the number of characters and the baud rate. Baud rates of 10 to 20 characters per second are usually the maximum, and operation is normally simplex, with a separate unit needed for transmission and reception.

The 202 systems are half-duplex modems that can run up to 1200 baud over the phone line but normally cannot simultaneously communicate in both directions unless a special four-wire system is used.

The 103 modems are full duplex and may be used at 110- and 300-baud rates. For the majority of tvt uses, this series, run at either baud rate, is the most practical. Unlike the other serial interface circuits of this chapter, proper design of a good 103-style modem circuit with reasonably good error performance is a major job, particularly if your circuit has to operate over the dial-up network for long distances and is to reliably communicate with commercial modems on the other end.

PHONE CHARACTERISTICS

A simplified schematic of a standard 500 telephone set is shown in Fig. 7-15. A carbon variable-resistance transmitter and a magnetic headphone-style receiver are connected to the line by way of a duplex coil, a normally closed dial contact, and a pair of open-when-unused hook-switch contacts.

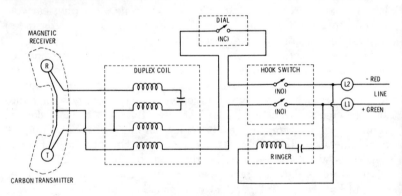

Fig. 7-15. Telephone receiver.

The duplex coil makes sure that outgoing signals reach the line and that ingoing signals reach the receiver with a minimum of interference. This is done by having two transmitter windings induce nearly equal and opposite signals into the receiver windings. This effectively cancels much of the local transmitter signal into the receiver. The net result is to keep transmitter energy from being wasted in its own receiver and to minimize a "hear yourself" *sidetone* that psychologically makes people speak much more quietly. The duplex coil attenuates the transmitted signal by 4 dB (to 60%

voltage), the received signal by 2 dB (to 80% voltage), and the sidetone by 17 dB (to 14% voltage).

The line is powered by a 48-volt central office battery supply, and the ac impedance of the line is nominally 600 ohms but varies with distance and quality of service. The audio signal levels at the line terminals are fractions of a volt. Normally, the loudest permissible modem tones are around a quarter of a volt, measured on the outgoing line. Received signals are lower still, typically one-half to one-tenth this value for local service, and less on long-distance loops.

When the phone is connected to the line by lifting the hook switch, the line voltage drops to around 6 V or so. The traditional dial-system signals by breaking this connection to deliver a group of mechanically spaced pulses that jump the line voltage between the open circuit and phone-off-the-hook values. Touch-tone systems replace the dial with a low impedance that sums the tones of the next section, (a pair of tones at a time) onto the line for signalling (see Fig. 7-15).

The ringer is capacitively coupled across the line and is resonant to some low frequency in the 20- to 47-Hz range. The ringing voltage is often an ac signal of 86-V rms. Selective ringing of a party line can be done in three-wire systems with a ground return by ringing one phone from one line to ground and the other one from the other line to ground. In two-wire systems, ringer circuits with different resonant frequencies can be selectively rung by changing the frequency of the ring signal.

For direct-entry modems, either a protective network or a data access arrangement, such as the Bell CBS or CBT units, can be used. These networks simulate the impedance of the telephone when activated and prevent any supply voltages from going onto or coming off the power line. Under no circumstances should dc power be applied to or removed from the phone-system lines, nor should any impedance that would degrade normal telephone services be placed across the line or to ground.

400-Style (Touch-Tone) Modems

Modems based on touch-tone signalling frequencies are usually limited to low data rates and often to a limited number of available characters. Touch-tone signalling simultaneously sends a pair of carefully chosen tones, following the code of Fig. 7-16.

The tone pair must exist for 40 ms, and the minimum time between tone pairs is 40 ms, with a resulting maximum character rate of 12 per second. Touch tones are normally entered at line signal levels some what higher than other voice and modern signals, being around three-quarters of a volt rms for the high frequencies and around half a volt for the low group. Line characteristics equalize these amplitudes by the time they get to recognition circuits.

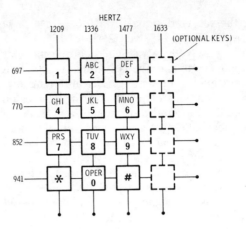

Fig. 7-16. Standard touch-tone frequencies. Each key simultaneously generates two tones as shown.

A touch-tone modem transmitter can simply be the touch-tone dial of a remote phone, or it can be a circuit that simultaneously generates two sine waves of proper amplitude and frequency. Integrated circuits to generate these tones are readily available. The Motorola MC14410 is typical. Unlike other modems, and much of the serial interface of this chapter, the code is activated directly by contact closures. One closure, rather than a serial code, is all that is needed to send one of twelve or one of sixteen separate pieces of information. Additional tones or three-tone combinations can be added, as is done in the Bell 401L or 402C systems that offer 99 or 256 characters.

Touch-tone reception consists of three parts. First, the signals need to be sharply filtered with bandpass group filters having responses of 650 to 1000 Hz for the low band and 1150 to 1700 Hz for the high band. Adequate prefiltering is absolutely essential for most tone detection schemes. Tones are then detected by using limiters and slicers, narrow-bandpass filters and detectors, or phase-locked loop tone detectors such as a Signetics 567 tone decoder. Finally, the detected tones are combined and output with suitable two-of-eight digital logic.

Additional information on touch-tone techniques appears in the March 1963 *IEEE Transactions on Applications and Industry,* the Signetics *Linear IC Applications Manual,* and various issues of the *Bell System Technical Journal.*

103-Style (300-Baud, Full-Duplex) Modems

The 103-style modems are often the best choice for tvt use, as they offer full-duplex, two-way, operation at 110- or 300-baud rates over the ordinary phone line. Fig. 7-17 shows a block diagram of this type of modem.

The circuits are used in pairs. The modem at the end that is doing the calling is called an *originate* modem. It sends a 1070-Hz sine wave for a space or 0 and a 1270-Hz sine wave for a mark or 1, usually at a phone-line level of −10 dbm, or around a quarter of a volt rms. The modem that is doing the receiving is called an *answer* modem, and it receives and responds to these two frequencies. In turn, the answer modem transmits a 2025-Hz sine wave for a space or a 0, and a 2225-Hz sine wave for a mark or a 1. These, in turn, are acceptable to the originate modem.

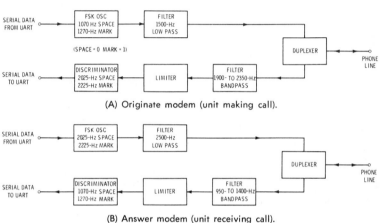

(A) Originate modem (unit making call).

(B) Answer modem (unit receiving call).

Fig. 7-17. Full duplex 300-baud modems.

These frequencies are carefully chosen to allow two-way conversation without interaction. The answer modem always transmits on the high frequency, since a 2025-Hz note is needed to automatically disable *echo suppressors* used on long-distance phone lines and to provide a standard recognition signal for automatic dialing equipment. (Echo suppressors effectively convert long-distance lines into voice-keyed, one-way lines. Two-way transmission on a long line is not possible unless these suppressors are defeated.)

There are several very important things to consider when you are designing a modem. The transmitted signal must be a low-distortion sine wave. Particularly, its second harmonic must be extremely low to prevent the originate modem transmitter from splattering its own receive spectrum with its second harmonic. When acoustical coupling is used, the transmit level must be held low enough that the rather bad second-harmonic distortion of the carbon mike does not raise harmonics to an intolerable level. This carbon-mike effect can be partially compensated for by summing a sine wave equal to the fundamental plus one half the third harmonic. This causes some second-harmonic cancellation and allows a higher level of transmission. Since most modem detectors use only the zero crossing information, it is important to *coherently* switch between these two frequencies, changing only when the sine wave goes through zero. The coherent operation eliminates "short cycles" that will jitter the received data.

Input signals to either modem *must* be strongly filtered to get rid of the other channel tones, as well as interference from speech, noise, touch-tone coding, and other signals. The duplex coil in the phone set reduces, but does not eliminate, sidetone coupling. If you build your own duplexer instead, the same cancellation is still only partial because of changing telephone-line impedances.

In addition to getting rid of unwanted signals, there is a second severe restriction to the input filter. Both the 1's and 0's going through the filter must be delayed by an equal amount. Otherwise the 1's and 0's will get out of step with each other and cause timing errors.

There are two basic ways to go about building this style of modem. An *analog* modem generates and decodes its signals, using gated oscillators, RC networks, and phase-locked loop detectors. A *digital* modem uses all digital logic for the frequency generation and detection. Analog modems should be avoided for several reasons. The transmitters inherently have less stability, potentially have a stronger second harmonic, and need calibration. They are harder to coherently switch at zero crossings to eliminate transients. Analog receivers also must be calibrated and able to accurately resolve a small frequency difference.

At this writing, there is no such thing as a modem on a chip. The Motorola MC6860 and MC14412 are two ICs that handle approximately one-third of the circuitry needed for a digital 103 modem. Quality active filters must be added to get those devices to have acceptable error rates. Two Exar chips, the 2207 FSK generator and the 2211 FSK demodulator, provide around half the circuitry for an analog system. A premium set of four hybrid integrated circuits from Cermetek Electronics is available that does almost the whole job in their Minimodem CH1213, 1214, 1252, and 1257 devices.

Figs. 7-18 through 7-21 show several techniques that might be of use in your own modem designs. Fig. 7-18 is a CMOS digital IC sine-wave generator; it produces a sine wave in response to a 10× digital clock input. It is based on summing phases of a walking ring or Johnson counter and has negligible harmonic output up to the ninth and eleventh, which are both 20 dB down ($\frac{1}{10}$ amplitude) and easily filtered. The output can also be used to coherently synchronize input

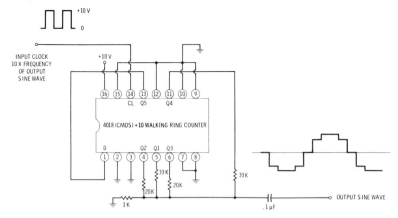

Fig. 7-18. Digital "sine-wave" modem transmitter is easily filtered. First strong harmonics (−20 dB) are the ninth and eleventh.

switching. Fig. 7-18 shows a digital timing sequence that starts with a crystal and produces all four modem frequencies needed for the Fig. 7-18 circuit. It can be built with a CMOS 4520 and a gate or two. Fig. 7-20 shows some active filters useful as prefilters with controlled group-delay distortion. Fig. 7-21 shows an adjustment- and calibration-free receiver digital discriminator. It is basically a digitally controlled monostable.

More information on 103-style modem designs is available in Motorola applications note AN731, Exar data sheets XR2211 and

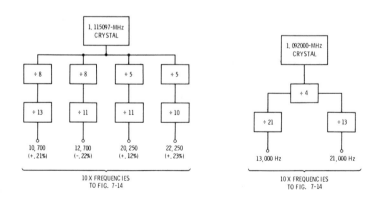

(A) 103:300-baud full duplex.   (B) 202:122-baud one way.

Fig. 7-19. Digitally derived modem frequencies.

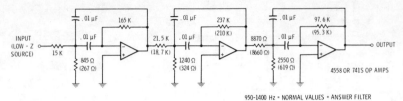

Fig. 7-20. Modem receive filter.

XR2207, the *Active Filter Cookbook* (published by Howard W. Sams & Co., Inc.), and Cermetek Microelectronics *Minimodem* data sheets.

202-Style (1200-Baud, Half-Duplex) Modems

The 202-style modem circuits are both faster and simpler than the 103 versions and may require less in the way of circuitry. Their big disadvantage is that most of them are strictly simplex or half-duplex devices when used on the ordinary two-wire phone line. Simultaneous transmission and reception are not ordinarily possible.

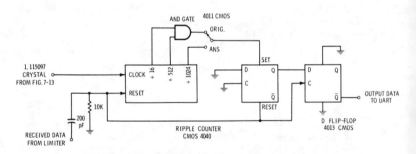

Fig. 7-21. Digital discriminator needs no adjustments or calibration.

Like the 103, 202 standards use frequency-shift keying. Bell standards call for a 1200-Hz mark or 1 and a 2200-Hz space or 0, while international standards call for a 1300-Hz mark or 1 and a 2100-Hz space or 0. An additional tone may have to be generated to provide for automatic answering. Commercial units also sometimes provide a back channel of four or five baud for acknowledgement.

The circuit design techniques for both types of modems are similar. Because of the faster baud rate, control of group-delay distortion in any filtering is extremely important. Detection circuitry must not differentially delay 1's with respect to 0's. The Rockwell 10371 Digital Telecommunications Data Interface handles many of the nonfiltering aspects of this type of modem. This IC also has a built-in UART.

Additional modem information may be found in various issues of *Data Communications and Telecommunications,* in the Microdata *Communications Handbook,* and in *Data Modem Evaluation Guide,* by V. V. Villips.

CHAPTER 8

Television Interface

We can interface a tv typewriter and a television-style display system by using either an rf *modulator* or a *direct-video* method.

In the rf modulator method, we build a miniature, low-power, direct-wired tv transmitter that clips onto the antenna terminals of the tv set. This has the big advantage of letting you use any tv set, and you end up with an essentially free display that can be used just about anywhere. No set modifications are needed, and you have the additional advantage of automatic safety isolation and freedom from hot-chassis shock problems.

There are two major restrictions to the rf modulator method. The first of these is that transmitters of this type must meet certain exactly spelled-out FCC regulations and that system type-approval is required. The second limitation is one of bandwidth. The best you can possibly hope for is 3.5 MHz for black and white and only 3 MHz for color, and many economy sets will provide far less. Thus, long character line lengths, sharp characters, and premium (lots of dots) character generators simply are not compatible with clip-on rf entry.

In the direct-video method, we apply the signal to the tv set immediately following the video detector but before sync is picked off. A few premium tv sets, and all monitors, already have a video input directly available, but these are still expensive and rare. Thus, you usually have to modify your tv set, either adding a video input and a changeover switch or dedicating the set to exclusive tv typewriter use. Direct video eliminates the bandwidth restrictions provided by the tuner, i-f strip, and video-detector filter. Response can be further extended by removing or shorting the 4.5-MHz sound trap and by making other modifications that will provide us with longer line lengths and premium characters. No FCC approval is needed, and several sets or monitors are easily driven at once without complicated distribution problems.

There are two limitations to the direct-video technique. One is that the set has to be modified to provide direct video entry. A second, and far more severe, restriction is that many television sets are "hot-chassis" or ac-dc sets with one side of the chassis connected to the power line. *These sets introduce a severe shock hazard and cannot be used as tv typewriter video entry displays unless some isolation technique is used with them.* If the tv set has a power transformer, there is usually no hot-chassis problem. Transistor television sets and IC sets using no vacuum tubes tend to have power transformers, as do older premium tube-type sets. All others (approximately half the sets around today) do not.

DIRECT-VIDEO METHODS

With either interface approach, we usually start by getting the dot-matrix data and the blanking, cursor, and sync signals together into one *composite video* signal whose form is useful to monitors and tv sets. A good set of standards is shown in Fig. 8-1. The signal is dc

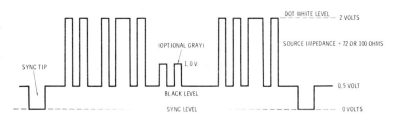

Fig. 8-1. Standard video interface levels.

coupled and always positive going. Sync tips are *grounded* and *blacker-than-black.* The normal open-circuit black level is positive by half a volt, and the white level is positive by two volts. In most tv camera systems, intermediate levels between the half-volt black level and the two-volt white level will be some shade of gray, proportionately brighter with increasing positive voltage. With most tv typewriter systems, only the three states of zero volts (sync), half a volt (black), and two volts (white dot) would be used. One possible exception would be an additional one-volt dot level when we want to dim but still present a portion of a message or a single word.

The usual video source impedance is either 72 or 100 ohms. Regardless of how far we travel with a composite video output, some sort of shielding is absolutely essential.

For short runs from board to board or inside equipment, tightly twisted conductors may be used, as may properly guarded pc runs. Fully shielded cables should be used for interconnections between the tvt and the monitor or tv set, and for other long runs. As long as the total cable capacitance is less than 500 pF or so (this is around 18 feet of RG178-U miniature coax), the receiving end of the cable need not be terminated in a 72- or 100-ohm resistor. When terminated cable systems are in use for long line runs or multiple outputs, they should be arranged to deliver the signal levels of Fig. 8-1 at their output under termination. Generally, terminated-cable systems should be avoided, since they need heavier drivers and extra supply power.

The exact width of the horizontal- and vertical-sync pulses is not usually too important, as long as the shape and rise time of these pulses are independent of position control settings and power-supply variations. One exception to this is when you are using a color receiver and a color display. Here, the horizontal-sync pulse should be held closely to 5.1 μs, so that the receiver color-burst sampling does in fact intercept a valid color burst. More on this later in the chapter.

Intentional Smear

Fig. 8-2 shows a typical composite video driver using a 4066 quad analog switch. It gives a 100-ohm output impedance and the proper signal levels. Capacitor C1 is used to *purposely* reduce the video rise and fall times. It is called a *smearing capacitor*.

Why would we want to further reduce the bandwidth and response of a tv system that is already hurting to begin with? In the case of a quality video monitor, we would not. But if we are using an ordinary run-of-the-mill tv set, particularly one using rf entry, this capacitor can very much *improve* the display legibility and contrast. Why?

Because we are interested in getting the most legible character with the highest contrast possible. This is not necessarily the one having the sharpest dot rise and fall times. Many things interact to determine the upper video response of a tv display. These include the tuner settings, the i-f response and alignment, the video-detector response, the video peaking, the sound-trap setting, the rf-cable reflections, and a host of other responses. Many of these stages are underdamped and will ring if fed a rise-time input that is too sharp, giving a ghosted, shabby, or washed out character. By reducing the video bandwidth going into the system, we can move the dot-matrix energy lower in frequency, resulting in cleaner characters of higher contrast.

For most tv displays, intentional smearing will help the contrast, legibility, and overall appearance. The ultimate limit to this occurs when the dots overlap and become illegible. The optimum amount of intentional smear is usually the value of capacitance that is needed to just close the inside of a "W" presented to the display.

Adding a Video Input

Video inputs are easy to add to the average television set, provided

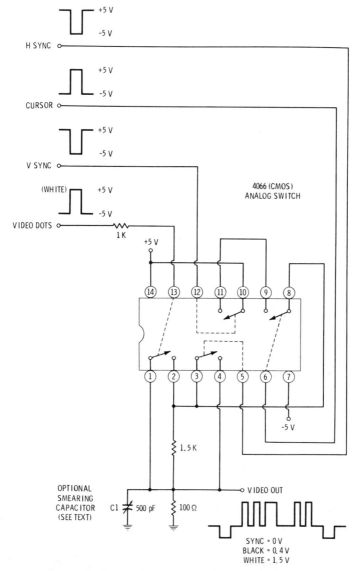

Fig. 8-2. Analog switch combiner generates composite video.

you take some reasonable precautions. First and foremost, you *must* have an accurate and complete schematic of the set to be modified, preferably a SAMS PHOTOFACT or something similar. The first thing to check is the power supply on the set. If it has a power transformer and if the chassis is properly safety-isolated from the power line, it is a good choice for a tvt monitor. This is particularly true of recent, small-screen portable tv sets. On the other hand, if you have a hot-chassis type with one side of the power line connected to the chassis, you should avoid its use if at all possible. If you must use this type of set, be absolutely certain to use one of the safety techniques outlined later in Chart 8-1.

A block diagram of a typical tv set appears in Fig. 8-3. The uhf or vhf signals picked up by the tuner are down-converted in frequency to a video i-f frequency of 44 MHz and then filtered and amplified. The output of the video i-f is transformer coupled to a *video detector,* most often a small-signal germanium diode. The video-detector output is filtered to remove the carrier and then routed to a *video amplifier* made up of one or more tubes or transistors.

At some point in the video amplification, the black-and-white signal is split three ways. First, a reduced bandwidth output routes sync pulses to the sync separator stage to lock the horizontal and vertical scanning to the video. A second bandpass output, sharply filtered to 4.5 MHz, extracts the fm sound subcarrier and routes it to a sound i-f amplifier for further processing. The third output is video, which is strongly amplified and then capacitively coupled to the cathode of the picture tube.

The gain of the video amplifier sets the contrast of the display, while the bias setting on the cathode of the picture tube (with respect to its grounded control grid) sets the display brightness. Somewhere in the video amplifier, further rejection of the 4.5-MHz sound subcarrier is usually picked up to minimize picture interference. This

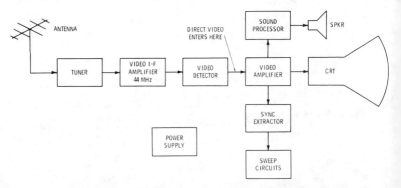

Fig. 8-3. Block diagram of typical black-and-white tv.

is called a *sound trap*. Sound traps can be a series-resonant circuit to ground, a parallel-resonant circuit in the video signal path, or simply part of the transformer that is picking off the sound for more processing.

The video-detector output is usually around 2 V peak to peak and usually *subtracts from* a white-level bias setting. The stronger the signal, the more negative the swing, and the blacker the picture. Sync tips are blacker than black, helping to blank the display during retrace times.

Fig. 8-4 shows the typical video circuitry of a transistor black-and-white television. Our basic circuit consists of a diode detector, a unity-gain emitter follower, and a variable-gain video output stage that is capacitively coupled to the picture tube. The cathode bias sets the brightness, while the video gain sets the contrast. Amplified signals for sync and sound are removed from the collector of the video driver by way of a 4.5-MHz resonant transformer for the sound and a low-pass filter for the sync. A parallel-resonant trap set to 4.5 MHz eleminates sound interference. Peaking coils on each stage extend the bandwidth by providing higher impedances and higher gain to high-frequency video signals.

Note particularly the biasing of the video driver. A bias network provides a stable source of 3 V. In the absence of input video, this 3 V sets the *white* level of the display, as well as establishing proper bias for both stages. As an increasing signal appears at the last video output transformer, it is negatively rectified by the video detector, thus lowering the 3 V proportionately. The stronger the signal, the blacker the picture. Sync will be the strongest of all, giving a blacker-than-black bias level of only 1 V.

The base of the video driver has the right sensitivity we need for video entry, accepting a maximum 2-V peak-to-peak signal. It also

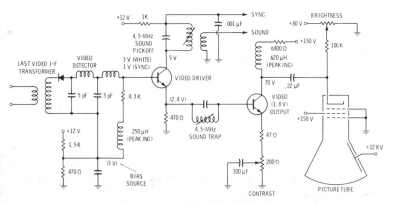

Fig. 8-4. Typical video circuitry of transistor black-and-white tv set.

has the right polarity, for a positive-going bias level means a whiter picture. *But, an unmodified set is already biased to the white level, and if we want to enter our own video, this bias must be shifted to the black level.*

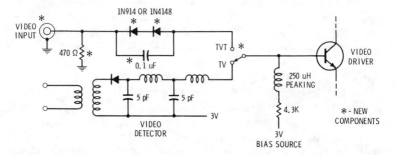

Fig. 8-5. Adding a video input to a transistor black-and-white set.

We have a choice in any tv of direct or ac coupling of input video. Direct coupling is almost always better because it eliminates any shading effects or any change of background level as additional characters are added to the screen. Fig. 8-5 shows how to direct-couple the video into a transistor black-and-white set. We provide a video input, usually a BNC or a phono jack and route this to a pair of series-connected silicon diodes. Each diode provides us with 0.6 volt of offset for a total of 1.2 volts of offset. The spdt switch selects either the video detector output or the new video input through this diode pair.

The two diodes add up to a 1.2 volts offset in the positive direction, so in the absence of video at the base of a sync tip, the video driver is biased to a blacker-than-black sync level of 1.2 volts. With a white video input of 2 volts, the video driver gets biased to its usual 3.2 volts of white level. Its important to keep the maximum input voltage at the white level low enough that the diodes are always conducting.

There are several other ways we can do the offsetting of the video input, such as by using a Darlington pnp emitter follower, a pair of ordinary pnp transistors connected as cascaded emitter followers, or a pnp transistor and a diode. If more or less offset is needed, extra diodes or transistors can be stacked up further to pick up the right amount of offset.

The important thing is that the video driver ends up with the same level for white bias and for black bias in either position of the switch.

Capacitively or ac-coupled video inputs should be avoided. Fig. 8-6 shows a typical circuit. The existing bias network is lowered in voltage by adding a new parallel resistor to ground to give a voltage

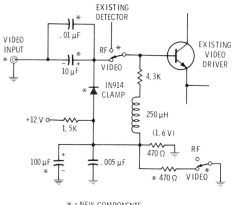

Fig. 8-6. Ac-coupled video needs shift of bias to black level, plus a clamping diode.

that is 0.6 V *more positive* than the blacker-than-black sync-tip voltage. For instance, with a 3-volt white level, and a 2-V peak-to-peak video, the sync-tip voltage would be 1 V; the optimum bias would then be 1.6 V. The input video is capacitively coupled by a fairly large electrolytic capacitor in parallel with a good high-frequency capacitor. This provides for a minimum of screen shading and still couples high-frequency signals properly. A clamping diode constantly clamps the sync tips to their bias value, with the 0.6-V drop of this diode being taken out by the extra 0.6 V provided for in the bias network. This clamping diode automatically holds the sync tips to their proper value, regardless of the number of white dots in the picture. Additional bypassing of the bias network by a large electrolytic may be needed for proper operation of the clamping diode, as shown in Fig. 8-6. Note that the bias network is used in both switch positions—its level is shifted as needed for the direct video input.

Tube-type sets are generally harder to interface than transistor sets. Fig. 8-7 shows us a typical direct-coupled tube interface. In the unmodified circuit, the white level is zero volts and the sync tip black level is *minus* two volts, bringing about the need for a *negative* two volts of offset. If we can find a negative supply (these are scarce in tube-type circuits), we could use the same diode or transistor offset techniques we did with the transistor sets, but going negative.

Instead of this, it is usually possible to *self-bias* the video amplifier to a cathode voltage of +2 V. This is done by breaking the cathode-to-ground connection and adding a small resistor (50 to 100 ohms) between cathode and ground to get a cathode voltage of +2 V. Once this value is found, a heavy electrolytic bypass of 100 μF or more is placed in parallel with the resistor, along with a good high-

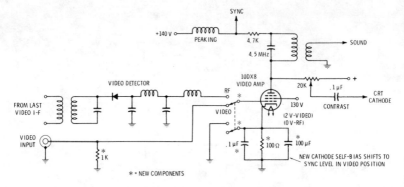

Fig. 8-7. Direct-coupled video added to tube-type black-and-white television.

frequency capacitor. Switching then ground the cathode in the normal rf mode and makes it +2 V in the cideo entry mode.

In the direct video mode, a sync-tip grounded input presents zero volts to the grid, which is self-biased −2 V with respect to the cathode. A white level presents +2 V to the grid, which equals 0 V grid to cathode.

Should there already be a self-bias network on the cathode, it is increased in value as needed to get the black-level rather than the white-level bias in the direct video mode Some shading may be introduced with the self-bias approach.

Hot-Chassis Problems

There is usually no shock hazard when we use clip-on rf entry or when we use a direct video jack on a transformer-powered tv. A very severe shock hazard can exist if we use direct video entry with a tv set having one side of the power line connected to the chassis. Depending on which way the line cord is plugged in, there is a 50-50 chance that the hot side of the power line is connected directly to the chassis.

Hot-chassis sets, particularly older tube versions, should be avoided entirely for direct video entry. If you absolutely must use one, some of the suggestions of Chart 8-1 may lessen the hazard. These include using an isolation transformer, husky back-to-back filament transformers, three-wire power systems, optical coupling of the video input, and total package isolation. Far and away the best route is to simply never attempt direct video entry into a hot-chassis tv.

Making the Conversion

Chart 8-2 explains how to modify a tv for direct video entry. Always have a complete schematic on hand and use a transformer-style tv set if at all possible. Late-model, small-screen, medium- to high-quality solid-state sets are often the best display choice. Avoid using junk sets, particularly very old ones. Direct coupling of video is far preferable to ac capacitor coupling. Either method has to maintain

Chart 8-1. Getting Around the Hot-Chassis Problem

Hot-chassis problems can be avoided entirely by using only transformer-powered tv circuits or by using clip-on rf entry. If a hot-chassis set must be used, here are some possible ways around the problem:

1. Add an isolation transformer.

A 110-V to 110-V isolation transformer whose wattage exceeds that of the set may be used. These are usually expensive, but a workable substitute can be made by placing two large surplus filament transformers back to back. For instance, a pair of 24-V, 4-A transformers can handle around 100 W.

2. Use a three-wire system with a solid ground.

Three-prong plug wiring, properly polarized, will force the hot-chassis connection to the cold side of the power line. This protection is useful only when three-wire plugs are used with properly wired outlets. A severe shock hazard is introduced if a user elects to use an adapter or plugs the system into an unknown or improperly wired outlet. The three-wire system should *not* be used if anyone but yourself is *ever* to use the system.

3. Optical-couple the input video.

Light-emitting diode and photocell pairs are low in cost and can be used to optically couple direct video, completely isolating the video input from the hot chassis. Most of these optoelectronic couplers do not have enough bandwidth for direct video use; The Litronix IL-100 is one exception. Probably the simplest route is to use two separate opto-isolators, one for video and one for sync, and then recombine the signals inside the tv on the hot side of the circuit.

4. Use a totally packaged and sealed system.

If you are only interested in displaying messages and have no other input/output devices, you can run the entire circuit hot chassis, provided everything is sealed inside one case and there is no chassis-to-people access. Interface to Teletypes, cassettes, etc., cannot be done without additional isolation, and servicing the circuit presents the same shock hazards that servicing a hot-chassis tv does.

the black-and-white bias levels on the first video amplifier stage. A shift of the first-stage quiescent bias from normally white to normally black is also a must. Use short, shielded leads between the video input jack and the rest of the circuit. If a changeover switch is used, keep it as close to the rest of the video circuitry as you possibly can.

Chart 8-2. How to Add a Direct Video Input to a TV Set

1. Get an accurate and complete schematic of the set—using either the manufacturer's service data or a *Sams Photofact* set. *Do not try adding an input without this schematic!*

2. Check the power supply to see if a power transformer is used. If it is, there will be no shock hazard, and the set is probably a good choice for direct video use. If the set has one side of the power line connected to the chassis, a severe shock hazard exists, and one of the techniques of Table 8-1 should be used. *Avoid the use of hot-chassis sets.*

3. Find the input to the first video amplifier stage. Find out what the white-level and sync-level bias voltages are. The marked or quiescent voltage is usually the white level; sync is usually 2 V less. A transistor tv will typically have a +3-V white level and a +1-V sync level. A tube-type tv will typically have a 0-V white level and a −2-V sync level.

4. Add a changeover switch, using the minimum possible lead lengths. Add an input connector, either a phono jack or BNC-type connector. Use shielded or twisted leads for interconnections exceeding three inches in length.

5. Select a circuit that couples the video and biases the first video amplifier stage so that the white and sync levels are preserved. For transistor sets, the direct-coupled circuit of Fig. 8-5 may be used. For tube sets, the circuit of Fig. 8-7 is recommended. Avoid the use of ac-coupled video inputs because they may introduce shading problems and changes of background as the screen is filled.

6. Check the operation. If problems with contrast or sync tearing occur, recheck and adjust the white and sync-input levels to match what the set uses during normal rf operation. Note that the first video stage must be biased to the *white* level during rf operation and to the *sync* level for direct video use. The white level is normally 2 V more positive than the sync level.

EXTENDING VIDEO AND DISPLAY BANDWIDTH

By using the direct video-input route, we eliminate any of the bandwidth and response restrictions of the rf modulator, tuner, video i-f strip, and video-detector filter. Direct video entry should bring us to a 3-MHz bandwidth for a color set and perhaps 3.5 MHz for a black-and-white model, unless we are using an extremely bad set. The resultant 6- to 7-million dot-per-second rate is adequate for short character lines of 32, 40, and possibly 48 characters per line. But the characters will smear and be illegible if we try to use longer line lengths and premium (lots of dots) character generators on an ordinary tv. Is there anything we can do to the set to extend the video bandwidth and display response for these longer line lengths?

In the case of a color tv, the answer is probably no. The video response of a color set is limited by an essential delay line and an essential 3.58-MHz trap. Even if we were willing to totally separate the chrominance and luminance channels, we would still be faced with an absolute limit set by the number of holes per horizontal line in the shadow mask of the tube. This explains why video color displays are so expensive and so rare. Later in the chapter, we will look at what is involved in adding color to the shorter line lengths.

With a black-and-white tv, there is often quite a bit we can do to present long lines of characters, depending on what set we start out with and how much we are willing to modify the set.

The best test signal to use for bandwidth extension is the dot-matrix data you actually want to display, for the frequency response, time delay, ringing, and overshoot all get into the act. What we want to end up with is a combination that gives reasonably legible characters.

A good oscilloscope (15-MHz or better bandwidth) is very useful during bandwidth extension to show where the signal loses its response in the circuit. At any time during the modification process, there is usually one response bottleneck. This, of course, is what should be attacked first. Obviously, the better the tv you start with, the easier the task will be. Tube-type tv's, particularly older ones, will be much more difficult to work with than a modern, small-screen, quality solid-state portable would be.

There are several things we can do: watch the control settings, get rid of the sound trap, minimize circuit strays, optimize spot size, control peaking, and shift to higher-current operation. Let's take a look at these in turn:

Control Settings

Always run a data display at the lowest possible contrast, using only as much brightness as you really need. In many circuits, low contrast means a lower video-amplifier gain and less gain-bandwidth restriction.

Eliminate the Sound Trap

The sound trap adds a notch at 4.5 MHz to the video response. If it is eliminated or switched out of the circuit, a wider video bandwidth automatically results. Fig. 8-8 shows the response changes and several positions for this trap. Generally, series-resonant traps are opened and parallel-resonant traps are shorted or bypassed through suitable switching or outright elimination. The trap has to go back into the circuit if the set is ever again used for ordinary program reception. Sometimes simply backing the slug all the way out on the trap will improve things enough to be useful.

Minimizing Strays

One of the limits of the video bandwidth is the stray capacitance both inside the video output stage and in the external circuitry. If the contrast control is directly in the signal path and if it has long leads going to it, it may be hurting the response. If you are using the tv set exclusively for data display, can you rearrange the control location and simplify and shorten the interconnections between the video output and picture tube?

Additional Peaking

Most tv sets have two peaking networks. The first of these is at the video-detector output and compensates for the vestigial-sideband transmission signal that makes sync and other low-frequency signals double the amplitude of the higher-frequency ones. The second of these goes to the collector or plate of the video output stage and raises the circuit impedance and the effective gain for very high frequencies. Sometimes you can alter this second network to favor dot presentations. Fig. 8-9 shows a typical peaking network and the effects of too little or too much peaking. Note that the stray capacitance also enters into the peaking, along with the video-amplifier output capacitance and the picture-tube input capacitance. Generally, too little peaking will give you low-contrast dots; too much will give you sharp dots but will run dots together and shift the more continuous portions of the characters objectionably. Peaking is changed by increasing or decreasing the series inductor from its design value.

Running Hot

Sometimes, increasing the operating current of the video output stage can increase the system bandwidth—*if* this stage is in fact the limiting response, *if* the power supply can handle the extra current,

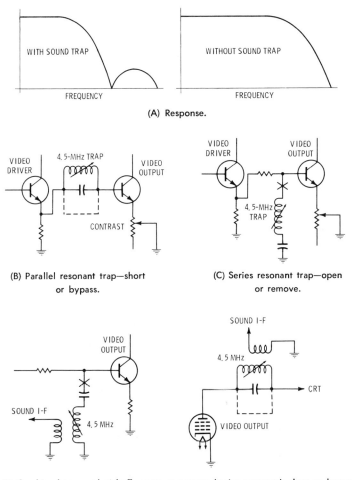

(A) Response.

(B) Parallel resonant trap—short or bypass.

(C) Series resonant trap—open or remove.

(D) Combined trap and pickoff—open or remove (series resonant), short or bypass (parallel resonant).

Fig. 8-8. Removing the sound trap can extend video bandwidth.

if the stage is not already at its gain-bandwidth peak, and *if* the extra heat can be gotten rid of without burning anything up. Usually, you can try adding a resistor three times the plate or collector load resistor in parallel, and see if it increases bandwidth by ⅓. Generally, the higher the current, the wider the bandwidth, but watch carefully any dissipation limits. Be sure to provide extra ventilation and additional heat sinking, and check the power supply as well. For major changes in operating current, the emitter resistors and other biasing components should also be proportionately reduced in value.

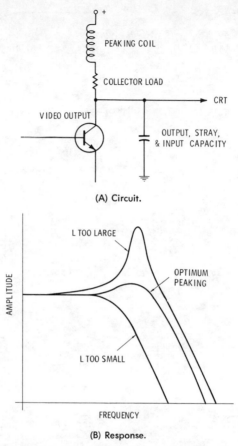

(A) Circuit.

(B) Response.

Fig. 8-9. Adjusting the peaking coil can extend video response.

Spot Size

Even with excellent video bandwidth, if you have an out-of-focus, blooming, or changing spot size, it can completely mask character sharpness. Spot size determines the ultimate limit to resolution, regardless of video bandwidth.

Once again, brightness and contrast settings will have a profound effect, with too much of either blooming the spot. Most sets have a focus jumper in which ground or a positive voltage is selected. You can try intermediate values of voltage for maximum sharpness. Extra power-supply filtering can sometimes minimize hum and noise modulation of the spot.

Anything that externally raises display contrast will let you run with a smaller beam current and a sharper spot. Using circularly polarized filters, graticule masks, or simple colored filters can minimize display washout from ambient lighting. Chart 8-13 lists several sources of material for contrast improvement. Much of this is rather expensive, from $10 to $25 per square foot being typical. Simply adding a hood and positioning the display away from room lighting will also help and is obviously much cheaper.

Chart 8-3. Contrast-Enhancing Filter Materials

Circularly Polarized Filters:	Light-Control Film:
Polaroid Corporation 547 Technology Square Cambridge, MA 02139	3M Visual Products Division 3M Center St. Paul, MN 55101
Antireflection Filters:	**Acrylic Plexiglas Filter Sheets:**
Panelgraphic Corporation 10 Henderson Drive West Caldwell, NJ 07006	Rohm and Haas Philadelphia, PA 19105

DIRECT RF ENTRY

If we want the convenience of a "free" display, the freedom from hot-chassis problems, and a "use it anywhere" ability, direct rf entry is the obvious choice. Its two big limitations are the need for FCC type approval and a limited video bandwidth that in turn limits the number of characters per line and the number of dots per character.

An rf interface standard is shown in Fig. 8-10. It consists of an amplitude-modulated carrier of one of the standard television-channel video frequencies of Chart 8-4. Channel 2 is most often used with a 55.250-MHz carrier frequency, except in areas where a local commercial Channel 2 broadcast is intolerably strong. Circuit cost, filtering problems, and stability problems tend to increase with high-frequency channels.

The sync tips are the strongest part of the signal, representing 100% modulation, often something around 4-mV rms across a 300-ohm line. The black level is 75% of the sync level, or about 3 mV for 4-mV sync tips. White level is less than 10% of maximum. Note that the signal is weakest when white, and strongest when sync. This is the exact opposite of the video interface of Fig. 8-1.

Radio-frequency modulators, suitable for clip-on rf entry tv typewriter use, are called *Class-1 tv devices* by the FCC. A Class-1 tv device is supposed to meet the rules and regulations summarized in Chart 8-5.

Fig. 8-11 shows a block diagram of the essential parts of a tv modulator. We start with a stable oscillator tuned to one of the Table 8-4

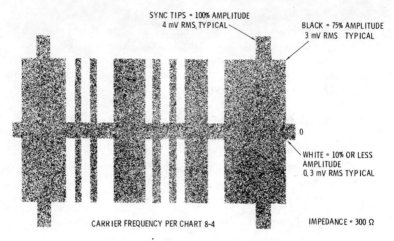

SYNC TIPS = 100% AMPLITUDE
4 mV RMS, TYPICAL

BLACK = 75% AMPLITUDE
3 mV RMS TYPICAL

0

WHITE = 10% OR LESS
AMPLITUDE
0.3 mV RMS TYPICAL

CARRIER FREQUENCY PER CHART 8-4

IMPEDANCE = 300 Ω

Fig. 8-10. Standard rf interface levels.

Chart 8-4. Television Picture-Carrier Frequencies

Channel 2	55.25 MHz
Channel 3	61.25 MHz
Channel 4	67.25 MHz
Channel 5	77.25 MHz
Channel 6	83.25 MHz

frequencies. A crystal oscillator is a good choice, and low-cost modules are widely available. The output of this oscillator is then amplitude modulated. This can be done by changing the bias current through a silicon small-signal diode. One milliampere of bias current makes the diode show an ac and rf impedance of 26 ohms. Half a milliampere will look like 52 ohms, and so on. The diode acts as a variable-resistance attenuator in the rf circuit, whose bias is set and changed by the video circuit.

Since diode modulators are nonlinear, we cannot simply apply a standard video signal to them and get a standard rf signal out. A differential amplifier circuit called a *video slicer* may be used to compensate for this nonlinearity. The video slicer provides three distinct currents to the diode modulator. One of these is almost zero for the white level, while the other two provide the black and sync levels. A contrast control that sets the slicing level lets you adjust the sync-tip

Chart 8-5. FCC Regulations on Class-1 TV Devices

1. A Class-1 tv device generates a video modulated rf carrier of a standard television channel frequency. It is directly connected to the antenna terminals of the tv set.

2. The maximum rms rf voltage must be less than 6 millivolts using a 300-ohm output line.

3. The maximum rf voltage on any frequency more than 3 MHz away from the operating channel must be more than 30 dB below the peak in-channel output voltage.

4. An antenna disconnect switch of at least 60-dB attenuation must be provided.

5. No user adjustments are permitted that would exceed any of the above specifications.

6. Residual rf radiation from case, leads, and cabinet must be less than 15 μV per meter.

7. A Class-1 tv device must not interfere with tv reception.

8. Type approval of the circuit is required. A filing fee of $1500 and an acceptance fee of $500 are required. More complete information appears in Subpart H of Part 15 and Subpart F of Part 2 of the Federal Communications Commission *Rules and Regulations*. It is available at many large technical libraries.

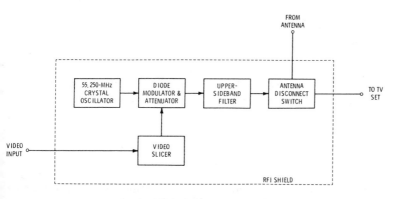

Fig. 8-11. Block diagram of rf modulator.

height with respect to the black level. The video slicer also minimizes the chances of rf getting back into the video. An attenuator to reduce the size of the modulated signal usually follows the diode modulator.

An upper-sideband filter removes most of the lower sideband from the a-m modulated output, giving us a *vestigial sideband* signal that stays inside the channel band limits. This same filter eliminates second-harmonic effects and other spurious noise. The filter output is usually routed to an antenna disconnect switch and the tv antenna terminals. A special switch is needed to provide enough isolation.

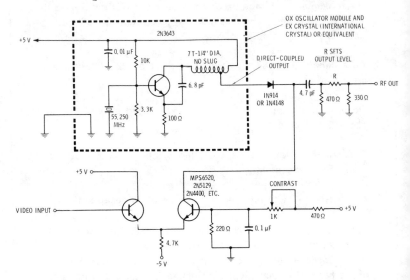

Fig. 8-12. Channel 2 oscillator, modulator, video slicer, and attenuator.

Some of the actual circuitry involved is shown in Fig. 8-12. The video slicer consists of a pair of high-gain, small-signal npn transistors, while the oscillator is a commercially available module.

Radio-frequency entry systems must always be direct coupled to the antenna terminals of the set and should never provide any more rf than what is needed for a snow-free picture. They should be permanently tuned to a single tv channel. Under no circumstances should an antenna or cable service hookup remain connected to the set during tvt use, nor should radiation rather than a direct rf cable connection ever be used.

HOLD SETTINGS

You may have to trim the receiver *horizontal hold* control, since tvt horizontal frequencies often differ slightly from broadcast standards. This control is usually found behind a hinged panel in front or at the bottom on the back of the set. Horizontal hold misadjustment results in a skewed, torn, or "S" shaped display.

Less often, the *vertical hold* control may also need touching up. Vertical hold misadjustment gives a rolling or jumping picture.

The hold controls will interact with the tvt position controls. Always set the hold controls first for a stable and undistorted picture, then center the picture as needed with the positioning controls internal to your tvt.

COLOR TECHNIQUES

We can add a full-color capability to a tv typewriter system fairly easily and cheaply—provided its usual black-and-white video dot rate is low enough in frequency to be attractively displayed on an ordinary color tv. Color may be used to emphasize portions of a message, to attract attention, to add interest to an electronic game or to give added value to a graphics display. Color techniques work best on tv typewriter systems having a horizontal frequency very near 15,735 Hz.

Basically, all we have to do is generate a subcarrier sine wave to add to the video output. To generate the various colors, the phase of this subcarrier (or its time delay) is shifted with respect to what the phase was immediately after each horizontal-sync pulse.

Fig. 8-13 shows the differences between normal color and black-and-white operation. Black-and-white baseband video is approximately 4 MHz wide and has a narrow 4.5-MHz sound subcarrier. The video is amplitude modulated, while the sound is narrow-band frequency modulated. This adds up to a 6-MHz rf channel with a vestigial lower sideband as shown in Fig. 8-13B.

To generate color, we add a new pilot or subcarrier at a frequency of 3.579545 MHz. (Fig. 8-13C). What was formerly the video is now called the *luminance,* and is the same as the brightness in a black-and-white system. The new subcarrier and its modulation are called the *chrominance* signal, and they determine what color gets displayed and how saturated it will be.

Since the black-and-white information is a sampled data system that is scanned at the vertical and horizontal rates, there are lots of discrete holes in the video spectrum that are not used. The color subcarrier is designed to stuff itself into these holes—exactly in a National Television System Committee (NTSC) color system and reasonably so in a tvt display. Both chrominance and luminance signals use the same spectral space, with the one being where the other one is not, overlapping comb style.

The *phase,* or relative delay, of the chrominance signal with respect to a reference determines the instantaneous *color,* while the

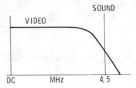

(A) Black-and-white— baseband video.

(B) Black-and-white—Channel 2 rf.

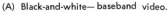
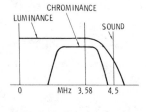
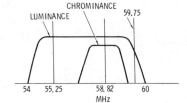

(C) Color—baseband video.

(D) Color—Channel 2 rf.

Fig. 8-13. Spectrum differences between color and black-and-white.

amplitude of this signal with respect to the luminance sets the *saturation* of the color. Low amplitudes generate white or pastel shades, while high amplitudes of the chrominance signal produce saturated and deep colors.

At least eight cycles of a reference or *burst* color phase are transmitted immediately following each horizontal-sync pulse as a timing reference, as shown in Fig. 8-14. The burst is around 25% of maximum amplitude, or about the peak-to-peak height of a sync pulse.

The tv set has been adjusted at the factory to sort all this out. After video detection, the set splits out the chrominance channel with a bandpass amplifier and then synchronously demodulates it with respect to an internal 3.58-MHz reference. The phase of this demodulation sets the color and the amplitude sets the saturation by setting the ratios of electron beam currents on the picture-tube red, blue, and green guns.

Meanwhile, the luminance channel gets amplified as brightness-style video. It is delayed with a delay line to make up for the time delay involved in the narrower-band color processing channel. It is then filtered with two traps—the 4.5-MHz sound trap and a new trap to get rid of any remaining 3.58-MHz color subcarrier that is left. The luminance output sets the overall brightness by modulating the cathodes of all three color guns simultaneously.

Just after each horizontal-sync pulse, the set looks for the reference burst and uses this reference in a phase detector circuit to keep its own 3.58-MHz reference locked to the version being transmitted.

Table 8-1 shows the phase angles related to each color with respect to the burst phase. It also shows the equivalent amount of delay

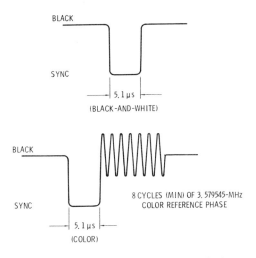

BLACK

SYNC

5.1 μs

(BLACK-AND-WHITE)

BLACK

SYNC

8 CYCLES (MIN) OF 3.579545-MHz
COLOR REFERENCE PHASE

5.1 μs

(COLOR)

Fig. 8-14. Adding a color reference burst to the back porch of the horizontal-sync pulses.

needed for a given phase angle. Since we usually want only a few discrete colors, it is far easier to digitally generate colors simply by delaying the reference through gates or buffers, rather than to use complex and expensive analog phase-shift methods.

Strictly speaking, we should control both the chrominance phase and amplitude to be able to do both pastel and strongly saturated colors. But, keeping the subcarrier amplitude at the value we used for the burst—around 25% of video amplitude—is far simpler and will usually get useful results.

Table 8-1. Colors are Generated by Delaying or Phase Shifting the Burst Frequency

Color	Approximate Phase	Approximate Delay
Burst	0°	0
Yellow	15°	12 ns
Red	75°	58 ns
Magenta	135°	105 ns
Blue	195°	151 ns
Cyan	255°	198 ns
Green	315°	244 ns

A circuit that can be used to add color to a tv typewriter is shown in Fig. 8-15. A 3.579545-MHz crystal oscillator drives a string of CMOS buffers that make up a digital delay line. The output delays caused by the propogation times in each buffer can be used as is,

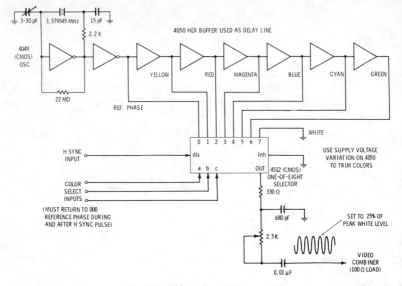

Fig. 8-15. Color subcarrier generator.

or they can be trimmed to specific colors by varying the supply voltage.

The reference phase and the delayed color outputs go to a one-of-eight data selector. The data selector picks either the reference or a selected color in response to a code presented digitally to the three select lines. The logic that is driving this selector must return to the reference phase position (000) immediately before, during, and, for a minimum of a few microseconds, after each horizontal-sync pulse. This gives the set a chance to lock and hold onto the reference color burst.

The chrominance output from the data selector should be disabled for the duration of the sync pulses and any time a white screen display is wanted. The output chrominance signal is RC filtered to make it somewhat sinusoidal. It is then cut down in amplitude to around one-quarter the maximum video white level and is capacitively coupled to the 100-ohm video output of Fig. 8-2 or otherwise summed into the video or rf modulator circuitry. For truly dramatic color effects, the amplitude *and* delay of the chrominance signal can be changed in a more complex version of the same circuit.

A RGB COLOR SYSTEM

Another interesting approach to color displays is to keep the three color channels totally separate. This is called the RGB or red-green-blue method. The RGB technique eliminates any need for multiplexing color information and does away with any bandwidth restrictions caused by the video processing circuitry.

The disadvantages of this route are that rf entry cannot be used, and that you either have to use an expensive color studio monitor with three channels of video available, or else you have to extensively modify a color tv receiver to allow direct entry into the color video amplifiers.

Sync can be provided on a separate line or optionally combined with the green video. *Ann Arbor Terminals* is one source of premium graphics tvt's using this technique.

More information useful in solving television interface problems appears in the *Television Engineering Handbook* by Donald Fink, and various issues of the *IEEE transactions on Consumer Electronics*.

CHAPTER 9

Hard Copy and Color Graphics

Two of the most important "add-on" techniques we would often like to use with tvt systems are *hard copy* and *color graphics*. Hard copy is any method of obtaining a permanent record, while graphics is any method that lets you display pictures as well as words. Advanced graphics techniques lead to video games and computer art synthesis applications. In this final chapter, we will take a detailed look at these add-on options, ending up with some important "what's next" suggestions on where you can go from here with advanced tv typewriter concepts.

HARD COPY

We need hard copy whenever we want a more or less permanent record of what the tvt is up to. In *word-processing* applications, such as form-letter writing, addressing, mailing-list generation, or typesetting, the hard copy is the main thing we are after in our system. In other tvt uses, hard copy can range from a convenience to an essential output.

Right now, hard copy is not cheap. And it is not likely to become cheap in the near future, particularly if final appearance is important. There are several good ways to solve the hard-copy problem. Whatever method you choose, you will end up evaluating the following tradeoffs:

* Cost of the printer
* Cost of the interface and support electronics
* Copy appearance, permanence, and legibility
* Length of line available

* Available character sets, case, and fonts
* Cost per copy
* Operating costs, including supplies
* Printing speed
* Ability to handle graphics
* Noise level
* Lifetime before major repair or replacement
* Skill needed to set up and interface
* Durability for student and public use

There is no known hard-copy system that is likely to optimize *all* of the above, particularly at tvt-compatible costs, so whatever you pick for hard-copy output will involve compromise, and probably quite a bit of it.

Generally, there have been several routes toward hard copy. You can build, rent, or buy (and buying further breaks down into new, used, and surplus).

Each of these routes has its own problems. Building may take both mechanical and electronic skills and can dramatically drive home the very high support costs of some deceptively simple and cheap printhead systems. Renting usually involves a 3- to 6-month minimum fee, plus installation and removal charges which can skyrocket the price of short-term usage. Buying new or used usually involves great expense, and you still might have interface problems. *American Used Computer Corp.* (Box 68 Kenmore Station, Boston, MA 02215) is one source of used equipment; others appear in the classified section of *Electronic News* and *Infosystems* magazines. Buying surplus can get you an unworkable and worn-out orphan in a nonstandard operating code without technical support or spare parts.

So, what can we do? We can usually dismiss computer-style line and chain printers outright because of their prohibitive costs—even as rentals—their expensive paper, and their less-than-perfect final appearance. This leaves us with computer Teletypes, surplus Baudot Teletypes, Selectric typewriters, electro-discharge printers, thermal printers, impact printers, photographic imaging, ink squirters, and nonprint alternatives. Let's take a closer look at these more or less viable techniques for acceptable-cost tvt hard copy.

COMPUTER TELETYPES

The Teletype ASR-33 of Fig. 9-1 has long been the mainstay of computer time-sharing services. It is made by the Teletype Corporation, 5555 Touhey Avenue. Skokie, IL 60076. The ASR-33 combines a mechanically encoded keyboard with a typewriter-like printer and a paper-tape punch. The printer and keyboard may be connected together in a *local* mode or may be used separately at half or full duplex in a *line* mode. The 33 series accepts the standard 8-bit ASCII serial code of Fig. 7-2 and may use the simple and inexpensive tvt interface of Fig. 7-6.

The format is normally 72 uppercase characters per line and ten lines per inch, printable on ordinary paper, a continuous roll, or a pin feed roll (holes along the edges). A graphics capability is also available but is restricted to 72 symbols per line and sequential line-by-line operation.

There are several different models available. The RO-33 is just a printer with no paper tape or keyboard. The KSR-33 is a combined keyboard and printer, while the ASR-33 adds a paper-tape punch and reader to the system. Integral 103-style modems are also available as options for phone line communications. The maximum speed rate of all units is 100 characters per second, equal to 100 words per minute. A newer and more expensive 35 series is also available that offers extreme durability and other advanced features.

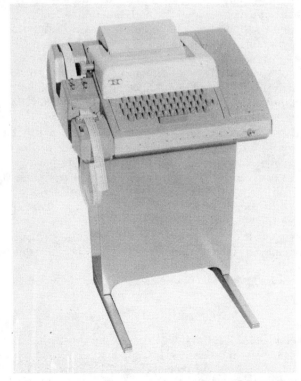

Courtesy Teletype Corp.

Fig. 9-1. ASR-33 Teletype.

Recent price reductions make the ASR-33 available for just under $1000 new, with the RO printer available for around $600. The paper tape can be used for program storage and retrieval, assembly and debug, and so on. Paper tape was the low-speed storage standard in minicomputers before the microprocessor revolution. Today, modern cassette techniques are far faster, quieter, and reusable, and they eliminate the paper-tape tendency to self-destruct. Paper-tape entry or punching takes place at an asynchronous 10 characters per second or slower. Long programs take forever to enter at this rate. The information is stored on the tape as a parallel ASCII word of eight bits, according to the code of Fig. 9-2. A hole is defined as a 1, and a no-hole is defined as 0. Parity makes the total number of 1's in the word an *even* number, by selectively punching or not punching the eighth bit.

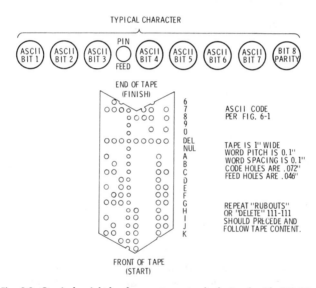

Fig. 9-2. One-inch, eight-level paper-tape standards (used with ASR-33).

Obvious advantages of the ASR-33 include its long history of reliable operation, its hassle-free tvt interface, and its wide availability. Its main limitations are its cost, its noisy operation, the absence of lowercase, the slowness of punched-tape entry, and the limited attractiveness of its character font for word-processing applications.

Rental and lease units are available from the phone companies and from various computer service firms. These usually advertise in telephone yellow pages. A local listing included General Electric, RCA Service, Teletype Corporation, and United Data Services. The going rental rate ranges from $35 to $80 per month, depending on the source, the purpose for which you are going to use the Teletype, and the length of rental time. There are usually stiff installation and removal charges for very short time users.

A lively exchange of new and used Teletypes usually appears in the classified pages of *Electronic News, Infosystems,* and other specialized data-processing trade magazines. Materials and supplies (tape, ribbons, paper, etc.) are usually available from the rental sources. One independent source is Robins Industries, 75 Austin Blvd., Commack, NY 11725.

Surplus (as opposed to used) 8-level Teletypes are extremely rare, with the possible exception of the older *Friden* Flexowriter system. Thus, any Teletype labeled "surplus" should be highly suspect—it's probably an obsolete 5-bit system or else something that may be totally unworkable.

BAUDOT TELETYPES

There are several obsolete Teletype machines currently available based on the Teletype 28, the Creed 75, and various Kleinschmidt units. These sometimes crop up as military surplus and are sometimes carried by surplus houses, particularly those that advertise in the ham radio magazines. (For military-surplus information, write to: Defense Supply Agency, Defense Logistics Center, Federal Center, Battle Creek, MI 49106.

These machines are widely used by hams for rtty and by deaf communications groups. As we saw earlier, the Baudot code is very limited since it needs a separate letters and figures shift to change case. The available character set is small, and the characters (and keycaps) do not directly map into ASCII without redefinition or code conversion. Older surplus units are likely to be badly in need of replacement parts and may not give a reasonable printout. While the continued use of these machines should be strongly discouraged, their low price (often from $50 upwards) and their compatibility with existing ham and deaf communications networks sometimes make them attractive for use.

The Baudot code is repeated in Table 9-1, and the serial format and paper-tape standards for 60- and 100-word-per-minute rates appear in Fig. 9-3. A standard UART may be programmed to do serial-to-parallel Baudot conversion as shown in Fig. 9-4. Newer versions of the UARTs automatically generate the needed 1.42 stop bits when programmed for only a 5-bit word.

There is a three-step process involved in using a Baudot machine with a tv typewriter. The first is to get the machine complete and clean and properly working in Baudot, with all characters legible and uniform. The second step is to provide a serial interface, either one similar to Fig. 7-6 or a higher-current version. Or, better yet, use a high-speed relay or opto-isolator. These machines work with higher currents than modern Teletypes and are notorious ground and spike noise generators, so complete isolation is strongly recommended. The third step of our process is to do the necessary Baudot-to-ASCII and ASCII-to-Baudot conversions to make them compatible with tvt use.

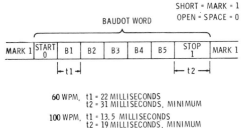

60 WPM, t1 = 22 MILLISECONDS
t2 = 31 MILLISECONDS, MINIMUM
100 WPM, t1 = 13.5 MILLISECONDS
t2 = 19 MILLISECONDS, MINIMUM

(A) Serial interface must match wpm rate of machine in use.

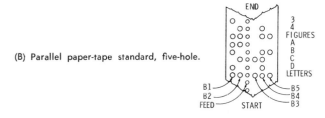

(B) Parallel paper-tape standard, five-hole.

Fig. 9-3. Baudot standards.

If we are starting with our own keyboard, we can use an ASCII keyboard encoder and simply redefine key positions and interconnections to produce a Baudot coding. This was shown in Fig. 6-13 and does take special keycaps and keyboard wiring.

If we are receiving our input information as Baudot, we would have to convert it to ASCII. This would be the case in ham rtty or on an existing data net, and would also be the case if the Teletype keyboard were the only data entry device. A read-only memory may be combined with a flip-flop to do the conversion, as shown in Fig. 9-5. The set-reset flip-flop precedes the ROM and keeps track of the letters and figures shifts for us. Depending on your system, the letters and figures commands can be ignored after coding or can be converted into unmappable ASCII characters (such as ">" and "<") for later retrieval. At this writing, preprogrammed low-cost ROMs are not readily available, so programming your own unit is a reasonable and low-cost route to the conversion.

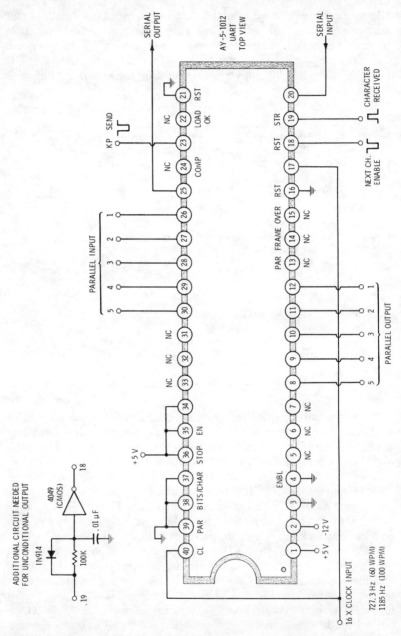

Fig. 9-4. UART connections for serial-parallel Baudot conversion (see Chapter 7).

Table 9-1. Baudot Code*

Code Bits					Letters	Figures	Code Bits					Letters	Figures*
5	4	3	2	1			5	4	3	2	1		
0	0	0	0	0	Blank	Blank	1	0	0	0	0	T	5
0	0	0	0	1	E	3	1	0	0	0	1	Z	"
0	0	0	1	0	Linefeed	Linefeed	1	0	0	1	0	L	)
0	0	0	1	1	A	—	1	0	0	1	1	W	2
0	0	1	0	0	Space	Space	1	0	1	0	0	H	#
0	0	1	0	1	S	Bell	1	0	1	0	1	Y	6
0	0	1	1	0	I	8	1	0	1	1	0	P	Ø
0	0	1	1	1	U	7	1	0	1	1	1	Q	1
0	1	0	0	0	Car. Ret.	Car. Ret.	1	1	0	0	0	O	9
0	1	0	0	1	D	$	1	1	0	0	1	B	?
0	1	0	1	0	R	4	1	1	0	1	0	G	&
0	1	0	1	1	J	'	1	1	0	1	1	Figures	Figures
0	1	1	0	0	N	,	1	1	1	0	0	M	.
0	1	1	0	1	F	!	1	1	1	0	1	X	/
0	1	1	1	0	C	:	1	1	1	1	0	V	;
0	1	1	1	1	K	(	1	1	1	1	1	Letters	Letters

* "Figures" punctuation may vary, depending on original use of machine.

Going backwards from ASCII to Baudot is a bit more tricky, although basically it takes the single read-only memory circuit of Fig. 9-6. The problem in the ASCII-to-Baudot conversion is that a shift of case may or may not be needed between each character if we are not careful.

There are several ways around this problem. One is to keep total track of the letters and figures shifts through the ASCII part of the system, perhaps by calling letters a "<" and figures a ">." The entire tvt and ASCII part of the system is restricted to being "Baudot transparent," with appropriate letters and figures shifts preceding every case rotation. Essentially, we have a continuous Baudot system this way, and there is no need to straighten things out after conversion. Unfortunately, this technique is very restrictive, particularly if you have other peripherals or a microprocessor in your circuit.

A second approach is simply to run the output Teletype at one half its normal speed, alternating between characters to be typed or letters-figures shifts. Before each character, the Teletype is shifted to make certain it is in the right case for that character. This means an output limit of 30 to 50 words per minute, but it is very easy to implement. All you need is a data selector or equivalent logic at the code conversion output that alternates between the word to be typed and a letters or figures command. System timing must be slow enough to prevent a new character from arriving before the two-step process is complete, or else you have to use a handshaking system in which the Teletype asks for each new character. Note that ASCII bit 6 is a 0 for letters and a 1 for figures.

Yet a better approach takes a little more logic. A circuit at the code converter remembers what the last typed character case was—letters or figures. It then compares this to the next character case. If the two are identical, no shift is needed, and the character gets printed

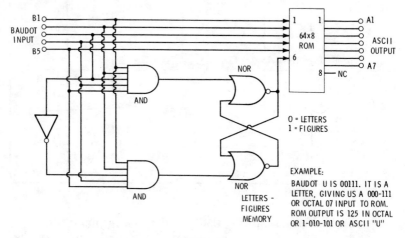

O = LETTERS
1 = FIGURES

EXAMPLE:
BAUDOT U IS 00111. IT IS A LETTER, GIVING US A 000-111 OR OCTAL 07 INPUT TO ROM. ROM OUTPUT IS 125 IN OCTAL OR 1-010-101 OR ASCII "U"

(A) Circuit.

IN		OUT	IN		OUT	IN		OUT	IN		OUT
00	NUL	000	20	T	124	40	NUL	000	60	5	065
01	E	105	21	Z	132	41	3	063	61	"	042
02	LF	012	22	L	114	42	LF	012	62	)	051
03	A	101	23	W	124	43	–	137	63	2	062
04	SP	040	24	H	110	44	SP	040	64	#	043
05	S	123	25	Y	131	45	BEL	007	65	6	066
06	I	111	26	P	120	46	8	070	66	0	060
07	U	125	27	Q	121	47	7	067	67	1	061
10	CR	015	30	O	117	50	CR	015	70	9	071
11	D	104	31	B	102	51	$	044	71	?	077
12	R	122	32	G	107	52	4	064	72	&	046
13	J	112	*33	FIG	000	53	'	047	*73	FIG	000
14	N	116	34	M	115	54	,	054	74	.	056
15	F	106	35	X	130	55	!	041	75	/	057
16	C	103	36	V	126	56	:	072	76	;	073
17	K	113	*37	LET	000	57	(	050	*77	LET	000
									*	SEE TEXT	

(B) Truth table for ROM (octal).

Fig. 9-5. Baudot-ASCII parallel code conversion.

immediately. If a case shift is needed, the circuit stops and produces a letters or figures shift, then goes on to print the character. The speed of this system depends very much on the mix of letters and figures in the message. But, if an occasional shift is all that is needed,

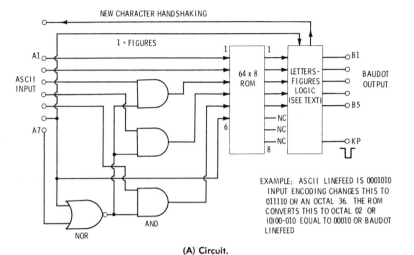

EXAMPLE: ASCII LINEFEED IS 0001010 INPUT ENCODING CHANGES THIS TO 011110 OR AN OCTAL 36. THE ROM CONVERTS THIS TO OCTAL 02 OR (0)00-010 EQUAL TO 00010 OR BAUDOT LINEFEED

(A) Circuit.

LF, CR AND BELL
CTRL ENCODING

IN		OUT	IN		OUT	IN		OUT	IN		OUT
00	⊕	00	20	P	26	40	SP	04	60	0	26
01	A	03	21	Q	27	41	:	15	61	1	27
02	B	31	22	R	12	42	"	21	62	2	23
03	C	16	23	S	05	43	#	24	63	3	01
04	D	11	24	T	20	44	$	11	64	4	12
05	E	01	25	U	07	45	%	00	65	5	20
06	F	15	26	V	36	46	&	32	66	6	25
07	G	32	27	W	23	47	'	13	67	7	07
10	H	24	30	X	35	50	(	17	70	8	06
11	I	06	31	Y	25	51	)	22	71	9	30
12	J	13	32	Z	21	52	*	00	72	:	16
13	K	17	*33	BEL	05	53	+	00	73	;	36
14	L	22	34	\	00	54	,	13	+ 74	<	00
15	M	34	*35	CR	10	55	-	03	75	=	00
16	N	14	*36	LF	02	56	.	34	+ 76	>	00
17	O	30	37	–	00	57	/	35	77	?	31

* ENCODED BY LOGIC GATES
+ SEE TEXT

(B) Truth table for ROM (octal).

Fig. 9-6. ASCII-Baudot parallel code conversion.

the technique runs almost at the full-speed capability of the Teletype.

There are three control commands in Baudot—*Bell, Linefeed,* and *Carriage Return.* We can directly recognize and convert these control words in ASCII with a large read-only memory, but the four gates preceding the ROM in Fig. 9-6 get us by with one half the size and cost.

This logic redefines Bell as an opening bracket "[," Return as a closing bracket "]," and Linefeed as an up arrow"↑," and stuffs these commands back into the smaller ROM for conversion. For proper Baudot operation, these three little-used symbols must be disallowed everywhere in the system. Note also that a separate Carriage Return and Linefeed command must be used in a two-step process to begin a new line, requiring at least a partial decoding of control functions in the rest of the tvt circuit.

Circuits of this type should be worked out in a full handshaking mode, with the Teletype asking for each new character. This prevents overspeeding if a long sequence of characters and shifts is needed at once.

Which circuit you decide on depends on what you want the machine to do. The two key things your output circuit must do are provide the proper shift for the proper character and prevent a new character from arriving till a previous one has been shifted (if needed) and printed.

Ads for Baudot products and conversion systems often show up in *73, Ham Radio, CQ, QST,* and similar magazines.

SELECTRIC TYPEWRITERS

One of the best-kept secrets in the computer industry is that all it takes to convert an ordinary Selectric *office* typewriter into a superb hard-copy printer is a small handful of cheap solenoids and some simple modifications that in no way impair the use of the machine as an ordinary typewriter. This gives us a printer that can handle uppercase and lowercase in any of dozens of quick-change type fonts, that handles a hundred or more characters per line, and that uses any shape and size of paper, at a cost that can be as little as $30 or so above the cost of the typewriter. Best of all, the final appearance tops *any* other hard-copy computer output system, regardless of cost.

The add-on conversion process is simplest and cheapest if the Selectric is to be used only as an ordinary typewriter or a tvt output printer and not used to enter data into the tvt system. When commercial Selectric conversions are done, the mechanical keyboard is usually replaced with an electronic one that has the usual Selectric keytops but directly encodes into ASCII. This allows the keyboard to be logically separated from the printing mechanism and eliminates the need for Selectric-ASCII conversion. If we are not going to heavily modify our machine, the printer-only route is perhaps best, entering data into the tvt from another keyboard located elsewhere.

A Selectric printing mechanism operates by dancing a golf-ball-shaped typing head across the paper. The ball can be shifted, tilted, and rotated to a given character position by using the compact 7-bit Selectric code shown in Fig. 9-7. A carriage under the ball advances one character position per character after impact and also provides for tab, repeat action, and return of the ball to the lefthand side of

R5 → T1 → T2 →	0 0 0	0 0 1	0 1 0	0 1 1	1 0 0	1 0 1	1 1 0	1 1 1	
S R2A R2 R1 ↓ ↓ ↓ ↓									
0 0 0 0	−	b	w	9					⎫
0 0 0 1	y	h	s	ϕ	/	l	o	4	
0 0 1 0									
0 0 1 1									⎬ lowercase
0 1 0 0	q	k	i	6	,	c	a	8	
0 1 0 1	p	e	'	5	;	d	r	7	
0 1 0 0	$=$	n	.	2	f	u	v	3	
0 1 1 1	j	t	$\frac{1}{2}$!	z	g	x	m	1	⎭
1 0 0 0	_	B	W	(					⎫
1 0 0 1	Y	H	S	)	?	L	O	$	
1 0 1 0									
1 0 1 1									⎬ UPPERCASE
1 1 0 0	Q	K	I	¢	,	C	A	*	
1 1 0 1	P	E	"	%	:	D	R	&	
1 1 1 0	+	N	.	@	F	U	V	#	
1 1 1 1	J	T	$\frac{1}{4}$ °	Z	G	X	M	‡[	⎭

⬚ = REDUNDANT OR NOT USED

Fig. 9-7. Selectric correspondence code.

the page. Unlike ordinary typewriters, the carriage is stationary; only the ball moves and only seven control bits are needed to select a character—compared to the one-per-key commands needed in a standard typewriter.

So, apparently, we need a few solenoids. We need seven for the ball-motion control. The first six of these are called TILT 1, TILT 2, ROTATE 1, ROTATE 2, ROTATE 2A, and ROTATE 5. They control the ball rotation and indexing. A seventh, called SHIFT, rotates the ball 180° for uppercase and lowercase.

An eighth solenoid is used to command printing, a ninth is needed for the nonprinting space, and a tenth for carriage return. In all, ten solenoids are needed for the basic motions. Optionally, extra solenoids could be added for index, bell, tab, backspace, etc., but these are rarely needed in most tvt applications.

Our conversion process consists of finding a suitable Selectric and some solenoids, tying them into safe and sane points in the machine, building the solenoid drive circuitry, and then providing ASCII-to-Selectrict conversion.

We found out how to convert ASCII to Selectric in Fig. 3-6 by using a programmed read-only memory. Suitable low-cost solenoids are available as the S series from *HI-G* or as the SP-650 series from *Electro-Mechanisms, Inc.* Other distributor-stocked solenoids are available at considerably more expense from Oak, Liberty, Guardian, Endicott, Phillips, and Ledex.

Fig. 9-8 shows a typical solenoid drive circuit that is CMOS and TTL compatible. A positive input voltage actuates the solenoid. The

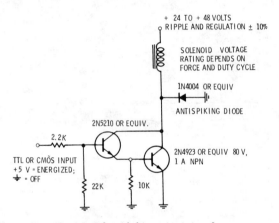

Fig. 9-8. Solenoid driver circuit interface.

diode eliminates reverse transient effects. Solenoids may be run at two or four times their rated continuous voltage for more pull, provided their duty cycle is restricted according to the manufacturer's recommendations. Note that a hot solenoid has considerably less pull than a cold one. The use of a 24- to 48-V supply for the solenoids is just about optimum, since it gets you by with relatively low-current drivers in the 100- to 500-mA range. This supply need not be tightly regulated, but the total ripple and no-load, full-load voltage difference should be under four volts or so. It is extremely important to arrange the supply ground returns so that ground noise is not sent back to earlier parts of the circuit. While opto-isolators are ideal, the noise problem can be minimized by careful layout and design without needing exotic parts.

Of course, a Selectric is a highly complex and precise piece of machinery. *Under no circumstances should any add-on changes be made anywhere in the machine except in the relatively "low precision" area immediately under and in front of the keyboard.* When working with a machine, particularly when its cover is off, be very careful not to interfere with the ball motion. The tapes and cords controlling the ball are easily damaged, and special tools and techniques are required to fix them.

The first part of any add-on modification usually consists of adding a false bottom an inch or two high. This goes between the real case bottom and the rest of the machine and gives working room for the solenoids and a place to put the electronics. A rigid subchassis is then added to the Selectric frame to stiffly hold the solenoids in their intended positions.

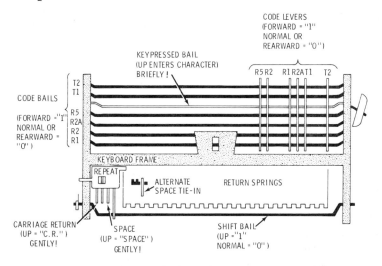

Fig. 9-9. Bottom of Selectric keyboard shows solenoid tie-in points.

Fig. 9-9 shows the bottom of a Selectric keyboard arranged upside down with the spacebar toward us. The ball position is set up with the six front-to-back code levers on the right side, arranged as groups of two, three, and one, from left to right. Again from left to right, these levers are (ROTATE 5, ROTATE 2); (ROTATE 1, ROTATE 2A, TILT 1); and finally (TILT 2). A logic 1 takes place with the levers toward the spacebar, and a logic 0 is toward the line cord. These code levers in turn are controlled by six dark bails that run the width of the keyboard. From front to rear, these bails are in a R1, R2, R2A, R5, T1, and T2 sequence, with a silver keypressed bail above and between R5 and T1.

In commercial Selectric conversions, the solenoids usually work directly with the front-to-back code levers. Often the levers are removed and replaced with ones that are directly attachable by a solenoid. The code levers are fairly easy to remove in newer Selectrics but are almost nonremovable in very early Model 72 machines.

If your mechanical precision capabilities are limited, it is probably better to control the six dark bails that encode the code levers. This is a low-technology area that is more forgiving, and the action can be conveniently distributed as much as needed. The added mechanical motion will slow the response somewhat, limiting in turn the maximum number of words per minute that you can put out as characters. The dark bails forward form a logic 1, while the bails unmolested or toward the rear are a 0. Your encoding process consists of adding a small solenoid in such a way that it does not interfere with normal typing but is strong enough to firmly encode the bail or lever as needed. For instance, to encode the letter A, we make ROTATE 1 a 0, ROTATE 2 a 0, ROTATE 2A and ROTATE 5 a 1, TILT 1 a 1, and TILT 2 a 0. To enter a 0, you do nothing; to enter a 1, you firmly hold the bail or lever toward the front of the machine.

The seventh shift bail is located in front under the spacebar, or any of a number of other obvious tie-in points could also be used. Shift might need a slightly heavier solenoid than that used for the code bails. Entering 1 shifts to uppercase.

First the code is entered; then a keypressed bail is tripped. Key pressed is the silver bail above and between the R5 and T1 bails. To type a character, *briefly* raise this bail a fraction of an inch. Note that the Selectric will enter multiple character hits if you hold this bail up instead of briefly pulsing it. When doing a conversion, be absolutely sure that all your solenoids drop back out of the way when the typewriter is to be used for normal typing.

If you look under the corner of the keyboard by the question mark, you will find a series of three or four additional short silver control levers pointing front to back. The leftmost is a carriage return, followed by index and space. Suitable solenoids may be added here for space and return. The ball and typing motion solenoids should be disabled when returning the carriage.

In a home-brew conversion, allow at least a second for carriage return and limit the typing rate to something very low, say 25 words per minute, until you are confident of the capabilities of your conversion. Lock out new characters by handshaking during carriage return.

At this writing, low-cost hobbyist Selectric conversion kits are not yet available, although they are an obvious and desirable product. Expensive commercial-quality conversions exist in the Wang 2200 i/o and various Tycom base adapters, and, of course, you can buy or rent heavy-duty computer i/o Selectrics such as the 735, 750, 820, or 850 directly from IBM. Their manual number OPD/241-5737-0 (about $4) is available from IBM's office products division and details maintenance and construction of the i/o Selectrics. Manual OPD 241-5615-2 (about $3) covers the office Selectrics. The Selectric, Selectric II and corrective Selectric office machines are all essentially the same mechanism.

ELECTROSENSITIVE PAPER

Special papers can often ease the cost and complexity of the mechanical end of a hard-copy system, but usually involve penalties such as poor appearance, extra materials costs, and format limitations. Typical examples are *electrosensitive* paper, *thermal* paper, *impact* (no carbon) *systems,* and the *photographic* papers of the following sections.

Electrosensitive papers consist of an aluminum-colored metallic coating on a paper base. A dark gray dot is produced whenever a wear resistant wire is brought in contact with the paper and a "spark" is applied. Fig. 9-10 shows the basic printhead concept. With modern low-voltage papers, a dot can typically be written in 50 μs with a 60-V supply. The peak current is some 400 mA and must be externally limited by a suitable 150-ohm resistor.

Some sources of electrosensitive paper are shown in Chart 9-1. The papers are supplied in adding-machine tape through full widths. Special papers sensitive to only 3 V are available; others respond to 1 mA of current at higher voltage.

The Telefunken SND20 is one example of an electrosensitive printhead (Fig. 9-11). It prints a row of 120 dots simultaneously. Each *sixth* dot position is missing, leaving us with the ability to do twenty 5-dot characters with one "undot" spacing between them. Each dot grouping is matrixed 10 × 2, so half of the printhead is activated at once.

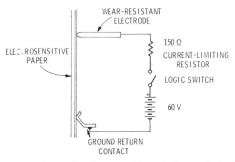

Fig. 9-10. Operating principle behind electrosensitive printheads. A dot is produced when the switch is closed, sparking the paper.

Chart 9-1. Sources of Electrosensitive Paper

> ASTRO-MED DIVISION
> ATLAN-TOL INDUSTRIES
> WEST WARWICK, RI 02893
>
> FITCHBURG COATED PRODUCTS
> Box 1106
> SCRANTON, PA 18501
>
> NICOLET PAPER COMPANY
> DE PERE, WI 54115

The cost of the SND20 is less than $10 when purchased in quantity. Major advantages of the system are that it is relatively quiet and that no horizontal motion is needed—all 20 characters (or more, with multiple printheads) go down essentially at once. A major disadvantage is that lots and lots of support circuitry is needed to get from ASCII characters to a sequence of dots. There are several possible ways to do this: with a lot of buffering and timing, with a custom IC, with extensive microprocessor software, or with elaborate

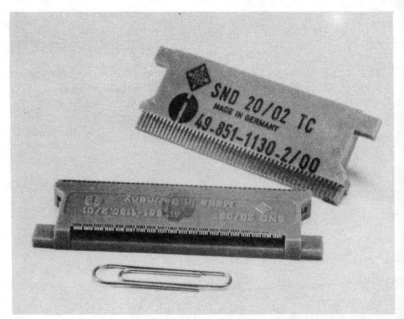

Courtesy Telefunken

Fig. 9-11. The Telefunken SND-20 is a low-cost electrosensitive printhead.

modification of the tvt for interfacing. Note that we can use the same character generator in the tvt if we use direct memory access and suitably time-share the character generator address lines. Additional buffering may be needed if a line of characters is to be simultaneously written.

The paper is indexed seven times vertically to pick up each row of dots, and then several additional times to get the space between character rows. This is the only mechanical motion needed in the printer. The indexing can be done with a rachet and pawl, with a geneva stop mechanism, or with a stepper motor. The ratchet and pawl route is cheap but is noisy and prone to wear. Geneva mechanisms are described well in most kinematics books; one premium source is Lavezzi Machine Works, who also has rollers, pin feeds, and other precision drive components. Suitable steppers would include the Molon LMS, Ledex series 50 devices, and the North American Philips 82000 series.

Note that the wires on the printhead are very easily bent. The utmost care must be used when experimenting with these printheads so that the print wires are protected during installation. Mechanical paper guides should further protect the print wires during final use.

One interesting way to get long line lengths with small printheads and narrow paper is to put the characters down *sideways*, perhaps

Courtesy Hycom

Fig. 9-12. Hycom DC2106 commercial electrosensitive printer.

using a 5×5 matrix. This way, there is no printhead limit to the number of characters per line, but the overall message is limited to 20 lines, or whatever the available width of the printhead is. A column-scan interface is required.

Complete, commercial electrosensitive printers include the Hycom DC 2106 (Fig. 9-12), the Elec-Trol PR 1011, the Copal SF-30 and others that are often advertised in *Computer Decisions, Modern Data, Datamation, Infosystems,* and other computer trade journals. Typically, the small-quantity costs of many of these systems are unrealistically high. Note also that the bare-printer cost usually does *not* include the extensive buffering, timing, software, and drive electronics. Either dedicated circuitry or extensive microcomputer software must be added to the printer mechanism to get a working system.

THERMAL PAPER

Thermal-paper printers use a special paper that darkens when heated, usually to a temperature of 65° to 100° C. Fig. 9-13 shows the basic operating principle. A small resistor is held against the paper and heats up when a current is briefly run through it. Bulk silicon is often a good resistance material to use because it has a

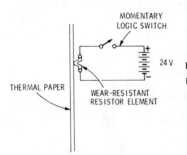

Fig. 9-13. Operating principle behind thermal printheads: a dot is produced when the switch is closed, heating the paper.

reasonably high resistance and good wear properties. Micaply *Omega* material has also been used successfully. With a silicon printhead, around 7 ms is needed for good dot density at a 24-V supply. Current is internally limited by the printhead resistance. Adequate heat sinking must be provided behind the elements to allow for cooling between character times.

Several sources of thermal paper are shown in Chart 9-2, and a typical printhead is shown in Fig. 9-14. The printhead arrangement can be a linear array for row-scan applications, vertical groupings of seven or nine elements for column scan, or complete 3×5 or 5×7 matrix systems for entry of an entire character at a time. The cost

GULTON PUTS IT
ON PAPER BETTER
THIS IS
AN EXAMPLE OF
THERMAL PRINTING

GULTON IND.
DM1101-40F12
7426

GULTON IND.
DM1101-40F12
7426

Courtesy Gulton Industries Inc.

Fig. 9-14. Gulton DM1101-40F12 thermal printhead.

of many of these systems is less than $20 when purchased in quantity, and thermal printheads made of bulk silicon have the potential for being an extremely low-cost device. Like the electrosensitive systems, thermal printing systems require extensive interface circuits or their software equivalents to get from a microprocessor or tvt into a usable printer format. Obviously, the type of circuitry used depends on the format of the printhead, the length of the line, and several other factors.

The thermal design of the printhead is usually a sticky problem—you have to provide enough heat sinking to let the individual elements cool off between character entry. Control of the duty cycle is also important. Under no circumstances should dc be applied to the printhead, or the elements will overheat and self-destruct. One way

Chart 9-2. Sources of Thermal Paper

Types 160, 161, 162
DUPLICATING PRODUCTS DIV.
3M CENTER
ST. PAUL, MN 55101

Types LT-1, LT-2, 2-3, HT
NCR
EASTERN SPECIALTIES CO.
Box 350
HOLYOKE, MA 01040

Type T-304
NASHUA CORP.
44 Franklin St.
NASHUA, NH 03060

Type PL100, PM100, PH100
MITSUBISHI INTERNATIONAL CORP.
7045 N. Ridgeway
LINCOLNWOOD, IL 60645

to get fail-safe operation is to use capacitor discharge for the source of printhead current.

Some representative thermal printing systems include the NCR T-7, the Copal SF-20, and the Gulton PS6151 (Fig. 9-15).

IMPACT SYSTEMS

Any printer that actually strikes the paper mechanically is an impact system. The Teletypes and Selectrics of the previous sections are impact systems. Another type of printhead is the *matrix impact printer*; its operating principle is shown in Fig. 9-16.

A group of seven solenoids is arranged so that seven pins corresponding to the height of the character can be impacted either against a ribbon or directly against a special "no carbon" paper. One advantage of the system is that you can get multiple copies, but potential limitations include noise and mechanical wear.

A typical printhead is the Practical Automation DM101 (Fig. 9-17). There are several approaches to printhead design. If the solenoid drives the impact pin against the paper, it is a *direct-impact* system. This is a simple system, but it does not wear well and may not yield uniform characters. If the solenoid drives the impact pin

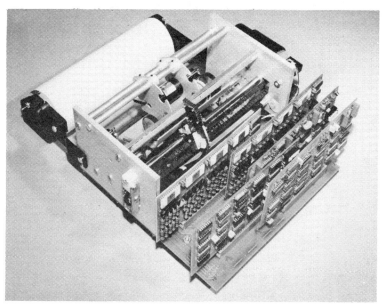

(A) NCR T-7.

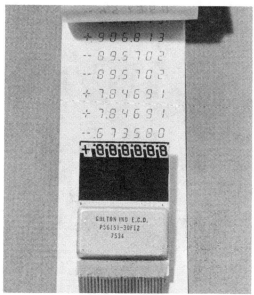

(B) Gulton PS6151.

Fig. 9-15. Complete thermal printers.

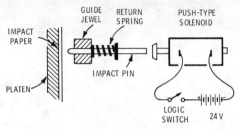

(A) Using impact-sensitive "no-carbon" paper.

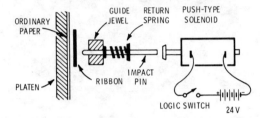

(B) Using a ribbon and ordinary paper.

Fig. 9-16. Operating principle behind matrix impact printhead. A dot is produced when impact pin hits ribbon or special paper.

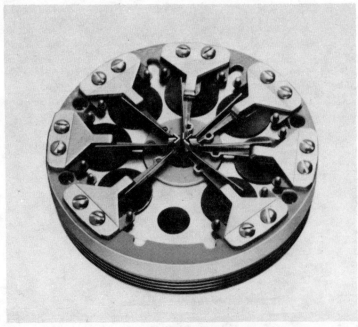

Fig. 9-17. DM101 impact printhead.

forward but stops before the pin hits the paper, we have a *ballistic* system. Here, the total kinetic energy is imparted into the pin before impact. This usually costs more but wears better and gives more controllable results, particularly with multiple copies.

In very large quantities, the printheads usually cost less than $35. Small-quantity pricing is usually very high, and extensive interfacing is needed with this type of system, just as it is with the electrosensitive and thermal matrix approaches.

Inking systems for ordinary paper impact printers can be a traditional typewriter ribbon or any of a number of newer "solid" roller-style systems. Two examples of these newer approaches to inking are the *Polypore* systems from Custom Inks and Coatings and the *Porelon* materials from Johnson Wax.

Impact-printer assemblies include the Amperex 60SR, the Seiko AN101-F, and the Victor IPM-130, shown in Fig. 9-18.

Courtesy Victor Comptometer Corp.

Fig. 9-18. IPM-130 impact printer.

OTHER HARD-COPY METHODS

There are several other approaches to hard copy that may or may not be suitable for low-cost tvt-oriented uses. Three of these include *ink squirters,* photographic techniques, and nonprint alternatives.

An ink squirter (Fig. 9-19) is a fast, quiet, and very expensive printhead that literally throws globs of ink at the paper. This is done by electrostatically charging the ink, modulating the flow into discrete droplets, and then vertically deflecting the droplets into seven or nine possible column positions. The only mechanical motion needed is a continuous bidirectional carriage travel. With suitable input buffering, the squirter can work in both directions, eliminating any pauses for carriage returns. The system is very quiet and there is no mechanical contact at the printhead, thus leading to inherently good reliability and freedom from wear. Any type of paper that is

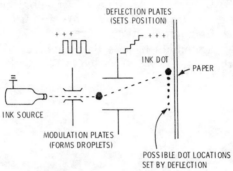

Fig. 9-19. Operating principle behind "ink slinger" printhead. Electrostatic acceleration and deflection literally throw ink dots toward paper.

compatible with the particular ink selected can be used, and the squirter approach lends itself very well to long line lengths, extensive graphics, and variable character fonts. Special inks minimize clogging problems. Like any matrix-style printhead, this one requires extensive buffering and formatting between the microcomputer or tvt. At present, the ink slinger is used only on very fast and very expensive printer mechanisms. Fig. 9-20 shows a typical unit.

One possible photographic technique might be to simply contact-print something—perhaps a piece of blueprint paper—directly from the face of the display. Unfortunately, this will not work, since the image is on the inside of the glass and the contact material is on the outside, making everything too fuzzy to use. If we get into lenses and imaging, we end up with an incredible loss of light (all the light you use has to be forced through a 3- or 4-inch lens placed a foot or more from the screen). This means we have to use very sensitive materials, dark processing, wet chemistry, and other complicated techniques.

Another photographic approach is to use a hand-held Polaroid camera such as the CR-9 of Fig. 9-21. This system is intended for oscilloscope use, so you can use it only on smaller screens. The cost of the camera is under $100. The final result is a Polaroid print. This

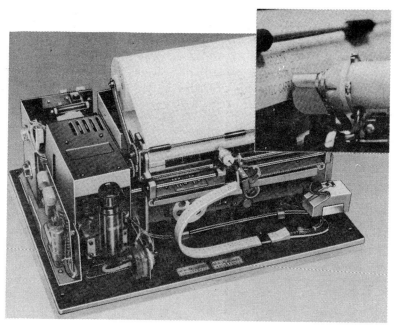

Fig. 9-20. The Casio 301 "Typuter" uses ink squirter techniques.

Fig. 9-21. CR-9 hand-held display camera.

can be handy as a record, but the format is very limited and the per-copy costs are very high compared with other print systems.

In any photographic system working with raster scans, one thing you have to watch carefully is the exposure time. If we expose for less than $1/60$ of a second, we will probably get only a partial display, unless the persistence of the phosphor in the tube is very long. If we expose for exactly $1/60$ of a second *and synchronize with the raster scan*, we will get a complete and uniform exposure. Somewhat longer times will give us a two-tone brightness effect in the screen, which diminishes with longer times. Finally, if we expose too long, the random variations in screen size, drift, etc., will blur the characters objectionably. Approximately $1/15$ of a second is often optimum.

We can also build an elaborate photographic system such as the kind used in phototypesetting. In this application, a cathode-ray flying spot scans a portion of a character mask, which in turn is imaged onto a suitable piece of film or paper and then developed. A special tube with very short persistence is needed, along with elaborate film drives. One interesting advantage of the system is that you can change fonts (the size and shape of the characters) simply by changing masks. Obvious disadvantages are the complexity and the wet chemistry usually involved.

Do we really need to have a printed hard copy the instant the tvt or microcomputer is in use? This brings out the possibility of non-print or not-immediate-print alternatives that will give us a permanent record without actually using a hard-copy printer. One possibility is to record the output on a suitable cassette system, which presently costs far less than any hard-copy system and still gives a permanent record. The recording can later be taken to someone who has a suitable printer (perhaps at a school, or one that is owned as a group by a computer club or is part of a larger system that can justify a printer's cost, etc.) and then converted into final copy. This technique lends itself particularly well to mailing lists and address generation, form letters, and other systems for which only a limited budget is available to do a lot of hard-copy output.

COLOR GRAPHICS

A *graphics display* lets us add pictures, lines, and symbols to the basic letters and numbers of an ordinary tv typewriter. Our graphics display can be entirely symbols, such as when it is used for a chess display, video art synthesis, a "super spirograph," or other similar games. Or, the display can be a mixture of symbols and words, such as when it is used to show a printed-circuit layout, a logic diagram, a chart, a circuit response, a game with scoring shown, and so on. In many tvt and microcomputer uses, the ability to display several colors at once is very important; in others, it is simply a convenience that may not be worth the extra complexity.

There are two fundamentally different approaches to graphics displays. One method is called the *stroke method*. Here, the display is told where to start each symbol or line, what direction to take it, what color to make it, and how far to go before stopping or changing direction. The *dot-matrix* method breaks the display down into as many raster-scanned boxes or dots as a backup storage memory can provide. These blocks are lit or not lit in a selected color, as needed, to form an image.

The stroke method somehow sounds better, particularly if we are interested in curved figures and nonragged edges on diagonal lines, but it has problems. Its most serious shortcoming is that it is not directly compatible with either a stock black-and-white or a stock color tv set. A special display is thus needed, although an oscilloscope can be substituted for single-color, low-resolution use. Another limitation is that the display and memory bandwidths have to be extremely wide, or else the display has to slow down its refresh rate as more and more symbols are added to the display. This can lead to unacceptable flicker, even with a special tube phosphor.

The raggedness of the dot-matrix system can be minimized by using enough memory to increase the resolution and by minimizing the curved or diagonal lines to be displayed. The dot-matrix technique has one major advantage in that we can easily and efficiently mix graphic and alphanumerics, simply by using a tvt system in a graphic mode on one field and in an alphanumeric mode on the second, merging the two separate displays as one. Besides giving more pleasing characters, this approach has an efficiency advantage—only six bits are needed to store an ASCII character, whereas 35 or more bits are needed to store and display the extended dot-matrix character in a 5×7 format.

It turns out that a dot-matrix graphics-only display is actually easier and simpler to do than an ordinary tvt, since the character generator is no longer needed and the high-frequency timing is usually very much simplified. This type of display lends itself very well to existing microprocessor organization without extensive interface.

One limitation of the graphics dot-matrix approach is that quite a lot of memory is needed, at least one bit corresponding to every possible dot location.

SOME TELEVISION LIMITATIONS

What are the limits to the matrix size we can display on a television set? First and foremost, this depends on the amount of memory you have available, for one bit will be needed for every potential dot position, and a fractional part of a bit (more on this later) will be needed for the location of that color information. If we are also interested in *gray scale* (brightness variations), more than one bit per dot position will probably be needed. Gray-scale techniques are usually not worth the added cost and complexity.

Black-and-white sets can allow very dense matrices. For instance, if we have a black-and-white set modified to display 72 characters in a 7 × 9 dot matrix with two undots between characters, we end up with a horizontal resolution of 648 dots over the active scan. (This does take direct video and some modifications as shown in Chapter 8.) The scan rate limits the dots vertically. Without interlace, we get 262-, 262½- or 264-dot resolutions. If we have to, we can go to full interlace and double these values. Thus, it is quite possible to have a 512 × 512 dot graphic display. The memory for this display would take 262,144 bits, or 32,768 eight-bit bytes. At 0.1 cent per bit, such a memory costs around $262. And, besides being expensive, a display this dense contains vastly more information than the human eye can process and pushes the line pair resolution of the tv display. So, we can conclude that black-and-white sets can handle just about anything we can afford to throw at them in the way of graphics.

Color sets are much more restrictive but still give us more than enough capability for very useful display matrices. An unmodified color tv has a maximum video bandwidth of 3 MHz, brought about by the need to eliminate a 3.58-MHz subcarrier in the color processing video (see Chapter 8). Video of 3 MHz is roughly equal to six million dots per second, which gives us around 380 or so dots per line. This does not include an allowance for horizontal retrace, so something around 256 dots displayed horizontally is a good limit. Similarly, if we do not use interface, 256 dots displayed vertically is also a reasonable limit. A 256 × 256 display contains 65,536 dot locations and costs us around $65 for a single-color display at 0.1 cent per bit, and somewhat more if multiple colors are to be added.

Even if we were to separate totally the luminance and chrominance channels on the color tv (a major job that totals the tv for anything else), we would still be limited by the number of holes in the shadow mask to resolutions only somewhat better than what we can get on an unmodified color tv.

One very important thing to note is that *the color bandwidth is far less than the dot resolution on a color tv set*. In addition, *the color bandwidth varies with the colors in use*. The available bandwidth ranges from a high of 1.5 MHz for an orange-cyan display to a low of 0.5-MHz for a red-blue-green tricolor display. Thus, *with a high-resolution display, it is not possible to change the color of each and every successive dot in the horizontal direction*. For full color presentation, something less than *fifty* color changes across the screen is pretty much an upper limit, particularly if we are to minimize fringing and edge shading effects and are using saturated colors.

The limited color bandwidth is both good and bad for graphics displays. The lower horizontal color resolution means that several dots in the horizontal direction must have the same color and that, *whenever possible, we should change colors on a black dot or blanked portion of the display.* At the same time, since this is the best we can do, we can use only a fraction of a bit per dot to specify the dot color. This means that our color storage will not add much to the basic memory size and cost. For instance, on an eight-bit word, two color bits can specify any of four colors to six different dot locations. Or, one color bit could specify a choice of two colors to seven different dot locations. Fortunately, black dominates and counts as wide bandwidth luminance video rather than color, so we can shift between black and colors and back again at full tilt.

SOME SIMPLE GRAPHICS DISPLAYS

An ordinary alphanumeric tvt can be converted into a very limited performance graphics display simply by adding one or gate as shown in Fig. 9-22. The or gate goes between the character-generator ROM

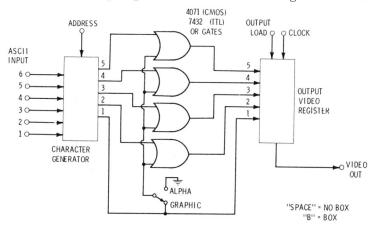

Fig. 9-22. Simple gate circuit converts ordinary tvt into limited graphic display.

outputs and the output video shift register. All it does is monitor the leftmost dot output and make the other dots a 1 if the leftmost dot is a 1. If you type a space, you get a blank location. If you type a *B* for box, you get a white box at each character location specified. There is nothing magic about using a *B*. Any character in which all leftmost dots are a 1 will do, such *D, E, F, H, K, L, M*, etc.

The resolution of your display depends on the original format, for you get one box per character. With a 32-character-per-line display of 16 lines, you get a total of 512 "black surround" boxes in your matrix. While this is not very attractive and does not give much in the way of resolution, it is handy for studying graphics techniques and is of limited use in games, displays, and simple video art applications, and for generating enormous alphanumeric characters.

Fig. 9-23 shows how we add color. Since we used only one bit of the word in which we stored the alphanumeric information, we have enough extra information left to handle quite a few different colors,

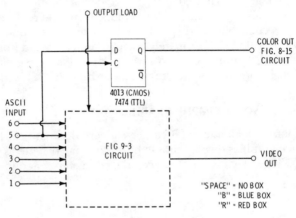

Fig. 9-23. Adding a second color.

ranging from 32 colors on a six-bit memory word to 128 on an eight-bit memory word. The color information is removed directly from the character-storage memory, monitoring bit 5. The color output is delayed and resynchronized to the output video with the flip-flop as shown. This delays the color to match the delay involved in the character generator. The color flip-flop output goes to a color subcarrier generator similar to that shown in Fig. 8-21. The subcarrier is programmed to produce a red output when bit 5 is a 1 and a blue output when bit 5 is a 0, and to return to the reference phase during horizontal retrace.

Now, for no box, we type a space. For a red box, we type an *R* and for a blue box, we type a *B*. The first bit of the character generator *output* decides box or no box (luminance), while the delayed fifth bit of the character generator *input* decides red or blue.

We can pull a trick to double the resolution in the vertical direction. We do this by making the top half of any box one color and the bottom half a second color. Better yet, we blank out enough of the middle of the box to exactly match what is blanked out *between* vertical boxes so that we get even spacing of all the boxes in the vertical direction. For instance, on a 5×7 dot matrix with three lines between vertical characters, we use only the two upper dots and the two lower dots, skipping the three middle ones.

Fig. 9-24 shows the details. We carefully search the dot patterns of all the displayed characters to come up with some useful combinations. With the circuit shown, the inverse of the bit 1 output is what counts in the double mode. By typing a B, we get neither an upper nor a lower box in a character location. Typing an A gets us an

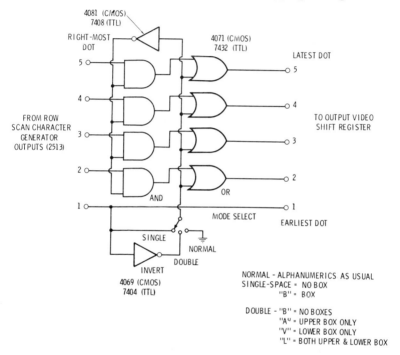

Fig. 9-24. Additional logic doubles horizontal resolution. A 32 × 32 array can be presented on a 32-character, 16-line tvt.

upper box but no lower box. A V gets us a lower box and no upper one. And a $<$ gives us both upper and lower boxes. Color may be added by using the circuit of Fig. 9-24 connected to the seventh and eighth memory bits.

A 96 × 96 FULL-COLOR DISPLAY

Let's look at the design problems involved in building a full-color display that uses a modest memory of 2048×8 bits for storage (costing $16.34 at 0.1 cent per bit) and that still has enough useful resolution for chess displays, pong-style games, video synthesis, creative art, and so on.

The central problem in designing a graphics display is proper *partitioning* of the memory. Partitioning simply decides which portion of the memory is related to the display in what manner. Three very important partitioning questions are:

* How many resolvable elements are supplied by a single memory word and in what positions and colors?
* How is graphic information separated from alphanumeric information, such as scores and printouts?
* How do we separate the "seldom-changing" memory portions of a display (such as the chess grid or a foul line) from the "often-changing" parts (such as a just captured rook or a fast-moving hockey puck) to simplify as much as possible the software and external control of the display?

For a 96 × 96 color display useful for chess and pong-style games, we might partition each memory word as shown in Fig. 9-25. The first

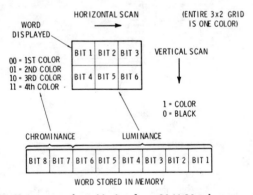

Fig. 9-25. Memory word partitioning for a 96 × 96 color game display.

six bits of our 8-bit word specify the luminance (black or not black) of six dot locations; the final two bits specify the color of all six of those locations simultaneously. This gives us up to four colors, plus black, and lowers the color change resolution enough that the color tv stays happy. In a pong-style game, the goal and sidelines can be one color, the opposing teams can be two other colors, and the ball or marker yet another color. For chess, we can use a two-color chessboard with two-color opponents.

While the first six bits could be arranged as six successive dots horizontally or vertically, a grouping of three horizontally by two vertically seems to work out well for both chess and many other

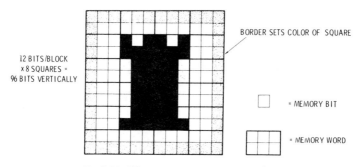

12 BITS/BLOCK x 8 SQUARES = 96 BITS HORIZONTALLY

12 BITS/BLOCK
x 8 SQUARES =
96 BITS VERTICALLY

BORDER SETS COLOR OF SQUARE

☐ = MEMORY BIT

⊞ = MEMORY WORD

Fig. 9-26. Chess square on a 96 × 96 grid.

games. The basic chess grid is shown in Fig. 9-26 and uses ⅛ of the 96 elements in both directions. The choice of a rectangular grouping is also handy in games, since the size of the ball or puck can be made double that of the goal and foul lines and still be specified with only one memory word.

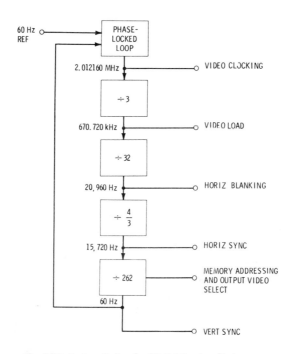

60 Hz REF

PHASE-LOCKED LOOP

2.012160 MHz — VIDEO CLOCKING

÷ 3

670.720 kHz — VIDEO LOAD

÷ 32

20,960 Hz — HORIZ BLANKING

÷ $\frac{4}{3}$

15,720 Hz — HORIZ SYNC

÷ 262 — MEMORY ADDRESSING AND OUTPUT VIDEO SELECT

60 Hz

VERT SYNC

Fig. 9-27. System timing for 96 × 96 color display.

Having chosen our basic word format, we can design our system timing, pretty much following the methods of Chapter 4. We start with a vertical rate of 60 Hz and use a 262-line noninterlaced system, for a total of 192 active scan lines and 70 retrace and blanking lines in the vertical direction. Thus, two vertical lines are used for each resolution box, and $96 \times 2 = 192$.

Our horizontal frequency will be $60 \times 262 = 15,720$ Hz, equal to a 63.6-μs horizontal line. With reasonable horizontal retrace, this gives us around 48 μs of live scan time for our 96 elements. The time per element is a relatively lazy half microsecond. There are three display elements per word horizontally, so each memory clocking will be needed at 1.5-μs intervals. One possible system timing setup is shown in Fig. 9-27.

The output video circuitry is simpler here than it is in an alphanumeric display, since we do not need a character generator. Fig. 9-28 shows one possible arrangement. The memory words are clocked once every 1.5 μs, and three bits are loaded into a four-bit shift register and clocked out at a 2-MHz rate. The other three memory bits are loaded into a second shift register, identical to the first. At

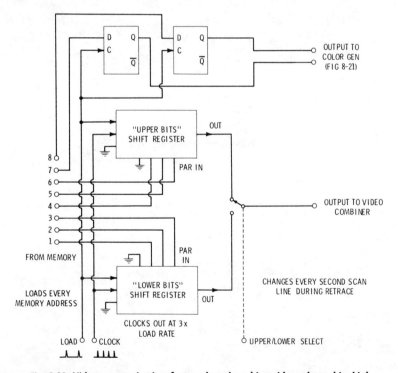

Fig. 9-28. Video output circuitry forms a box three bits wide and two bits high.

242

the same time, the two color bits are decoded and sent to the color subcarrier system.

On alternate pairs of scan lines, the registers are alternately selected. This automatically selects the first three bits for the upper three boxes, and the second three for the lower three boxes of each memory. Note that we can use a data selector since we change it only during the horizontal retrace time. If we tried to do the whole job with selectors, the glitch and settling time problems would probably make it too bad to use. Note also that we get the same memory words back in the same sequence for *four* consecutive scan lines, two to display the first three bits and two to display the second three bits. This is similar to the readdressing that takes place on an alphanumeric tvt when we get each horizontal line back at least seven times to produce an entire dot-matrix character.

The output of the data selectors is routed out as brightness-style video to a typical video combiner such as the one shown in Fig. 8-2. The color information is routed to the subcarrier circuit similar to that in Fig. 8-15. Be sure that the color circuitry returns to the reference phase during the horizontal retrace time. Try to design the display so that most of the color changes take place on a black or blanked location. If color fringing becomes a problem, a slight additional amount of video delay (with respect to the color changes) may minimize this effect.

Fig. 9-29 shows one possible arrangement of the chessmen for a chess display, while the program of Fig. 9-30 shows us the starting

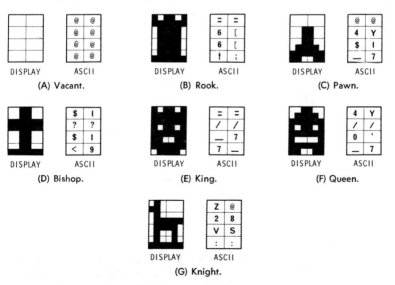

Fig. 9-29. Chessmen and their subprograms.

position for a chess game. A basic hockey or pong setup and program are shown in Fig. 9-31.

We can add scoring or other alphanumerics most simply by using an ordinary tvt with the graphics display and alternating frames, as shown in Fig. 9-32A, or by summing video, as shown in Fig. 9-32B.

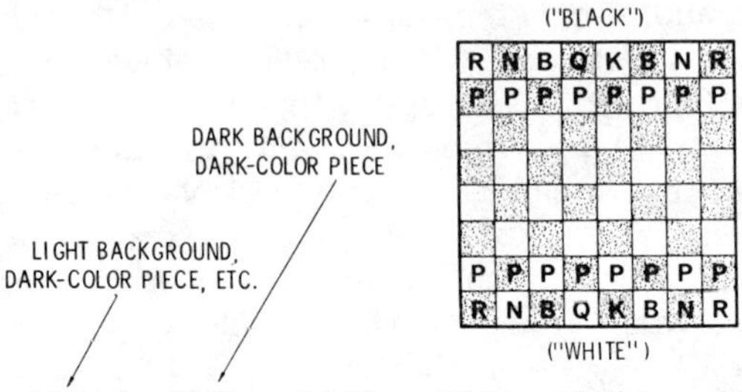

("BLACK")

R	N	B	Q	K	B	N	R
P	P	P	P	P	P	P	P
P	P	P	P	P	P	P	P
R	N	B	Q	K	B	N	R

("WHITE")

DARK BACKGROUND, DARK-COLOR PIECE

LIGHT BACKGROUND, DARK-COLOR PIECE, ETC.

```
O G G '     O G G '     O G G '     O G G '     O G G '     O G G '     O G G '     O G G '
C = = $     C Z @ $     C $ I $     C 4 Y $     C = = $     C $ I $     C Z @ $     C = = $
C 6 [ $     C 2 8 $     C ? ? $     C / / $     C ? ? $     C 2 8 $     C 6 [ $
C 6 [ $     C V S $     C $ I $     C 0 ' $     C _ 7 $     C $ I $     C V S $     C 6 [ $
C ↑ ; $     C : : $     C < 9 $     C _ 7 $     C 7 _ $     C < 9 $     C : : $     C ↑ ; $
9 8 8 <     9 8 8 <     9 8 8 <     9 8 8 <     9 8 8 <     9 8 8 <     9 8 8 <     9 8 8 <

O G G '     O G G '     O G G '     O G G '     O G G '     O G G '     O G G '     O G G '
C @ @ $     C @ @ $     C @ @ $     C @ @ $     C @ @ $     C @ @ $     C @ @ $     C @ @ $
C $ I $     C $ I $     C $ I $     C $ I $     C $ I $     C $ I $     C $ I $     C $ I $
C 4 Y $     C 4 Y $     C 4 Y $     C 4 Y $     C 4 Y $     C 4 Y $     C 4 Y $     C 4 Y $
C _ 7 $     C _ 7 $     C _ 7 $     C _ 7 $     C _ 7 $     C _ 7 $     C _ 7 $     C _ 7 $
9 8 8 <     9 8 8 <     9 8 8 <     9 8 8 <     9 8 8 <     9 8 8 <     9 8 8 <     9 8 8 <

O G G '     O G G '     O G G '     O G G '     O G G '     O G G '     O G G '     O G G '
C @ @ $     C @ @ $     C @ @ $     C @ @ $     C @ @ $     C @ @ $     C @ @ $     C @ @ $
C @ @ $     C @ @ $     C @ @ $     C @ @ $     C @ @ $     C @ @ $     C @ @ $     C @ @ $
C @ @ $     C @ @ $     C @ @ $     C @ @ $     C @ @ $     C @ @ $     C @ @ $     C @ @ $
C @ @ $     C @ @ $     C @ @ $     C @ @ $     C @ @ $     C @ @ $     C @ @ $     C @ @ $
9 8 8 <     9 8 8 <     9 8 8 <     9 8 8 <     9 8 8 <     9 8 8 <     9 8 8 <     9 8 8 <

O G G '     O G G '     O G G '     O G G '     O G G '     O G G '     O G G '     O G G '
C @ @ $     C @ @ $     C @ @ $     C @ @ $     C @ @ $     C @ @ $     C @ @ $     C @ @ $
C @ @ $     C @ @ $     C @ @ $     C @ @ $     C @ @ $     C @ @ $     C @ @ $     C @ @ $
C @ @ $     C @ @ $     C @ @ $     C @ @ $     C @ @ $     C @ @ $     C @ @ $     C @ @ $
C @ @ $     C @ @ $     C @ @ $     C @ @ $     C @ @ $     C @ @ $     C @ @ $     C @ @ $
9 8 8 <     9 8 8 <     9 8 8 <     9 8 8 <     9 8 8 <     9 8 8 <     9 8 8 <     9 8 8 <
```

(ONE HALF OF PROGRAM SHOWN — OTHER HALF IS MIRROR IMAGE EXCEPT BOTH QUEENS LEFT OF CENTER; BOTH KINGS RIGHT OF CENTER, AND ALL LOWER PIECES LIGHT COLORED, AND ALL SQUARES ALTERNATE COLORS.)

Fig. 9-30. Chess display and ASCII program.

Both system timing circuits must be locked together and have the same number of horizontal lines, and the same amount of horizontal retrace must be provided in both modes if the television is to recognize a continuous program. Another possibility is to use simple box "stroke-style" characters and store them directly in the memory matrix.

When only an extremely limited amount of alphanumeric or numeric-only information is to be added to a graphics display, dedicated circuitry similar to that used to display time on a television set (Fig. 9-34) *may* prove cheaper and simpler than a full tvt-style circuit. Additional advantages of this technique are a completely variable character size and position. Details of an early eight-character tv time or message display system appeared in the September 1974 issue of *Radio Electronics* magazine. This system is easily

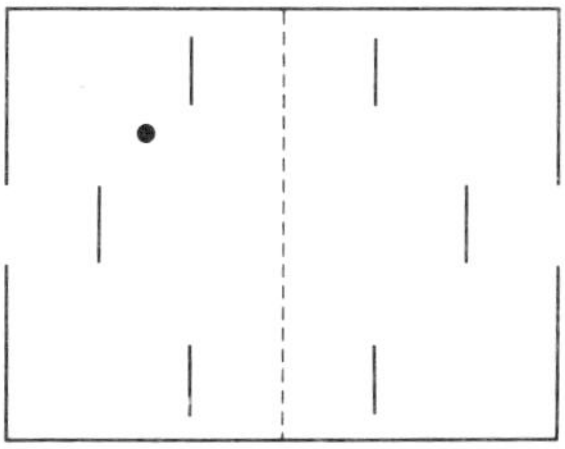

```
O G G G     G G G G     G G G G     G G G V     G G G G     G G G G     G G G G     G G O @
I @ @ @     @ @ @ @     @ @ @ @     @ @ @ J     @ @ @ @     @ @ @ @     @ @ @ @     @ @ I @
I @ @ @     @'@ @ @     @ @ @ @     @ @ @ @     @ @ @ @     @ @ @ @     @ @ @ @     @ @ I @
I @ @ @     @ @ @ @     @ @ @ J     @ @ @ @     @ @ @ J     @ @ @ @     @ @ @ @     @ @ I @
I @ @ @     @ @ @ @     @ @ @ J     @ @ @ J     @ @ @ J     @ @ @ @     @ @ @ @     @ @ I @
I @ @ @     @ @ @ @     @ @ @ J     @ @ @ J     @ @ @ J     @ @ @ @     @ @ @ @     @ @ I @

I @ @ @     @ @ @ @     @ @ @ J     @ @ @ @     @ @ @ J     @ @ @ @     @ @ @ @     @ @ I @
I @ @ @     @ @ @ @     @ @ @ J     @ @ @ @     @ @ @ J     @ @ @ @     @ @ @ @     @ @ I @
I @ @ @     @ @ @ @     @ @ @ J     @ @ @ J     @ @ @ J     @ @ @ @     @ @ @ @     @ @ I @
I @ @ @     @ @ @ @     [ @ @ @     @ @ @ J     @ @ @ @     @ @ @ @     @ @ @ @     @ @ I @
I @ @ @     @ @ @ @     @ @ @ @     @ @ @ @     @ @ @ @     @ @ @ @     @ @ @ @     @ @ I @

I @ @ @     @ @ @ @     @ @ @ @     @ @ @ J     @ @ @ @     @ @ @ @     @ @ @ @     @ @ I @
I @ @ @     @ @ @ @     @ @ @ @     @ @ @ J     @ @ @ @     @ @ @ @     @ @ @ @     @ @ I @
I @ @ @     @ @ @ @     @ @ @ @     @ @ @ @     @ @ @ @     @ @ @ @     @ @ @ @     @ @ I @
@ @ @ @     J @ @ @     @ @ @ @     @ @ @ @     @ @ @ @     @ @ @ @     @ @ J @     @ @ @ @
@ @ @ @     J @ @ @     @ @ @ @     @ @ @ J     @ @ @ @     @ @ @ @     @ @ J @     @ @ @ @
@ @ @ @     J @ @ @     @ @ @ @     @ @ @ J     @ @ @ @     @ @ @ @     @ @ J @     @ @ @ @
```

(ONE HALF OF PROGRAM SHOWN - - - OTHER HALF IS MIRROR IMAGE
EXCEPT FOR BALL "[" LOCATION.)

Fig. 9-31. "Pong"-style display and ASCII program.

adapted to scoring on a "pong-style" game. (Note that the sync signals, which originally needed tv modification, are already available elsewhere in the tvt.) The National 5841 is a single-IC version of this circuit.

Fig. 9-33 shows several approaches to the third partitioning problem, the separation of often and seldom changing data. Most often, a graphics tvt display will be used in association with a microprocessor to get extensive game capabilities. This has a tremendous advantage over hard-wired logic in that we can rapidly change a game format simply by changing programs.

The object of memory partitioning is to trade off specialized timing against the total number of memory bits involved with every computation and update. For instance, in Fig. 9-33A, we simply use the entire 2 K × 8 memory in one brute force piece. While conceptually the simplest and the most flexible, it takes extensive software and a long time to initially fill the display and then specify any changes.

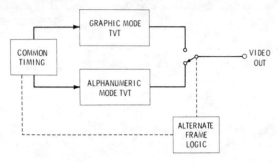

(A) By alternating graphic and alphanumeric frames.

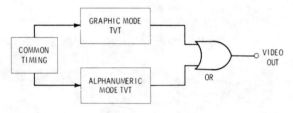

(B) By summing output video.

Fig. 9-32. Two ways to mix graphics and alphanumerics. Both tvt circuits have to use the same number of total scan lines.

In Fig. 9-33B, we have added some dedicated timing that separates the chess playing spaces from the board spaces. This is done with some "cross-hatch" logic gates that select the places where the chessmen are to go. Now a much smaller portion of memory is involved in specifying piece locations. With the system shown in Fig. 9-33A, 1536 words of our memory were involved. With that shown in Fig. 9-33B, only 512 words are involved.

Can we do better? In Fig. 9-33C, we have broken our memory into three distinct areas and selected the areas with hard-wired add-on logic. The main area is the board background, which can be a ROM or a RAM that is loaded once and never changed. The second area is a "file" where we have stored the programs for the seven chessmen involved (pawn, bishop, knight, rook, king, queen, and vacant). This file is sort of a "subroutine" that can *repeatedly be addressed to go in different locations in the main graphics display.*

Finally, we have a small "active" memory that decides what chess piece of what color (or the option of no piece) goes in what location. This active portion of our memory can be made up of as few as 32

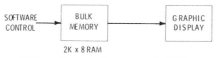

(A) Brute-force—entire memory is RAM.

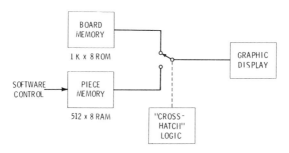

(B) Separating board memory as ROM takes "cross-hatch" logic.

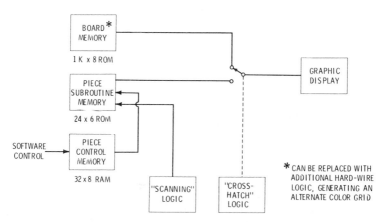

(C) Storing piece shapes as subroutines need "scanning" logic but slashes RAM and software needs.

Fig. 9-33. As these chess display examples show, a small amount of dedicated hard-wired timing logic can drastically simplify the amount of RAM and software backup used.

words, since there are only 64 squares and since only four bits are needed to specify any chessman or blank of either color. Software to work with only 32 words is obviously much more reasonable than software that has to handle 2048 words. Only a small amount of hard-wired, dedicated logic is needed for this tremendous simplification.

In a pong-style game, the ball is specified as four bits of the six-bit word, making it twice the size of the background, foul, and goal lines. Ball motion can usually be computed during the vertical retrace time. For instance, if our microprocessor has a 10-μs cycle time and we have around 4 ms of vertical retrace time, up to 400 machine cycles are available to compute the new ball location.

The 96 × 96 format seems to lend itself well to game graphics and seems easy and reasonable to build. It is by no means the only possible organization for graphics displays. (See the February, 1976 issue of *Popular Electronics* for some other format possibilities.) The basic partitioning problems will change for different types of graphics displays. Two important partitioning rules are (1) to use the absolute minimum grid size you can for your particular display and (2) to use hard-wired timing logic to break down the memory locations into an always-there background, a subroutine file for repeatedly used characters or symbols, and a small active file involved with only the computed *changes* from field to field.

WHERE TO FROM HERE?

When this book was started, there was only one low-cost hobby microcomputer (the Mark-8) and only one very dated tvt (the

Courtesy Radio Electronics

Fig. 9-34. Circuit to display scores or time on a tv display.

TVT-1). If you could get them, 2102's were $30 each and nonexistent microprocessor chips were advertised for $300 to $400 each, without documentation, and the key interface and support chips were a figment of the data-sheet writer's imagination. Peoples Computer Company (PCC) and the Amateur Computer Society (ACS) were voices crying in the wilderness.

An incredibly short time later, the hobbyist and experimenter are literally swamped with microprocessor computers and CPU evaluation kits. Well-documented and supported CPUs are now available for $20 each in single quantities. The 2102's are available as surplus for $1.50 each, only slightly over a tenth of a cent per bit. PROMs have dramatically dropped in price to half a cent per bit and less.

Computer and tvt-user clubs and groups exist by the dozens. Besides PCC (Peoples Computer Company, Box 310 Menlo Park, CA 94025), and the numerous smaller newsletters, major computer hobbyist magazines now exist with excellent editorial materials, professional graphics, and wide distribution. These include BYTE, Interface and Microtek. Universities, junior colleges, industries, and even high schools now offer microprocessor courses. There are now dozens of retail computer stores.

Now what? Where do we go from here? The answer literally changes by the minute. In fact, if things continue at their present explosive rate, many of the basic principles in this book may seem quaint or primitive by the time you read this. Let's suppose that for an instant we could freeze time at November, 1975. Suppose further that your main interest was not in experimenting with a CPU and software like everyone else, but was aimed at bringing tvt's and other truly low-cost peripherals as near to reality as possible, so that something useful could be done cheaply with the CPUs everyone else was building. Here, as I see it, are the major tvt-related questions that you can help answer at this instant in time:

* Can a basic low-cost tv typewriter with cursor and memory be built to retail at the hobbyist level for $39.95?
* Can a miniature calculator-style ASCII keyboard and encoder with quality features (2KRO, choice of strobe, tactile response, two shot keys) be built to retail at the hobbyist level for $14.95?
* What is the longest length and highest character quality that can be obtained with direct rf entry of an unmodified tv set?
* Can you build a *legal*, universal, single-channel rf modulator to retail at the hobbyist level for $4.95?
* What is the minimum possible cost for a snap-on Selectric base-plate adapter and converter? How fast will it operate? Can it be made to enter as well as print?
* How do you add light-pen feedback to graphic and tvt displays?

Can a single microprocessor such as an MOS Technology 6502 provide *all* the timing and control for a stand-alone tvt?

* What are the most effective software and algorithms needed for graphic display games and puzzles?
* Can you design a simple CPU backup for a graphics tvt that will move chessmen following chess notation, e.g., Bishop to King's Rook 5?
* Can you build a *basic* compiler on a chip or two?
* What is the setup needed for a tvt-oriented word-processing system to be used for addressing, printing form letters, and so on? Can this be done without a CPU?
* What is the simplest and cheapest dedicated "super front panel" tvt configuration you can come up with that will read out the *entire* memory contents of a microcomputer a page at a time? Can you make it sequentially read out locations in hex or octal instead of ASCII?
* Can you come up with a simple and universal locking system for video titling and superposition on existing EIA sync programs, both for studio and home video-recording uses? Can you make it crawl, have variable character size and shape, etc.?
* How do you use a tvt for printed-circuit and schematic layouts?
* What is the best way a CPU and tvt can interact with an electronic music synthesis system?
* What about video art synthesis? Can you build a super spirograph? Make it follow music?

Where to from here? Get literature. Pour over trade journals. Join a club. Subscribe to *PCC, Interface* and *BYTE*. Collect newsletters. Take some courses. *Read. Read. Read.*

Index

TV TYPEWRITER COOKBOOK

Want to put your own words and pictures on an ordinary tv set? **TV Typewriter Cookbook** shows you how to accomplish this economically and easily.

Starts with the basics—what a tv typewriter is, and what its uses, configurations, and principles of operation are. Includes the terminology involved with tvt's and microcomputer interface.

Covers three basic types of memories: you-program PROMs, factory-programmed ROMs, and RAMs that let you selectively store and retrieve information..

Cursor and update circuitry techniques range from the traditional count and compare and the McFadden system, to "super front panel" tvt's that work directly from microcomputers. Update systems include both frame-rate and direct memory access systems.

Also covered are hard-copy techniques, color graphics, and games such as "chess" and "pong."

TV Typewriter Cookbook is for the computer hobbyist, the professional data processor, the video game "freak," the electronics technician, and those working with video recording, cable tv, or studio broadcasting. The book is also useful as a text for teaching microprocessors on the high school through university levels.

Don Lancaster is head of Synergetics-Arizona, an electronics design and consulting firm. He has written numerous articles on electronics applications, both for technical journals and for hobby magazines. His nonelectronic interests include ecological studies, firefighting, cave exploration, and bicycling. Don's other Sams books include **Active-Filter Cookbook, Cheap Video Cookbook, CMOS Cookbook, The Hexadecimal Chronicles, The Incredible Secret Money Machine, RTL Cookbook, Son of Cheap Video, TTL Cookbook,** and **User's Guide to TTL** (poster).

Howard W. Sams & Co., Inc.
4300 WEST 62ND ST. INDIANAPOLIS, INDIANA 46268 USA

$11.95/21313

ISBN: 0-672-21313-3